Teaching multiliteracies across the curriculum

Teaching multiliteracies across the curriculum

Changing contexts of text and image in classroom practice

Len Unsworth

Open University Press

Open University Press
McGraw-Hill Education
McGraw-Hill House
Shoppenhangers Road
Maidenhead
Berkshire
SL6 2QL

email: enquiries@openup.co.uk
world wide web: www.openup.co.uk

and
Two Penn Plaza
New York, NY 10121-2289, USA

First Published 2001
Reprinted 2004

A catalogue record for this book is available from the British Library.

ISBN 0 335 20604 2 (pb)   0 335 20605 0 (hb)

Library of Congress Cataloging-in-Publication Data
Unsworth, Len.
    Teaching multiliteracies across the curriculum : changing contexts of text and image in classroom practice / Len Unsworth.
        p. cm.
    Includes bibliographical references and index.
    ISBN 0-335-20605-0 – ISBN 0-335-20604-2 (pbk.)
    1. Visual literacy.   2. Visual education.   3. Learning.   I. Title.

LB1068.U58   2001
370.15′23–dc21   00-052452

Typeset by Graphicraft Limited, Hong Kong
Printed and bound in Great Britain by Biddles Ltd, King's Lynn, Norfolk

For Loraine

Contents

List of figures

Acknowledgements

The author and publisher wish to thank the following for permission to use previously published material:

Illustrations from *The Tunnel* © 1989 Anthony Browne. Reproduced by permission of the publisher, Walker Books Ltd., London.

Cover of *Dan's Grandpa* by Bronwyn Bancroft, published by Sandcastle Books (Fremantle Arts Centre Press, children's imprint), 1996.

Figure 3.3 taken from *Science Workshop: Magnetism*, first published 1992; Figure 3.10 taken from *Life Guides: Alcohol Abuse*, first published 1987; Figure 3.24 and 3.37 taken from *Hands on Science: Sparks to Power Stations*, first published 1989; Figure 3.26 taken from *Hands on Science: Seeds to Plants*, first published 1990; Figure 3.28 taken from *Killing for Luxury*, first published 1988; Figure 3.35 taken from *Hands on Science: Jellyfish to Insects*, first published 1990; Figure 3.36 taken from *Today's World: Insects and Simple Creatures*, first published 1988; Figure 3.37 taken from *Science Through Energy*, first published 1992; Figure 3.38 taken from *Science Starters: Air and Flying*, first published 1991; Figure 3.39 taken from *Science Starters: Water at Work*, first published 1990; Figure 3.40 taken from *Hands on Science: Burning and Melting*, first published 1990; Figure 3.43 taken from *Vanishing Habitats*, first published 1987; Figure 3.44 taken from *Saving the Whale*, first published 1987. All the above published by Franklin Watts, a division of The Watts Publishing Group Ltd, 96 Leonard Street, London EX2A 4XD.

Figure 3.29 taken from *I, the Aboriginal* by D. Lockwood, published by Landsdowne, with permission from Ruth Lockwood and New Holland Publishers.

Figures 3.1 and 3.5 courtesy of Yarra Valley Water Ltd., Australia.

For Figures 3.8, 3.21, 3.34, 3.41 and 4.6, every effort has been made to trace the copyright owner in each instance. Anyone claiming copyright should contact the author.

Introduction

Central to the orientation of this book is a view of literacies, learning and teaching as completely interconnected social processes. As the theoretical and research bases for this position became more established in the 1980s and 1990s, some tertiary textbooks (Unsworth 1993d) dealt with the detailed practical classroom ramifications of these theoretical understandings about the social construction of literacies. While there is a strong and continuing consensus about the more 'socially responsible' practices in literacy pedagogy explicated at the time, the parameters of school literacies have been significantly extended with the rapid cultural and technological changes in literate forms of communication in recent years. Predominant among these are the growing impact of images in an increasing range of texts and the shift from page to screen-based literacies. Learning materials in school subject areas are changing, texts of popular culture are being seen as important curriculum resources and traditional resources like children's literature are being influenced by intermodal comparisons and transformations.

There have been some useful publications dealing separately with some issues arising from these changes. However there remains a need to address the bi-directional impact of research and practice from the perspectives of both beginning and experienced classroom teachers. Teachers are looking for a coherent and practical framework for classroom work, which consolidates fundamental aspects of traditional literacy pedagogy and also encompasses the multiliteracies competencies that children will need to negotiate in the new millennium. This book extends the trajectory of the 1993 edited work, *Literacy Learning and Teaching: Language as Social Practice in the Primary School* (Unsworth 1993d), to attempt such an enterprise, focusing on primary and junior secondary schooling.

There are three broad stages in the structure of this book as indicated in Figure 0.1.

Framing perspectives in Chapter 1 introduces sociocultural, semiotic and pedagogic perspectives on key issues in literacy learning and teaching and emerging dimensions of change. It addresses the theoretical and practical bases of contemporary literacy pedagogy and foreshadows the subsequent chapters' explorations of both consolidation and transformation in the development of a pedagogy of multiliteracies.

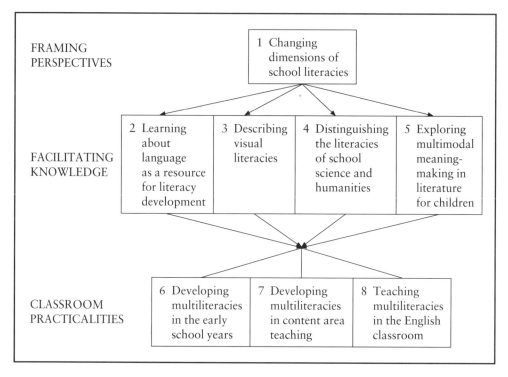

Figure 0.1   Stages in the structure of this book

Facilitating knowledge deals with a number of areas of detailed technical knowledge teachers need to have. Chapter 2 is concerned with the grammatical, cohesive and generic structures of language. Chapter 3 addresses the meaning-making structures and features of images. Chapter 4 delineates the distinctive textual forms and literate practices of different school subject areas, including some of the ways in which computer technology mediates characteristic screen-based literacies. Chapter 5 describes the multimodal meaning-making of literature for children.

Accessible accounts of these areas of knowledge are important since most students and many teachers, due to the curriculum they experienced, have very little systematic knowledge about language structures. Nor have they studied visual semiotic systems. They frequently do not appreciate the distinctive literacies of subject areas and are novices in the field of computer-based literacies.

This knowledge about how semiotic resources are deployed to make meanings in a variety of contexts facilitates teachers' informed and effective intervention in children's learning. Underlying the accounts of the meaning-making resources of language and image in conventional and electronic modes across curriculum areas is the understanding that the ways in which these resources are deployed are mediated by the cultural and socioeconomic positioning of the participants. From this perspective the issue of critical social literacies is integrally linked to the actual descriptive accounts of the meaning-making systems.

Classroom practicalities shows how the knowledge of meaning-making systems informs the design and implementation of teaching/learning activities in different school curriculum areas in classroom contexts from infancy to adolescence. Chapter 6 is concerned with teaching children in the early years of schooling. Chapter 7 deals with the development of multiliteracies in curriculum area teaching and learning in the upper primary and junior secondary school, while Chapter 8 focuses on work in the English classroom at these levels. It is important that teachers have not only the sound understandings that will inform their practice at the particular school level of their current teaching, but that they also understand the differences and continuities of teaching and learning literacies across primary and junior secondary schooling. As well as articulating general principles and providing guidelines for the practical classroom teaching of multiliteracies, sample programs and detailed lesson material are included.

The importance of the bi-directionality of theory and practice in negotiating the teaching and learning of emerging multiliteracies is a major premise of the approach in this book. The intention has been to provide sufficient detail to demonstrate the advantages of engagement with this kind of theory–practice orientation to classroom work. Although selected key learning areas have been addressed in some detail, a conscious decision was made not to attempt the kind of panoramic survey that could deal only superficially with the full range of learning areas. What is gained is a thorough introduction to informing theoretical understandings and detailed accounts of their impact on practical day to day planning of classroom activities. It is hoped that this book will stimulate critically constructive revision and renewal of what it advocates as teachers and researchers together explore the kinds of interrelated theoretical and practical understandings needed in negotiating changing contexts of text and image in the social construction of multiliteracies in classroom practice.

PART I

Framing perspectives

CHAPTER 1

Changing dimensions of school literacies

OLD AND NEW LITERACIES: NEGOTIATING CHANGE, CONTINUITY AND COMPLEMENTARITY

The textual habitat, the textual environment which affects us and which we affect, has experienced remarkable changes in the twentieth century and will continue to do so in the twenty-first century, as the students we teach grow to adulthood. While many of the fundamentals of established, language-based literacy pedagogy will remain necessary, they are by no means sufficient for the development of the kinds of literacy practices that already characterize the continuously evolving information age of the new millennium. We know that many young children have already functionally and critically engaged with electronic and conventional format texts in ways which they do not encounter in their classrooms when they begin school (Green and Bigum 1993; Mackey 1994; Smith *et al.* 1996).

Many instances can be cited from the professional literature and from everyday experience of children intensely involved in multimodal textual practices outside their school experience, which are rarely reflected or acknowledged as part of school literacies. For example, fifth grade students Max and James are avid users of the animation program Microsoft 3D Movie Maker. As well as making their own 30-minute movies, they download from the Internet similar movies made by other children, send both finished cartoons and 'work in progress' internationally, swap ideas and communicate by e-mail about style and effect (Davidson 2000). Christian, also in year five at school, is described (Wilson 2000) as a studious reader of his prolific collection of N64 (Nintendo 64) magazines. His adult interviewer was initially concerned that one of his favourite sections is 'cheats', which turned out to be a list of strategic shortcuts in procedures for achieving success in playing the electronic games. The adult interviewer was also bemused by Christian's electronic games discourse like 'I've clocked Banjo Kazooie.' However, Christian subsequently revealed that he was also reading a recent novel by well-known Australian author of literature for children, Victor Kelleher. This serves to remind us that the advent of the digital datasphere as part of the textual habitat does not necessarily mean the extinction of page-based literacies. Christian's devoted reading of N64 magazines reflects the burgeoning bookstore shelves of computer magazines (often with CD ROM included), manuals, enhanced practice guides etc. But Christian's reading of N64 does not preclude his attention to the fictional narrative in the conventional novel format, and this would appear to be reflected more broadly in the phenomenal commercial success of J.K. Rowling's 'Harry Potter' books (1997, 1998, 1999, 2000).

Although there is no doubt that multimedia and electronic information sources are quickly taking up the communication of much information previously presented solely in traditional text formats, rather than being displaced by computer text, conventional literacies are maintaining a complementary role as well as being both co-opted and adapted in the evolution of our textual habitat (Goodwyn 1998; Rassool 1999; Lankshear *et al.* 2000; Leu and Kinzer 2000). In the twenty-first century the notion of literacy needs to be reconceived as a plurality of literacies and *being* literate must be seen as anachronistic. As emerging technologies continue to impact on the social construction of these multiple literacies, *becoming* literate is the more apposite description. If schools are to foster the development of these changing multiple literacies, it is first necessary to understand the bases of their diversity. These include not only the affordances of computer technology but also the increasing prominence of images in both electronic and conventional formats, the differentiation of the distinctive literacy demands of different school curriculum areas, and the distinguishing among forms of reproductive and critically reflective literacy practices. In the next section the nature of these parameters of diversity are outlined and their interactive effects are described as producing multidimensional, multiple literacies – multiliteracies.

In order to become effective participants in emerging multiliteracies, students need to understand how the resources of language, image and digital rhetorics can be deployed independently and interactively to construct different kinds of meanings. This means developing knowledge *about* linguistic, visual and digital meaning-making systems. This kind of knowledge about how meanings are made requires meta-language – language for describing language, images and meaning-making intermodal interactions. Of course, meta-language in the form of a range of different types of grammar and descriptions of text structure is not new. Various forms of meta-language describing technical aspects of images and their production are also well known. What is needed, however, is a meta-language which recognizes that ultimately the forms of multimodal meaning-making resources that are available, take the forms that they do because of the functions they have evolved to fulfil, which are largely determined by the cultural forces at work within any society. In a later section (p. 16) such 'socially responsible' descriptions of visual and verbal grammar and discourse will be outlined as the basis of a functional and accessible meta-language of multiliteracies.

What students learn about multiliteracies and meta-language is inextricably intertwined with the how of their learning. That, of course, is influenced by the interaction of a multitude of complex individual and social factors within the classroom, the school, the community and the broader cultural and political contexts. Although the nature of classroom practices cannot be realistically decontextualized from this complexity of influences, pedagogic frameworks for managing multiliteracies development that optimize learning and teaching need to be identified. To conclude this chapter, some key features of such frameworks will be discussed (see p. 19).

MULTILITERACIES: MULTIDIMENSIONAL, MULTIPLE LITERACIES

The relationships between visual and verbal representations – visual literacies

Written texts have always been multimodal. They are produced using a particular script or typeface, of a particular size or in varying sizes, laid out in a particular way and on certain types and quality of paper or other materials. On the whole we have been taught to overlook this kind of multimodality except in cases where students have been chided for 'untidy' work on 'scrappy' paper or rewarded for 'excellent presentation' of an essay (Kress 1995b: 26). But today the multimodality of print is being exploited in a wide range of texts. In her discussion of 'visual English' Sharon Goodman illustrates the role of typographic variation in representing multiple voices in texts and the increasing use of what she calls visual puns, which rely on the interaction of visual and verbal elements to bring their meaning to the fore (Goodman and Graddol 1996). Computer technology facilitates not only effortless use of wide typographic variation in terms of font, colour, size etc., but also the use of dynamic text which can 'appear', 'fly' across the screen, 'rotate', 'flash on and off' etc. The verbal forms of the computer screen also have a strong intertextual function (alluding to or echoing other texts) when they appear in other contexts such as signs on shopfronts identifying businesses like 'Newtown.freshfruit@Georges.com'. The graphology of written language needs to be read multimodally. In so doing the ways in which these multimodal features of written language make different kinds of meanings need to be understood because they are fundamental to a text's positioning of the reading with respect to how it might be interpreted.

Texts are also becoming increasingly multimodal in their incorporation of images with written language. This is very obvious in contemporary newspapers, although there is some variation across different types of publications (Kress 1997). Even in the case of picture story books the nature and the role of images have undergone major changes with the advent of the postmodern picture book (Lonsdale 1993; Stephens and Watson 1994; Hollindale 1995; Watson 1997; Prain 1998). In the case of school textbooks the latter part of the twentieth century has seen a significant shift to the prominence of images (Kress 1995a, 1997). The situation has changed from one where language as writing was dominant as the vehicle for all of the information deemed important, to the current situation where writing is far from dominant. In contemporary texts the majority of the space is given to images and they have a significant role together with language in communicating the essential information about the topic (Kress 2000).

Kress has argued that the contemporary integrative use of the visual and the verbal has produced a new code of writing *and* image, in which information is carried differentially by the two modes (Kress 1997). Information that *displays* what the world is like is carried by the image, consistent with the logic of the visual as arrangement and display. Written language on the other hand, tends to follow the logic of speech in being oriented to action and event, and is thus oriented to the recording/reporting of actions and events and the ordering of procedures. Lemke has also pointed out that in scientific texts, images like abstract graphs and diagrams on the one hand, and written text on the other hand, contribute differentially to the construction of meaning (Lemke 1998b). He argues that in these texts meanings are made 'by the *joint* co-deployment of two or more semiotic modalities' suggesting further that, 'It is the nature of scientific concepts that they are semiotically multimodal in this sense, and this may well be true in other systems of semiotic practices as well' (Lemke 1998b: 111).

As well as recognizing that all texts need to be read multimodally, we need to understand how these different modalities separately and interactively construct different dimensions of meaning. These dimensions include the 'ideational' dimension, concerning the people, animals, objects, events and circumstances involved; the 'interpersonal' dimension, concerning the issues of relative power, attitude, affect etc., defining the relations among the participants in the communication; and the textual dimension, concerning the channel of communication and the relative emphasis and information value of aspects of what is being communicated. To understand how these dimensions of meaning are constructed by the elements and structures of language and image requires knowledge of the kind of visual and verbal grammar that relates such elements and structures to meanings and ultimately to the nature of the context in which the visual and verbal texts function. Such a meta-language of multiliteracies is addressed later in this chapter (see p. 16).

The differentiation of subject-specific literacy demands – curriculum literacies

Multiple literacies can be differentiated not only on the basis of the channel and medium of communication (print, image, page, screen), but also according to field or subject area (history, geography, science, maths etc.). Research from a variety of theoretical perspectives has shown that school subject areas have their own characteristic language forms and hence entail distinctive literate practices (Richards 1978; Applebee 1981; Davies and Greene 1984; Street 1984; Gee 1990; Martin 1993b). A study of the literacy demands of the enacted curriculum in the secondary school (Wyatt-Smith and Cumming 1999) showed that the literacy demands were dynamic, varying significantly both within lessons and across school subject areas. The researchers concluded that it is no longer appropriate to talk about 'literacy across the curriculum'. Instead there is a need to delineate 'curriculum literacies', specifying the interface between a specific curriculum and its literacies rather than imagining there is a singular literacy that could be spread homogeneously across the curriculum.

Descriptions of differentiated curriculum literacies of a range of school subject areas has resulted from systemic functional linguistic research (Halliday and Martin 1993; Coffin 1996, 1997; Humphrey 1996; Rothery 1996; Veel and Coffin 1996; Martin and Veel 1998; Unsworth 1999a; Veel 1999). This work has identified the genres (types of texts like explanations, reports, procedures, narratives etc.) that are prominent in the reading materials and writing demands of different subject areas, specifying the organizational structures of such text types. For example, explanations and procedures are very frequent in science but rare in English and, while explanations also occur in history, procedures are much less frequent. The schematic structures of these genres are quite different. A report begins with a general statement that classifies the object of the report, then describes it, then details its behaviours or uses. An explanation begins with an identification of the phenomenon to be explained and then proceeds through a series of implication sequences showing how or why something is the way it is. What has also been documented is the variation in the deployment of grammatical resources in different genres and in the language of different subject areas. One example is the use of 'nominalization'. That is the formation of a noun from the verb form, like 'compress' → 'compression'. In sequential science explanations (which show how something came to be through a sequence of events) like the formation of coal, there is negligible use of nominalization. On the other hand in explanations where cause is also linked to increasing levels of technicality like how sound travels, nominalizations like 'compression', 'rarefaction', 'series' etc. are integral (Unsworth 1997c). In history nominalizations also occur but rarely to construct subject-specific technical terms like 'rarefaction' etc. In history nominalizations are prominent in explanatory genres, but they are usually abstract nouns that are not history-specific like 'widespread unemployment' and 'intolerance of religious dissent' (Martin 1993b; Coffin 1996; Veel and Coffin 1996).

Understanding the grammatical forms of written English and how these are characteristically deployed in the genres of school subject areas is a crucial resource for enhancing students' comprehension and composition of the distinctive discourse forms of different school subject areas. What is required to mobilize this resource is a meta-language shared by students and teachers. A number of professional development programs for teachers in Australia have incorporated the explicit teaching of functional grammar and genre to provide such a meta-language (National Professional Development Program 1997; Polias 1998). This kind of meta-linguistic understanding positions students not only to comprehend and compose the text forms of their school subjects but also to critique the perspectives on knowledge they construct (see Chapter 4).

Once teachers understand the orientation and basic concepts of systemic functional grammar and discourse and genre, their use in classroom work can be quite well

aligned with meeting the government mandated syllabus requirements concerning knowledge of grammar and text form. An outline of key concepts in systemic functional
grammar and discourse is provided in Chapter 2. The ways it has informed differentiation of curriculum literacies in science and humanities is detailed in Chapter 4 and its
application to classroom work is demonstrated in Chapters 6, 7 and 8.

The affordances of computer technologies – cyberliteracies

Some of the affordances of computer-based and networked technologies for information and communication are exclusive to this digital datasphere. These include hypertext and hypermedia links, windows or frames, 'chat rooms' of various kinds, e-mail
and certain 'search' capabilities. Such features have generated new kinds of literacy
practices. Multimodality is not an exclusive feature of electronic texts, but the range
of modalities, the extent of their use, and the nature and quality of their articulation,
have significantly increased in electronic formats. The interaction of the peculiar
affordances of computer-based and networked technologies and the multimodality of
electronic format texts has the effect of multiplying potentially new literacy practices.
Because of the digital dimension of these new practices and growing access to multimodal
authoring software, individuals are now more likely to be able to be equally engaged
as constructors and consumers of textual materials, closely articulating comprehend-
ing and composing behaviours. Clearly the impact of the new technologies cannot
be understood as an add-on tool for learning and teaching literacies. Rather than trying to squeeze new technologies into familiar literacy education procedures, we need
to attend to the reality of new and emerging literacies. As in the case of curriculum
literacies, central to understanding the new dimensions of multiliteracies afforded by
information technology is meta-semiotic knowledge – understanding the systematic
nature of the digital rhetorical resources that are available to make meanings and having the meta-language to describe them. Although theoretical descriptions of digital
rhetorical systems remain in their infancy, brief comment will be made about the
nature and potential of hypertext links and windows and the relative significance of
multimodal features of cybertexts. Then, having noted the need to attend to the reality
of new and emerging literacies, it will be important to acknowledge that the conventional, hard-copy forms of 'linear' texts will continue to coexist with the textual
matrixes of electronic hypertext for some time, and that in many electronic texts, less
than optimal use is made of the potential of digital rhetorics.

   The rhetorical role of the hypertextual link is routinely regarded as a kind of
neutral 'connection', which facilitates readers being able to choose among various
permutations and combinations of 'non-linear' pathways through one or more texts. But
attention has been drawn to the need to problematize this view and develop a more
sophisticated account of the meaning-making potential of links (Foltz 1996; Burbules
1997; Kamil and Lane 1998). The use and placement of links is one of the vital ways
in which the tacit assumptions and values of the designer/author are manifested in a

hypertext – yet they are rarely considered as such (Burbules 1997: 105). Burbules proposes several categories of links based on the kinds of meanings they imply. For example, a link from a page dealing with 'political organizations' to one dealing with 'Catholic Church' could be read as a metaphor, encouraging the reader to think about politics and religion in a different way. If a page on 'human rights violations' is linked to pages on 'corporal punishment in schools', this suggests categorical inclusion.

> Links make such associations, but do so in a way that is seldom made problematic; yet because such categorical links are often the gateway that controls access to information, clustering and relating them in one way rather than another is more than a matter of convenience or heuristic – it becomes a method of determining how people think about a subject.
>
> (Burbules 1997: 113)

The use of frames or windows makes it possible to have two different texts and/or images on the screen at the same time. This provides new ways for designers/authors to structure their texts and may be considered a significant advance in the potential use of the Internet for educational purposes (Moore 1999). But again the semiotic significance of the use of and placement of these frames to achieve these parallelisms goes beyond a neutral resource for juxtaposing related information. Critical reading of digital rhetorical structures necessitates a capacity to 'make strange' or problematize the apparent 'naturalness' or 'invisibility' of the rhetorical choices designers/authors have made, questioning why certain links and juxtapositions are included and to imagine connections of a similar kind that could have been made but weren't. This requires meta-knowledge of digital rhetorical devices – such as understanding how hyperlinks are made and multiframes included; 'the more one is aware of how this is done, the more one can be aware that it was done and that it could have been done otherwise' (Burbules 1997: 119).

In view of the potential for non-linear text structuring and the inclusion of multimedia 'pages' or screens, it is remarkable that so much electronic publishing features written text and makes strong demands on conventional reading skills (Garton 1997). Nevertheless, the potential of electronic texts for enhanced multimodal presentation has had an obvious impact and it has been argued that visual literacies may be pre-eminent in negotiating multimedia electronic texts.

> The most popular and successful websites are not necessarily elaborately linked hypertexts, but they are visually interesting. Literacy in electronic environments may have more to do with the production and consumption of images than the reading and writing of either hypertextual or linear prose.
>
> (Bolter 1998: 7)

The nature, extent and rhetorical use of images in electronic publishing however, also warrants critical attention. Some literary narratives for young readers on CD

ROM use multimedia and hypertextual elements to draw the reader into the story in ways that are not available in conventional format books (James 1999). On the other hand some such narratives are replete with gratuitous hypermedia links to images and text that are at best peripheral to the story (Miller and Olsen 1998). In an investigation of science topics for primary school students (Unsworth 1999b) sections in conventional trade books were compared with presentations of the same topics on the CD ROMs: *Encarta 95* (Microsoft 1994) *The Eyewitness Encyclopedia of Science* (Kindersley 1994) and *The Way Things Work* (Macaulay 1994). There were many more, and a greater variety of images in the trade books. In some topics on some of the CD ROMs there were no images at all. On the other hand some CD ROMs on some topics provided animations that were not possible in the books. The significance of the type of animation also needs to be considered, however. For example, the *Encarta 95* CD ROM provides a realistic animation of the water cycle, but there is no synoptic, schematic diagram simultaneously depicting all stages of the water cycle. Current work comparing science explanations on CD ROM and on Internet websites suggests that learners attempting to work from less complex to more complex explanations need to adopt different reading strategies depending on the format of the material they are using. For example the *Encarta 95* CD ROM entry for the greenhouse effect presents the more technical version as the main text and the second version as a hyperlinked oral explanation accompanying an animation. On the other hand on the *USA Today* website (http://usatoday.com.weather/tg/whrmng.htm) the simpler explanation with animated images is presented first with a hyperlink to the more technical version and a more complex, static image.

In Chapter 7 sample lesson materials address the complementary use of conventional and computer-based texts in curriculum area teaching. These deal with developing critical understanding of the resources of electronic texts. They also incorporate explicit teaching of verbal and visual grammar using the meta-language drawn from systemic functional linguistic and visual analyses, which is introduced in the next section and described in detail in Chapters 2 and 3.

The challenge of alternative perspectives – critical literacies

What is involved in critical literacy defies simple definition (Lankshear 1994; Muspratt *et al.* 1997) but work from a variety of theoretical perspectives suggests a common recognition of critical literacy practices that can be distinguished from routine decoding of textual information and from compliantly participating in the established, institutionalized textual practices of a culture. These different aspects of literate practice will be categorized here as 'recognition literacy', 'reproduction literacy' and 'reflection literacy'. The relationship of these categories to those published elsewhere is indicated in Figure 1.1.

Recognition literacy involves learning to recognize and produce the verbal, visual and electronic codes that are used to construct and communicate meanings. It can also refer to the literacy practices that are very familiar to members of a culture as they

Dimensions of Literate Practice	(Green 1988)	(Freebody and Luke 1990)	(Hasan 1996)	(Macken-Horarik 1996)
Recognition	Operational	Code-breaker	Recognition	Functional
Reproduction	Cultural	Text participant Text user	Action	Reproductive
Reflection	Critical	Text analyst	Reflection	Critical

Figure 1.1 Distinguishing critical literacy – comparing typologies of literate practice

are ubiquitous and integral to common experiences of everyday life. Reproduction literacy involves understanding and producing the conventional visual and verbal text forms that construct and communicate the established systematic knowledge of cultural institutions. Reflection literacy necessitates an understanding that all social practices, and hence all literacies, are socially constructed. Because of this, literacies are selective in including certain values and understandings and excluding others. Reflection literacy means learning how to read this inclusion and exclusion. Interpreting and constructing texts entails the text analyst role, interrogating the visual and verbal codes to make explicit how the choices of language and image privilege certain viewpoints and how other choices of visual and verbal resources could construct alternative views.

This triadic categorization carries the risks of its neatness. In practice there is likely to be some degree of overlap and interweaving. Nor is the triad a simple developmental progression. Even those quite proficient in a range of literacies need to deal with code-breaking or operational mechanics in contexts of literacy practices that are novel to them. It has also been shown that quite young learners can engage productively in reflection literacies (Knobel and Healy 1998). Nevertheless, it has been argued (Hasan 1996; Macken-Horarik 1996) that, regardless of the age or experience of the learner, reflection literacy presupposes reproduction literacy, which presupposes recognition literacy. These three facets of literate practice are not linked by temporal sequence but by logical inclusion: reflection literacy includes a well-developed range of reproductive literacy practices, and these include recognition literacies, but the reverse is not the case. In Chapter 6, sample lesson materials indicate how to address these three facets of literacy with young children and in Chapters 7 and 8 examples of classroom materials indicate how they are practically managed in working with students in the upper primary or junior secondary school.

What is being increasingly recognized is the importance of meta-language in developing all three facets of literacy but particularly critical literacies (Lankshear 1997; Rassool 1999; Luke 2000). In fact, although not a sufficient resource, some argue that meta-language is a priority resource for critical literacy development.

A rudimentary working definition of critical literacy entails three aspects. First, it involves a meta-knowledge of diverse meaning systems and the socio-cultural contexts in which they are produced and embedded in everyday life. By meta-knowledge I mean having an understanding of how knowledge, ideas and information 'bits' are structured in different media and genres, and how these structures affect people's readings and uses of that information.

(Luke 2000: 72)

Since the 'critical dimension' of literate practice fundamentally involves awareness that all literacies are socially constructed (Lankshear *et al.* 2000), an essential feature of the meta-language to be adopted would seem to be a clear theoretical link between the descriptions of the visual and verbal elements of texts and how they make meanings, and their relationship to the parameters of the social contexts in which they function. This is at the heart of systemic functional linguistics and the verbal semiotic analyses extrapolated from it, contributing a sound basis for a meta-language of multiliteracies.

A META-LANGUAGE OF MULTILITERACIES

The importance of a meta-language for developing multiliteracies is very widely acknowledged, and there seems to be growing consensus about the kind of meta-language that is needed. A group of 10 academics, identifying themselves as 'The New London Group', and including members from the UK, the US and Australia addressed this issue in their proposal for a pedagogy of multiliteracies (New London Group 2000).[1] They emphasized that the meta-language needed to support a sophisticated critical analysis of language and other semiotic systems yet not make unrealistic demands on teachers and students. Above all, however, the meta-language needed to derive from a theoretical account that linked the meaning making elements and structures of semiotic systems like language and image to their use in social contexts: 'the primary purpose of the metalanguage should be to identify and explain differences between texts, and relate these to the contexts of culture and situation in which they seem to work' (New London Group 2000: 24).

This aligns with a fundamental premise of systemic functional linguistics (SFL) – the complete interconnectedness of the linguistic and the social (Halliday 1973, 1978; Halliday and Hasan 1985; Martin 1991, 1992; Hasan 1995; Halliday and Matthiessen 1999). SFL approaches the description of social context by interpreting it as two interrelated levels: context of situation and context of culture. The context of situation is the immediate context in which the language is used. The 'same' context of situation may be very different in different cultures. For example, purchasing food in a western supermarket where prices are not negotiable is quite different from purchasing fresh food in a market in Bangkok or Singapore, where bargaining is expected. Some contexts of situation are quite culture-specific. The context of culture can be thought of as the full range of systems of situational contexts that the culture embodies.

In order to be able to achieve social purposes one needs to be familiar with the ways in which culturally recognized situation types are typically structured to achieve those purposes. These structured, goal oriented social processes have been referred to by Martin as genres (Martin 1984, 1989, 1993a, 1997) and the stages or steps by which they are organized are known as their schematic structure or generic structure. For example, in visiting a local doctor in Australia, one arrives at the medical centre, approaches the receptionist, shows a medicare card, then the receptionist retrieves (or generates) a patient file, and you wait your turn in the waiting room for the doctor to emerge, greet you and take you into the consulting room. If you are writing a review of a novel or film in a junior secondary school English class in Australia, you will probably begin with a 'context' stage in which you give the cultural/historical context of the work together with a brief synopsis. The next stage will be the 'text description' in which you will introduce the main characters and summarize key incidents. The final stage will be the 'judgement' in which you will evaluate the text and make a recommendation to potential readers/viewers. (For a more elaborated introduction to the relationship between context and culture and genre and the associated meta-language see the first chapter in *Researching Language in Schools and Communities: Functional Linguistic Perspectives*, Unsworth 2000.) Specifying the genres of school literacies and identifying the stages of schematic structure that characterize these genres have been a major contribution of SFL to literacy pedagogy. The meta-language of these genres or text types and their stages are now included in mandatory school syllabuses in New South Wales (New South Wales Board of Studies 1998b) and Queensland (Queensland Department of Education 1994). Genres and school literacy development are further discussed in Chapters 5 to 8 of this book.

As well as the context of culture influencing the genres and their staging, key features of the particular context of situation are related to the grammatical and discourse forms that are used. Any context of situation is described in terms of three main variables that are important in influencing the choices that are made in the language that is used. The first of these, *Field*, is concerned with the social activity, its content or topic; the second, *Tenor*, is the nature of the relationships among the people using language; and the third, *Mode*, is the medium and role of language in the situation – whether spoken or written, accompanying or constitutive of the activity, and the ways in which relative information value is conveyed. These situational variables are related to three overarching areas of meaning – 'ideational', 'interpersonal' and 'textual' meanings. For example, if I say 'My daughter is coming home this weekend', ideationally this involves an event, a participant and the circumstances of time and place associated with it. Interpersonally it constructs me as a giver of information and the reader/listener as a receiver (as well as perhaps suggesting I have at least some acquaintance with the listener). Textually, it locates 'my daughter' as the orientation or point of departure for the interaction, simultaneously suggesting that 'my daughter' is given information that we both know about and the new information is that she is coming home 'this weekend'. If I say 'Is my daughter coming home this weekend?', the ideational meanings remain the same – the event, the participant, the circumstances have not changed – but the interpersonal meanings have certainly changed. Now I am demanding information, not giving it (and there may be some suggestion of estrangement between the listener and me). Similarly, if I say 'This weekend my daughter is coming home', the ideational meanings are still the same, but this time the textual meanings have changed. Now the orientation is the weekend and this is the given or shared information. What is new or unknown concerns what my daughter is doing. So the different structures reflect different kinds of meaning, which in turn reflect different aspects of the context. The meta-language of systemic functional grammar derives from this linking of language structure, meaning and context. Basic concepts of this grammar are outlined in Chapter 2. Its use in distinguishing curriculum area literacies is explained in Chapter 4 and in interpreting literature for children in Chapter 5. Then the incorporation of this grammar in teaching is demonstrated in Chapter 6 in work with young children, in Chapter 7 in teaching in curriculum areas and in Chapter 8 in enhancing teaching in the English classroom.

Extrapolating from systemic functional descriptions of language, researchers have developed a corresponding functional account of 'visual grammar' (Kress and van Leeuwen 1990, 1996; O'Toole 1994; Lemke 1998b). This work recognizes that images, like language, realize not only representations of *material reality* but also the interpersonal interaction of *social reality* (such as relations between viewers and what is viewed). The work also recognizes that images cohere into textual compositions in different ways and so realize *semiotic reality*. More technically, functional semiotic accounts of images adopt from systemic functional linguistics the meta-functional organization of meaning-making resources:

- *representational/ideational* structures verbally and visually construct the nature of events, the objects and participants involved, and the circumstances in which they occur;
- *interactive/interpersonal* verbal and visual resources construct the nature of relationships among speakers/listeners, writers/readers, and viewers and what is viewed;
- *compositional/textual* meanings are concerned with the distribution of the information value or relative emphasis among elements of the text and image.

The basic concepts of the functionally oriented 'grammar of visual design' proposed by Kress and van Leeuwen (1990, 1996) are described in Chapter 3. Their use in interpreting literature for children is explained in Chapter 5, the incorporation of visual literacy into teaching is demonstrated in Chapter 6 in work with young children, in Chapter 7 in teaching in curriculum areas and in Chapter 8 in enhancing teaching in the English classroom.

The New London Group (2000: 24) indicated that what is needed to support a pedagogy of multiliteracies is

an educationally accessible functional grammar; that is, a metalanguage that describes meaning in various realms. These include the textual and the visual, as well as the multimodal relations between different meaning-making processes that are now so critical in media texts and the texts of electronic multimedia.

The descriptions of verbal and visual grammar used in this book clearly address these requirements. Current research is developing functionally oriented intermodal descriptions relating visual and verbal semiotic resources (O'Halloran 1999; van Leeuwen 2000; Martin in press) as well as those relating to movement (Martinec 1999), sound and music (van Leeuwen 1999). This work will extend and enhance the current visual and verbal bases of a meta-language of multiliteracies as described here.

MULTILITERACIES AND MANAGING CLASSROOM PRACTICE

In dealing with the practicalities of implementing multiliteracies in learning and teaching, three dimensions of classroom learning contexts will be addressed. These are the knowledge dimension, the pedagogic dimension and the multiliteracies dimension. The multiliteracies dimension has been outlined in the previous sections and will be further developed in the next four chapters. In this section the knowledge and pedagogic dimensions will be briefly outlined. The three dimensions will be brought together in the context of sample classroom programs in the final three chapters of the book.

The knowledge dimension distinguishes among informal, systematic and transformative knowledge. Informal or commonsense knowledge is the understanding individuals develop largely incidentally through personal and/or communal experience. Knowledge of this kind is often passed on through casual interaction or at points of perceived need and is frequently also acquired through observation and trial and error. It may and may not be accurate, but it is the knowledge students often bring to school learning situations. Systematic knowledge is the specialized learning of societal institutions reflected in the content of formal school curricula. It includes the fundamental concepts and hegemonic perspectives within recognized disciplines like maths, science, geography, history, economics, etc. Systematic knowledge builds up an alternative construction of reality alongside that of commonsense experience. Transformative knowledge initially involves questioning the taken-for-grantedness of systematic knowledge, understanding that what appears to be the 'natural' view of phenomena is actually a view produced by particular combinations of historical, social, political influences, and that alternative combinations of these influences could produce different views. Transformative knowledge extends beyond critique, however, to a remaking of understanding emerging from the negotiation of conflicting and complementary perspectives. The result may be enduring tension rather than resolution, but it is transformative knowledge that leads to new understandings and the potential for social action. Classroom work needs to address all aspects of the knowledge dimension for all students. These kinds of knowledge are constructed and communicated by multiliteracies practices and it is the pedagogic dimension of classroom learning contexts that articulates students' access to the intersections of multiliteracies and learning and hence to different kinds of knowledge.

The pedagogic dimension involves the strategic use of student-centred, discovery learning as well as teacher directed, overt teaching and intermediate guided investigations of various kinds. Managing classroom learning also includes designing learning experiences based on collaborative small group activities, individual independent work and common whole class tasks. The teacher at times will be a facilitator and guide or a co-researcher, but at other times will be an authoritative (but not authoritarian) leader and direct instructor. Initial work on a topic for example may involve sharing of informal knowledge, observations, and opportunities and suggestions for extending understanding. This may be highly student-centred and exploratory but as the teacher begins to bridge toward negotiating more systematic knowledge, the pedagogic dimension shifts to more guided investigation and direct instruction. On the basis of students' greater familiarity with systematic knowledge of the topic, the teacher then moves to emphasize more critical framing to provoke critical questioning by students and a shift toward transformative knowledge. This kind of work may entail more collaborative group work and independent research and may also require a shift back to more student-centred, student-initiated learning. As the classroom work progresses through these phases, teaching is differentiated to optimize the engagement of all students in essentially the same learning tasks. This means sophisticated planning and preparation. It might include providing scaffolded learning guides for some students. It could also involve grouping students with high support needs together to 'prime' their understanding of subsequent tasks through direct teaching while more proficient learners operate independently, then regrouping students heterogeneously so that highly proficient students and high support students are able to work productively together on collaborative tasks. These kinds of articulations are explained more fully in the Curriculum Area Multiliteracies and Learning (CAMAL) framework and accompanying examples of classroom work detailed in the final three chapters.

NOTE

1 Courtney Cazden (Harvard, USA); Bill Cope (University of Technology, Sydney); Norman Fairclough (Lancaster University, UK); Jim Gee (Clark University, USA); Mary Kalantzis (James Cook University of North Queensland); Gunther Kress (University of London, UK); Allan Luke (University of Queensland); Carmen Luke (University of Queensland); Sarah Michaels (Clark University, USA); Martin Nakata (James Cook University of North Queensland).

PART II

Facilitating knowledge

CHAPTER 2

Learning about language as a resource for literacy development

INTRODUCTION

At the same time as governments in the United Kingdom and Australia have mandated the teaching of grammar in school curricula, linguists, teacher educators and innovative teachers have generated a fresh and inviting perspective on the nature and role of grammar in teaching. The use of systemic functional descriptions of English grammar has formed the basis of very significant advances in the theory and practice of literacy development and English teaching. The melding of functional and traditional descriptions of English grammar is evident in Australian syllabuses, e.g. New South Wales English K–6 (New South Wales Board of Studies 1998b) and Queensland English 1–10 Frameworks (Queensland Department of Education 1994), and is eminently applicable to the National Curriculum in the United Kingdom and its implementation frameworks like 'The Literacy Hour' (DfEE 1998).

The purpose of this chapter is to provide an introduction to basic concepts of systemic functional grammar, relating these to more traditional grammatical descriptions and to the types of texts (genres) children need to negotiate in school curricula. The grammatical descriptions provided here are not intended to be comprehensive accounts of systemic functional descriptions of English grammar (for more detailed coverage see Eggins 1994; Halliday 1994b; Bloor and Bloor 1995; Matthiessen 1995; Thomson 1996; Derewianka 1998). The level of detail in the discussion of systemic functional grammar in this chapter is intended to provide a sufficient basis for showing how it can resource an enhanced approach to addressing the grammatical requirements of current mandatory syllabuses in school systems. What we want to show is the usefulness of these grammar descriptions in facilitating literacy learning and teaching. This will be initiated here by using examples of children's writing and excerpts from books and other texts for children to illustrate the language descriptions. (For related reading on the application of this grammar to literacy teaching see Williams 1993;

Collerson 1994, 1997; Butt *et al.* 1995; Polias 1998; Unsworth 2000). Subsequent chapters will show how the grammatical concepts and genre descriptions are incorporated into teaching/learning activities.

WHY IS GRAMMAR ALWAYS SO CONTROVERSIAL?

There are two broad dimensions to persistent controversy surrounding English grammar and its teaching in schools. The first is a belief among some powerful groups that there is a 'standard' grammatical form of English, which is considered 'correct' English, and that public use of English should adhere to this 'correct' grammatical form. It is assumed that use of grammatical forms that depart from this standard will erode the language. Such fears have been voiced almost continuously from the early seventeenth century (see Carter 1990 and Sealey 1996 for accounts of this 'complaint' tradition in the history of the study and teaching of grammar). Historical and contemporary expressions of this view have sometimes aligned lack of attention to 'correct' grammar with a general decline in standards of behaviour and social discipline. Under the influence of these kinds of views the traditional teaching of grammar insisted on adherence to the grammatical conventions of formal written English regardless of the context of language use. The traditional teaching of grammar, sustained by textbooks and successive generations of teachers, included many grammatical rules that were not consistent with widely accepted common usage (Martin and Rothery 1993; Collerson 1997). These included:

- You *can*not use the word *can* to seek permission. The word *may* is used in seeking permission.
- A preposition is something you should never end a sentence *with*.
- It is quite wrong *to carelessly split* infinitives.
- *And* you should never begin a sentence with a conjunction.

But, as Geoff Williams points out, such rules are often honoured more in the breach than the observance in well established literary texts;[1] for example:

from Shakespeare's *Macbeth*:

Banquo:	Were such things here as we do speak about?
	Or have we eaten of the insane root
	That takes the reason prisoner!
Macbeth:	Your children shall be kings.
Banquo:	You shall be king.
Macbeth:	**And** thane of Cawdor too: went it not so?

from Nadine Gordimer – 'The defeated' in 'Why haven't you written?' (1972): (Gordimer is a South African writer and recipient of the Nobel Prize for Literature).

My mother didn't want me to go near the Concession stores because they smelled, and were dirty, and the natives spat tuberculosis germs into the dust. She said it was no place for little girls.

But I used to go down there sometimes, in the afternoon, when static four o'clock held the houses of our Mine, and the sun washed over them like the sea over sandcastles.

Unfortunately, these kinds of 'rules' are still being enforced in many currently marketed traditional grammar workbooks for primary school children – often with 'basic skills' somewhere in the title. For example:

7 **Like** is never a **conjunction**.

He walks **like** I do. (wrong – like is used here as a conjunction)
He walks **as** I do. (correct – as is a conjunction)
My cousin looks **like** me (right – like is a preposition)

(Howard 1993)

To critique these kinds of rules is not to say that use of the conventions of the grammar of formal or 'standard' English has no social consequence. Let's take the convention of agreement between subject and verb in terms of person and number, as shown in the following example:

I am going to start a course in customer relations.

The next two versions of this statement demonstrate lack of the conventional subject/verb agreement:

I are going to start a course in customer relations.
I is going to start a course in customer relations.

Anyone who said or wrote one of these versions would very probably find that this kind of grammatical usage would inhibit their employment or advancement prospects in certain commercial contexts. What counts as 'correct' grammar and how this might vary in different contexts of language use then, remains a somewhat vexed issue.

The second broad dimension to the controversy about English grammar teaching is a history of research suggesting that it has no effect on students' results in written composition or their ability to interpret texts (Braddock *et al.* 1963; Elley *et al.* 1976; Hillocks and Smith 1991). The following statement is indicative:

School boards, administrators, and teachers who impose the systematic study of traditional school grammar on their students over lengthy periods of time in the name of teaching writing do them a gross disservice which should not be tolerated by anyone concerned with the effective teaching of good writing.

(Hillocks 1986: 248, quoted in Hillocks and Smith 1991: 596)

Until the 1990s this view was reflected in many syllabus documents and in teaching practice, which eschewed the teaching of grammar. However, in a number of Australian states in the early 1990s, syllabus documents re-emphasized the explicit teaching of grammar and the current 'National Literacy Strategy' mandated in the United Kingdom (DfEE 1998) represents a return to the teaching of aspects of traditional school grammar. The controversy remains however. Some still resist the systematic and explicit teaching of any kind of grammar, and others accept the teaching of traditional grammar as a statutory requirement. However, advocates of a relatively new form of grammar – a meaning-oriented, functional grammar developed principally by Professor Michael Halliday (1973, 1985, 1994a) – have proposed changes to the teaching of traditional school grammar in the light of these functional grammatical descriptions of language developed since the 1960s. These were the kinds of changes developed in the Language in the National Curriculum (LINC) materials in the United Kingdom (Carter 1990), which were not adopted by the British government. They are the kinds of changes that have been an integral basis for the Queensland State English 1–10 syllabus for schools adopted in 1994 (Queensland Department of Education 1994). They are also the kinds of changes that were integral to New South Wales English K–6 syllabus published in 1994, but then revised in 1998 (New South Wales Board of Studies 1998b) in favour of a melding of both new functional and traditional school grammar. The intense public and professional interest in debates about the teaching of grammar in schools is evident in the media whenever any kind of change to the curriculum is mooted. What is crucial is that these debates are informed by ongoing developments in linguistic and educational research so that practices in schools can benefit from our evolving understanding of grammar as a meaning-making resource and how it is best mediated to students.

WHAT ARE CLAUSES IN ENGLISH?

In the grammatical analysis of texts both functional and traditional approaches make use of categories of language like 'clause', 'group' or 'phrase' and 'word'. Here we will provide very basic information about the nature of clauses. More detailed accounts from the perspective of traditional grammar abound (see for example Quirk and Greenbaum 1993) and as well there are a large number of detailed accounts from the perspective of functional grammar (Collerson 1994; Eggins 1994; Halliday 1994a; Bloor and Bloor 1995). Our approach will be to accommodate the more traditional grammatical orientation of some syllabus documents and at the same time to indicate how this can be enhanced by a functional orientation to grammar (Derewianka 1998).

Clauses, clause complexes and types of sentences

A clause is a pattern of wording built up around a verb. Informally we can think of the concept of a verb in terms of some kind of process. That process might be material action (run, fix, shut); some kind of mental event (understand, hear, see, hate, adore); or some kind of process of relating as in 'A kangaroo is a mammal'; 'A koala is not a bear'; 'A spider has eight legs'. The process, expressed by a verb or verbal group, is the nucleus of the clause and one or more participants may be associated with the process. In the clause 'A spider has eight legs', the verb 'has' expresses the relational process of possession and the participants are 'A spider' and 'eight legs'.

A process may have circumstances (adverbs or adverbial phrases) as well as participants associated with it. For example,

Feral cats hunt indigenous species in the bushland at night.

The verb 'hunt' is the nucleus of the clause, the participants are 'Feral cats' and 'indigenous species' and the circumstances are 'at night' and 'in the bushland'. Clauses like these can exist by themselves as simple sentences. They are referred to as independent clauses:

Jumping spiders have extremely good eyesight.

Clauses can also combine:

Jumping spiders have extremely good eyesight ‖ and can judge distances well.
Mother spiders guard the eggs ‖ or wrap them in a protective web or in a silken cocoon.

In this case the clauses are joined by coordination and you cannot reverse the order of the clauses. When clauses are joined by coordination, both clauses are said to be independent. Clauses joined in this way are called clause complexes. Clause complexes joined by coordination form compound sentences.

Clauses can also be joined by subordination:

When a predator attacks, ‖ a spider runs down into its burrow.
Because the eucalypt forests are being destroyed, ‖ the Australian koala is endangered.

In this case you can reverse the order of the clauses:

A spider runs down into its burrow, ‖ when a predator attacks.
The Australian koala is endangered, ‖ because the eucalypt forests are being destroyed.

Clauses joined by subordination are also clause complexes and they form complex sentences. The clauses beginning with conjunctions like 'when' and 'because' are known as dependent or subordinate clauses and the clauses without the conjunctions are known as the independent or principal clauses.

Sometimes sentences contain several clauses – some joined by coordination and some by subordination:

When a spider is touched, ‖ it runs down into its burrow ‖ and presents its 'shield' to the attacker.

Finite and non-finite clauses

In the examples used so far all of the clauses have the process located in the present with respect to the time of speaking – they are in the present tense. Of course processes can also be located in the past with respect to the time of speaking – in the past tense (The spider ate the fly), or in the future (The frog will eat the spider). (For an account of more complex tense selections see Halliday 1994a: 200–7.) But not all processes have this indication of tense. Processes expressed by verbs consisting of the 'ing' form only, do not indicate tense. Consider the following examples:

Hiding near the web with a signal thread, ‖ the spider detects its prey.
Hiding near the web with a signal thread, ‖ the spider detected its prey.
Hiding near the web with a signal thread, ‖ the spider will detect its prey.

The clause containing the 'ing' verb is non-finite. It depends on the second clause for location in time with respect to the time of speaking. It is the second clause in each case that signals the tense as present, past or future.
    Another form of non-finite clause is where the process is expressed by the verb form of the 'to + lexical verb' type.

To make the web, ‖ the spider works for many hours.
To make the web, ‖ the spider worked for many hours.
To make the web, ‖ the spider will work for many hours.

Both types of non-finite clause may be found together with a finite one in a text:

To make the web, ‖ the spider works for many hours, ‖ moving from branch to branch.

Included clauses

Included clauses are those that 'interrupt' another clause:

The spider, having sprayed its prey with a mixture of poison and gum from its fangs, walks up to its victim and kills it with its bite.

In this sentence there are three clauses:

1 The spider walks up to its victim
2 having sprayed its prey with a mixture of poison and gum from its fangs
3 and kills it with its bite.

The second clause interrupts the first clause. The convention for displaying this when analysing texts using functional grammar is << >>, so the clauses in this example would be shown as follows:

The spider, <<having sprayed its prey with a mixture of poison and gum from its fangs>>, walks up to its victim || and kills it with its bite.

1 The spider <<2>> walks up to its victim
2 <<having sprayed its prey with a mixture of poison and gum from its fangs>>
3 and kills it with its bite.

Clauses quoting and reporting

In many narrative texts authors rely on *quoting* and *reporting* what characters say and think. This usually occurs in a sentence consisting of two or more clauses (a clause complex).

'Did you really pay a hundred thousand for the house?' ‖ he said.	Quoting speech
'Snoopy little fellow,' ‖ Elaine *thought* angrily.	Quoting thought
My dad says ‖ you were taken for a ride.	Reporting speech
Elaine *realized* ‖ that he would be hard to shake off.	Reporting thought

BELOW THE CLAUSE

The clause itself has component parts. These are called groups or phrases

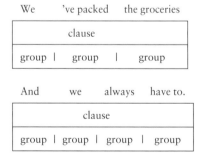

These groups or phrases in turn are made up of words. That is,

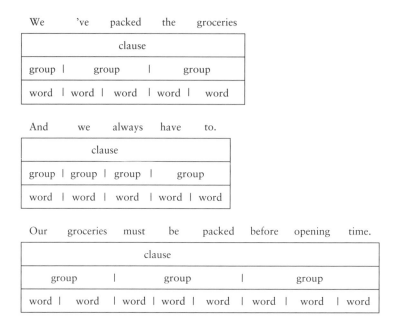

These units (clause, group/phrase and word) form the *rank scale*, the hierarchical arrangement of grammatical constituents. Clauses are made up of groups and phrases, which are made up of words. Below the rank of word, it is also possible to look at morphemes, that is, the component structures of words, but we will not pursue that level of analysis here.

One complication to the notion of rank is that of *rankshift*, also called *embedding*. This occurs when a unit of one rank is itself made up of a unit from the same rank or from the rank above. Consider the nominal group, 'Your investment in Telstra shares'. Notice that both the nominal group 'Your investment' and the prepositional phrase 'in Telstra shares' define the entity being referred to. They belong together. Here is a prepositional phrase acting inside a nominal group. The prepositional phrase has been rankshifted to form part of a complex nominal group. Clauses can also be rankshifted. Consider the clause,

The suit I bought for my brother's wedding is now very old-fashioned.

What is very old-fashioned? – 'The suit I bought for my brother's wedding'. This is the nominal group required to identify the entity in question. But this nominal group has an embedded or rankshifted clause ('I bought for my brother's wedding') as part of it. Double brackets are used to indicate such clauses in analyses: 'The suit [[I bought for my brother's wedding]] is very old-fashioned'. (for further information on embedding or rankshift see Eggins 1994; Halliday 1994a; Matthiessen 1995; Ravelli 2000).

Grammatical units are identified in two ways: by class and by function. The class of a unit refers to the formal characteristics of that unit, the patterns it enters into. Major word classes include the following:

verb: is, receive, make, do, declare, pop . . .
noun: week, customers, invitation, St George, envelope, box . . .
adjective: eligible, genuine, special, best, friendly . . .
adverb: simply, always, importantly, possibly, really . . .
determiner: a, the, this . . .
numeral: one, two, first, second . . .
pronoun: we, it, you, us, your, our . . .
preposition: in, at, of, as, for, before . . .
conjunction: because, and, or . . .

Some words belong to more than one class, thus 'pack' could be a verb ('we pack our groceries') or a noun ('his pack was very heavy'), so it can be necessary to refer to context in order to identify class.

Many of the word classes have equivalent classes at group and phrase rank; for example:

verbal group: have made; will pack; must be packed . . .
nominal (noun) group: his pack; all perishable discounted groceries . . .
prepositional phrase: before opening time; in paper bags; at the counter . . .

Identifying grammatical units by class, however, enables us to say very little about meaning. Compare the following examples, which have been identified in terms of their group classes:

The plantlife	grew	abundantly.
nominal group	verbal group	adverbial group

Pollution	killed	the plantlife.
nominal group	verbal group	nominal group

In both examples, 'the plantlife' is a nominal group, but the groups are playing different roles. In the first example, 'the plantlife' is the responsible element, the one actually doing the action; in the second, it is the object of the action. The label 'nominal group' does not allow us to draw the distinction; additional labelling is necessary, in terms of representing the *function* of the constituent in constructing meaning. Functional labels are an interpretation of meaning, and so can only be analysed in context; out of context, it is impossible to say what the function of 'the plantlife' would be (although it's possible to suggest a range of alternatives). Traditional grammar certainly entails a smattering of functional labelling (such as subject and object), but this kind of labelling still does not distinguish, in the examples below, the kinds of processes the children are engaged in, or the kinds of roles they are fulfilling.

The children	loved	the stories.
nominal group	verbal group	nominal group
subject	verbal group	object

The children	built	a cubbyhouse.
nominal group	verbal group	nominal group
subject	verbal group	object

A more informative kind of functional labelling is required. In the following section we will show that, simultaneous with class information and traditional grammatical labelling, there can be up to three sets of functional labels, in order to draw out the full meaning potential of a clause. This results in a complex grammar, but the complexity is well worth the effort because it enables detailed analyses of language, which are focused on meaning. (Systemic functional grammar also provides functional labelling of the components of groups and phrases, that is at the word level, but space does not permit discussion here. For further information see Halliday 1994a and for application to teaching see Unsworth 1997b.)

HOW DOES THE GRAMMATICAL STRUCTURE OF LANGUAGE REFLECT ITS SOCIAL CONTEXT?

Systemic functional grammar is based on a view of the complete interconnectedness between the grammatical structures people select in using language and key variables of the situation in which they are using the language. These situational variables are field, tenor and mode.

Field refers to the subject matter, or activity of which the language is a part. Examples of fields are tennis, rock music, genetic engineering, Tudor England, futures trading etc. The meaning dimension associated with field is known as ideational meaning. Ideational meanings concern entities and their relationships, events in which they are involved and the circumstances that obtain. The ideational meanings in all fields are modelled in these terms, but the entities, events etc. involved in one field like chemistry are obviously different from the entities, events etc. involved in other fields like cricket or music. Sometimes fields overlap, so some of the entities, events and circumstances, in baseball and cricket for example, are the same (bat, run, catch). In systemic functional grammar, the grammatical system that realizes these categories of ideational meaning is known as the transitivity system. It consists of participants, processes and circumstances as shown in the following analysis:

Feral cats	kill	many small indigenous animals	in the bushland	every night.
Participant	Process	Participant	Circumstance	Circumstance

They	are	a pest.
Participant	Process	Participant

A lot of nature-lovers	detest	these cats.
Participant	Process	Participant

This basic analysis can be refined to show the different types of processes and the particular functional roles of the participants distinctively associated with each of these process types, as shown in the following more detailed analysis of the feral cats text:

Feral cats	kill	many small indigenous animals	in the bushland	every night.
Actor	Process: material	Goal	Circumstance: location in space	Circumstance: location in time

They	are	a pest.
Carrier	Process: relational	Attribute

A lot of nature-lovers	detest	these cats.
Senser	Process: mental	Phenomenon

Tenor refers to the nature of the relationships among the people involved in using the language. These relationships include their roles as information givers or demanders and their roles in using language to provide or demand goods and services. It also includes their status as subordinate/superior, novice/expert, the relative power that participants have in the context of situation, the extent of their contact and the nature of the affective relations among them. The dimension of meaning associated with tenor is known as interpersonal meaning. Interpersonal meanings are mainly realized grammatically by the systems of mood and modality. For example, in the feral cats text above, the writer/speaker is providing information. Grammatically this means that the finite element of the verbal group follows the subject of the clause:

Feral cats	k-	ill	many small indigenous animals	in the bushland	every night.
Subject	Finite[2]	Predicator	Complement	Adjunct	Adjunct

If the relationship between the writer/speaker and the reader/listener changed so that the writer/speaker were demanding instead of giving information, the finite element of the verb would precede the subject. In the case of the feral cats example, the finite is then no longer conflated with the lexical verb:

Do	Feral cats	kill	many small indigenous animals	in the bushland	every night?
Finite	Subject	Predicator	Complement	Adjunct	Adjunct

When the writer/speaker is giving information about feral cats, she or he adopts the view that the veracity of this information is unproblematic. If the writer/speaker wanted to qualify his or her position on this, a modal adjunct may be introduced:

Feral cats	probably	k-	ill	many small indigenous animals	in the bushland	every night.
Subject	Mood Adjunct	Finite	Predicator	Complement	Adjunct	Adjunct

This could also be achieved by the use of a modal verb:

Feral cats	may	kill	many small indigenous animals	in the bushland	every night.
Subject	Finite: modal	Predicator	Complement	Adjunct	Adjunct

Notice that these changes to the grammar realizing interpersonal meaning do not change the ideational meanings of the text, so we can analyse the text simultaneously for transitivity and for mood and modality to show the realization of the ideational and interpersonal meanings respectively. In the following examples the ideational meanings and the transitivity analysis remain the same but the interpersonal meanings and the mood analysis is different:

Feral cats	k-	ill	many small indigenous animals	in the bushland	every night.
Subject	Finite	Predicator	Complement	Adjunct	Adjunct
Actor	Process: material		Goal	Circumstance: location in space	Circumstance: location in time

Feral cats	may	kill	many small indigenous animals	in the bushland	every night.
Subject	Finite: modal	Predicator	Complement	Adjunct	Adjunct
Actor	Process: material		Goal	Circumstance: location in space	Circumstance: location in time

Mode is concerned with a number of factors such as the physical channel used for communication (graphic/aural) and the medium or the extent to which the language uses the grammatical forms conventionally culturally associated with each channel. Mode then, accounts for the differences that result from communicating face-to-face, rather than over distance or in writing. The dimension of meaning associated with mode is known as textual meaning. One of the issues involved in textual meaning is how the information value of elements of the communication is indicated. In face-to-face communication these kinds of emphases can be achieved intonationally. In written English a principal grammatical resource for this purpose is word order. Here we will consider how the writer indicates his/her point of departure, orienting the reader to what the clause is 'about'. In English this is achieved by location at the beginning of the clause and is referred to as the Theme/Rheme system in systemic functional grammar. In the feral cats text the Theme is feral cats – this is what the clauses are 'about':

Feral cats	kill many small indigenous animals in the bushland every night.
Theme	Rheme

They	are a pest.
Theme	Rheme

Notice however, that if we change the Theme in the first clause, the orientation is quite different. The text is now 'about' the bushland of which the activity of feral cats is one feature.

In the bushland	feral cats kill many small indigenous animals every night.
Theme	Rheme

Again notice that this change in textual meaning does not change the ideational or interpersonal meaning.

In systemic functional grammar then, we always have three distinctive analyses of each clause – transitivity, mood and modality, and Theme/Rheme.

	Feral cats	k-	ill	many small indigenous animals	in the bushland	every night.
Transitivity	Actor	Process: material		Goal	Circumstance: location in space	Circumstance: location in time
Mood and Modality	Subject	Finite	Predicator	Complement	Adjunct	Adjunct
Theme/ Rheme	Theme	Rheme				

These grammatical analyses indicate the realization of different dimensions of meaning – ideational meaning, interpersonal meaning and textual meaning. These dimensions of meaning derive from the the key variables in the social context of the language use – field, tenor and mode. The interrelationships among grammar, semantics and social contextual variables are represented in Figure 2.1.

Language bridges from the cultural meanings of social context (with its contextual variables of field, tenor and mode, reflecting the institutional activities, the social hierarchies and role relationships, and the related use of language within these) to sound or writing. It does this by moving from higher orders of abstraction to lower ones. These orders of abstraction are organized into three levels or strata – semantics, lexicogrammar and phonology (or graphology). The stratal role of semantics is that of an interface between social context and lexicogrammar: ideational meanings realize field, interpersonal meanings realize tenor, and textual meanings realize mode.

Lexicogrammar is a resource for wording meanings, that is realizing them as configurations of lexical and grammatical items. Textual meanings, construing mode, are realized largely by the grammatical systems of theme and information focus. Interpersonal

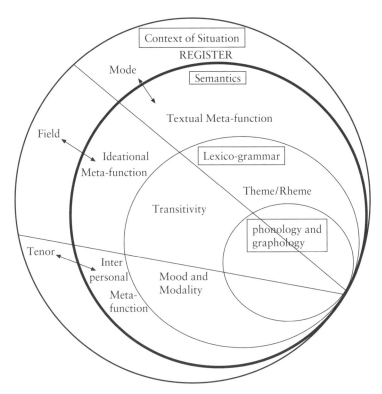

Figure 2.1   Language and register

meanings, construing tenor, are realized by the grammatical systems of mood and modality. Ideational meanings are realized grammatically by the system of transitivity. We will now describe each of these three grammatical systems and how they are used to analyse texts.

HOW DOES FUNCTIONAL GRAMMAR MODEL EXPERIENTIAL MEANING?

We have considered briefly how functional grammar models experiential meaning in terms of participants, processes and circumstances. In this section we will look in more detail at how the grammatical system of transitivity constructs the reality of the material and mental worlds we experience through language (example texts for analyses are taken or derived from Katherine Paterson's novel *Bridge to Terabithia* (1977) and a number of factual texts for children).

As well as analysing experience into its component parts and combining these into configurations of processes, participants and circumstances, the grammar of

Domain of experience	Process type	Example
Consciousness – internal – external	mental verbal	You have just *seen* a number of sources of sound. We *say* the air is saturated.
Doing and happening	material	As the prong *moves* outwards ...
Being and having	relational	Coal *is* another important biochemical sedimentary rock. Microscopes *have* two lens systems.

Figure 2.2   Major process types in systemic functional grammar

experiential meaning also classifies the world into domains of experience such as consciousness, happening and doing, and being and having. In the grammar of transitivity, the system Process Type is concerned with the particular domain of experience of processes. Figure 2.2 illustrates the classification of process types noted in Matthiessen (1995: 203).

We will distinguish two further subcategories of process types discussed by Halliday (1994a) – *behavioural* processes and *existential* processes. The domain of experience of behavioural processes is that of physiological or psychological behaviour and grammatically they are intermediate between material and mental or verbal processes.

behavioural *Look at* the prong of the tuning fork.
         Listen to the sound it makes.

Existential processes assert directly the existence of something. The most common form is 'There is . . .' The other obvious realization is the verb 'exist'.

existential On the moon or in space *there is* not air (or any other substance) to carry the sound.
         A whole city in miniature *exists* in a pond.

The Process is the 'nucleus' of the clause. The selection of the Process determines the types of Participants. Each Process type has its own particular set of Participants. Circumstances, however are independent of Process type and hence the same Circumstances can occur with different Process types. However some types of Circumstance occur more frequently with a specific process type than others (for example Circumstances of matter occur more frequently with Verbal Processes – 'They talked about their families'). The types of Circumstances are illustrated in Figure 2.3.

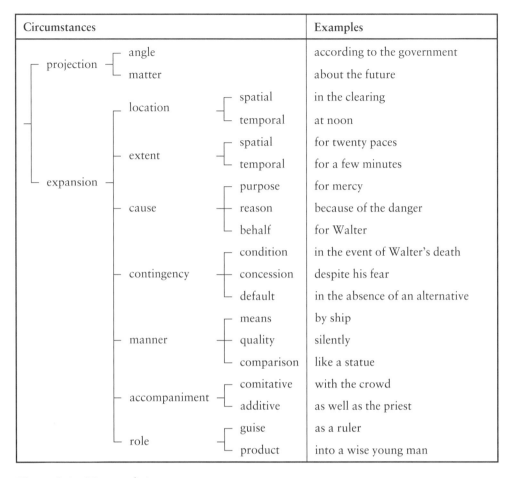

Circumstances			Examples
projection	angle		according to the government
	matter		about the future
expansion	location	spatial	in the clearing
		temporal	at noon
	extent	spatial	for twenty paces
		temporal	for a few minutes
	cause	purpose	for mercy
		reason	because of the danger
		behalf	for Walter
	contingency	condition	in the event of Walter's death
		concession	despite his fear
		default	in the absence of an alternative
	manner	means	by ship
		quality	silently
		comparison	like a statue
	accompaniment	comitative	with the crowd
		additive	as well as the priest
	role	guise	as a ruler
		product	into a wise young man

Figure 2.3 Types of circumstances

The main Process types are: material, mental, verbal, behavioural, relational, and existential. We will discuss each of these in turn and the participant roles associated with them.

Material processes

- one participant – Actor

May Belle	was standing	in the kitchen door.
Actor	Process:material	Circ:location:space

- two participants – Actor, Goal

Jess	pushed	his damp hair		out of his face.
Actor	Process:material	Goal		Circ:loc:space

He	dumped	two spoonfuls of sugar	into his cup.
Actor	Process:material	Goal	Circ:loc:space

- additional participants – Beneficiary (Recipient/Client)

Thy right arm	hast given	us	the victory.
Actor	Process:material	Beneficiary:Recipient	Goal

Get	me	a shirt	May Belle.
Process:material	Beneficiary: Client	Goal	Vocative (interpersonal) – not part of transitivity

Notice that the Beneficiary role can occur with a preposition:

Get a shirt for me, May Belle.
Thy right arm has given the victory to us.

But these are not Circumstances because they can occur without the preposition and can be the Subject. For example the last clause can be reformulated as:

We have been given the victory by thy right arm.

Now, if we add a 'tag question' to that clause it indicates the Subject:

We have been given the victory by thy right arm, haven't we?

'We' is the Subject, because it is 'picked up' in the tag question. So, since 'us' can be made into a Subject, it is a participant, in this case a Beneficiary, and not a Circumstance.

- additional participants – Range

He'd	play	football	until Christmas	and
Actor	Process:material	Range: Process	Circ:extent:time	

baseball	until June	with the rest of the big guys.
Range: Process	Circ:extent:time	Circ: accompaniment

In this case the Range is the name of the actual Process. There is no such thing as football without the playing of it. This is the same as 'take a bath', 'do a dance' etc. The Range can also be the domain over which the Process takes place:

Leslie ran the full length of the cow paddock.[3]

Here 'the full length of the cow paddock' is the Range:Entity.

Mental processes

• cognitive

He	couldn't remember
Senser	Pro:mental:cognition

• perceptive

where	he	'd heard	that one.
Circ:loc:space	Senser	Pro:mental: perception	Phenomenon

• reactive

Jess	didn't like	his older sisters' behaviour[4]
Senser	Pro:mental: reaction	Phenomenon

Verbal processes

Verbal Processes may be used to project or report a locution:

• Project locution

but instead		she	said
Conjunctive – not part of transitivity		Sayer	Process:Verbal

you	shouldn't ought to beat	me	in the head.
Actor	Pro:material	Goal	Circ:loc:space

Who	do	we	thank
Goal		Actor	
	Process:		material

he	whispered.
Sayer	Process:Verbal

- report locution

she	said
Sayer	Process:Verbal

that		he	shouldn't ought to beat	her	in the head.
Textual – not part of transitivity		Actor	Pro:material	Goal	Circ:loc:space

- additional participants – Verbiage

She	shouted	a warning.
Sayer	Pro:Verbal	Verbiage

He	whispered	a question.
Sayer	Pro:Verbal	Verbiage

Note that the Verbiage is a speech act – story, joke, poem, lie etc.

- additional participants – Receiver

She	shouted	him	a warning.
Sayer	Process:Verbal	Receiver	Verbiage

He	whispered	a question	to her.
Sayer	Process:Verbal	Verbiage	Receiver

- passive form

He	was shouted	a warning	by her.
Receiver	Process:Verbal	Verbiage	Sayer

Behavioural processes

These are 'in between' Material and Mental/Verbal processes. They are Mental/Verbal processes as physical activity. Behavioural processes require a human participant (or a participant endowed with consciousness), but unlike Mental processes, they realize ongoing activity with the present continuous rather than the simple present tense: 'I'm watching the cricket on TV' **not** 'I watch the cricket on TV' (indicates habitual rather than ongoing).

Behavioural processes also cannot report ideas and facts: 'I watched that they came late.'

His mother	was looking	now.
Behaver	Pro:Behavioural	Circ:loc:time

Jess	tried not to smile.
Behaver	Pro:Behavioural

Existential processes

These indicate the existence of something. The most common form is 'There + is . . .'

There	wasn't	a muscle in his body that didn't ache.
	Process:Existential	Existent

There are two main types of Relational Process:

1 attributive type – classifies or describes a participant;
2 identifying type – defines or identifies a participant uniquely.

We will deal first with the attributive type.

Relational attributive processes

There are three subtypes in this category:

- intensive

classifying

and	he	(was)		only	a fourth grader.
▮	Carrier	Pro:Rel:intensive:attributive		▮	Attribute

describing

Lord	he	was		tired.
▮	Carrier	Pro:Rel:intensive:attributive		Attribute

- circumstantial

but	this year	Wayne Pettis	would be	in the sixth grade.
▮	Circ:loc:time	Carrier	Pro:rel:intensive: attributive	Attribute/Circumstance

perhaps	Terabithia	was	like a castle ...
▮	Carrier	Pro:rel:intens:attrib	Attribute/Circumstance

- possessive

Jess	had	a little sister, May Belle.[5]
Possessor	Pro:relational:possessive:attributive	Possessed

Some verbs other than the verb 'to be' may function as an attributive process:

become	Jess and Leslie became inseparable.
turn	He turned pale.
grow	In Terabithia you grew strong.
turn out	The day turned out badly.
start out	They started out enemies.
end up	He ended up very confident.
keep	She kept quiet.
stay	The dog stayed still.

seem	Leslie seemed invincible.
appear	Jess appeared stunned.
look	Jess looked tired.
sound	The voice sounded awful.

In descriptions and in Report genres (whose function is to classify and describe phenomena) the frequency of relational attributive clauses is usually quite high. We can see this in the following student's report on whales (the relational attributive and existential clauses are shaded).

Whales

Whales	live, feed and	often	play	in groups	in many different oceans.
Actor	Pro:mat			Circ:accomp	Circ:loc:space

Whales	travel	far.
Actor	Pro:mat	Circ:loc:space

They	are	always	moving	looking	for food.
Actor	Pro:mat			Pro:behav	Circ:purpose

They	have	large, flat, tail-like flukes.
Possessor	Pro:rel:poss:attrib	Possessed

Their flukes	help	them	move	through the water.
		Actor		
Initiator	Pro:mat			Circ:loc:space

Whales	are	mammals.
Carrier	Pro:rel:intens:attrib	Attribute

All mammals	are	warm-blooded.
Carrier	Pro:rel:intens:attrib	Attribute

They	have	hair or fur and lungs.
Possessor	Pro:rel:poss:attrib	Possessed

Their young	are born	and	drink	milk	from their mother's body.
Actor	Pro:mat		Pro:mat	Goal	Circ:loc:space

A whale	has	smooth skin and a few bristles of hair around its mouth.
Possessor	Pro:rel:poss:attrib	Possessed

Whales	breathe	through blowholes in the top of their heads.
Behaver	Pro:behav	Circ:manner:means

Blowholes	are	tightly	shut.
		Circ:manner	
Goal	Pro:mat		

There	are	two main groups of whales.
	Pro:existential	Existent

One	has	teeth	and	the other	does not.
Possessor	Pro:rel:poss:attrib	Possessed		Possessor	Pro:rel:poss:attrib

Baleen whales	have	no teeth.
Possessor	Pro:rel:poss:attrib	Possessed

Sheets of hornlike baleen	hang	from the roofs of their mouths.
Actor	Pro:mat	Circ:loc:space

A baleen whale	has	two blowholes	in the top of its head.
Possessor	Pro:rel:poss:attrib	Possessed	Circ:loc:space

The largest toothed whale	is	smaller than the largest baleen whales.
Carrier	Pro:rel:intens:attrib	Attribute

Relational identifying processes

We looked at the three subtypes of relational attributive processes. The same subtypes exist for the relational identifying processes, but we will only look at the first – the relational:intensive:identifying (for an account of the other subtypes of relational identifying processes see Halliday 1994a: 130–8 and Matthiessen 1995: 297–326).

Relational:intensive:identifying processes define or uniquely identify a participant.

. . . he [Jess] had been that crazy little kid [[that draws all the time]].

For the rest of the day and until after lunch on the next he [Jess] had been the fastest kid in the third, fourth and fifth grades.

Since these processes set up a relationship of 'identity' or 'equivalence', they are reversible.

that crazy little kid that draws all the time had been him [Jess].

For the rest of the day and until after lunch on the next the fastest kid in the third, fourth and fifth grades had been him [Jess].

Notice that the attributive type is not reversible:

. . . and only a fourth grader was he.

Lord, tired was he.

The participant roles in relational identifying processes are Value and Token.

Value		Token
His name was		Jess.
His best friend was		the new girl.

To determine which Participant is the Token we need to use the concept of Subject, and also the concept of active and passive voice. The method of identifying the Subject is indicated in Figure 2.4. The Subject is the element referred to in the Mood Tag.

One approach to understanding the difference between active and passive voice is that in the passive voice, in the simple present or past tense, the verb usually has the form finite + lexical verb + ed + by. For example:

Peace is symbolized by the white dove.

is	symbolized	by
Finite	lexical verb + ed	by

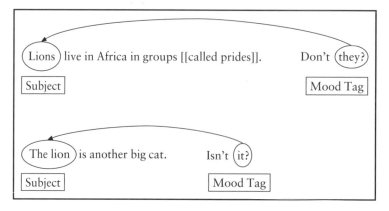

Figure 2.4 Method of identifying the subject

In the active voice the finite is fused with the lexical verb:

The white dove *symbolizes* peace.

So the participant which is 'agentive' (The white dove) is the Subject.

In Relational Identifying clauses, if the verb is active the Subject is the Token. In the example above, we know that the clause is Relational Identifying because it is reversible. In the active form we can see that 'The white dove' is the Subject (Figure 2.5). So in this clause 'The white dove' is the Token and 'peace' is the Value:

The white dove	symbolizes	peace.
Token	Process: relational: identifying	Value

In the case of the verb 'to be' it is difficult to see whether the clause is active or passive:

His name was Jess.

His best friend was the new girl.

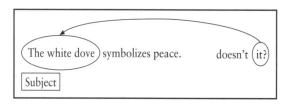

Figure 2.5 Subject as Token in active identifying clauses

So change the verb 'to be' to another identifying verb like 'represent' or 'symbolize' or 'identifies' and the passive form becomes explicit:

His name was represented by Jess.

His best friend was represented by the new girl.

These clauses are passive so the order is Value^Process^Token.
In the active form, however:

Jess was [represented] his name.

The new girl was [represented] his best friend.

The order is Token^Process^Value.

he [Jess]	had been	that crazy little kid [[that draws all the time]]
Token	Pro:rel:intens:ident	Value

For the rest of the day and until after lunch on the next	he [Jess]	had been	the fastest kid in the third fourth and fifth grades.
Circ:extent:time	Token	Pro:rel:intens:ident	Value

Some verbs other than the verb 'to be' may function as an identifying process:

equal	His time equalled the county record.
stand for	The clenched fist stands for black power.
symbolize	The white dove symbolizes peace.
indicate	The three stripes indicates sergeant rank.
refer to	The humidity index refers to the amount of water vapour in the air.
call	This is called osmosis.
mean	Red means stop.
play	Gary Sweet plays 'Mickey' in the new police drama series.

In the following excerpt from an explanation of bird flight (Hemsley 1990) we can see the use of relational:identifying clauses (shaded) to construct definitions. Notice that there are fewer relational clauses in this Explanation genre than in the earlier example of the Report genre dealing with whales. Notice also that the relational: identifying clauses tend to come at the end of component stages of the explanation text, summing up the explanation sequence realized by mainly material processes in the preceding clauses.

There	are	three main sorts of flight.
	Pro:Existential	Existent

Birds	use	all three types.
Actor	Pro:mat	Range

In gliding flight	a bird	holds	its wings	out	without	moving	them.
			Goal			Pro:mat	Goal
Circ:loc:temp	Actor	Pro:mat					

The wings	work	in the same way [[as the wings of an aircraft]].
Actor	Pro:mat	Circ:manner

Because of the wings' shape	air	passes	more quickly than underneath	over the top of the wings.
Circ:reason	Actor	Pro:mat	Circ:manner	Circ:loc:space

This	means	[[that air pressure on top of the wings is less than underneath]].
Token	Pro:rel:id	Value

The result	is	an upwards force [[called lift]] on the wings.
Value	Pro:rel:id	Token

The bird	keeps moving	forward	because	it	is dropping
Actor	Pro:mat	Circ:loc:space		Actor	Pro:mat

under the force of gravity	so	the power of flight	comes from	the bird's own weight.
Circ:reason		Value	Pro:rel:id	Token

The problem with gliding	is	[[that the bird must start high up and will eventually reach the ground]].
Value	Pro:rel	Token

In soaring flight	a bird's wings	work	in the same way [[as in gliding flight]].
Circ:loc:time	Actor	Pro:mat	Circ:manner

However	the bird	places	itself	in rising currents of air.
	Actor	Pro:mat	Goal	Circ:loc:space

The rising air	lifts	the bird	so that	it	gains	height
Actor	Pro:mat	Goal		Actor	Pro:mat	Range

rather than	losing	it.
	Pro:mat	Range

The rising currents	are	often	[[what is known as thermals]].
Value	Pro:rel:id		Token

Thermals	are	columns of warm air [[that have been heated by areas of hot ground]].
Token	Pro:rel:id	Value

Rising currents of air	also	occur	where	wind
Existent		Pro:existential		Actor

hits	sharply rising ground such as a cliff.
Pro:mat	Goal

It	is	mostly	large birds with big wings	[[that soar]].
	Pro:rel:id		Token	
Value				

HOW DOES GRAMMAR CONSTRUCT INTERPERSONAL MEANING?

Interpersonal meanings are realized grammatically by the systems of Mood and Modality. Mood structures reflect speaker–listener (and reader–writer) relationships. If

I say, 'Close the door please', the directive indicates that I have power over the person I am speaking to. The structure of the clause indicates the selection of the *imperative* mood. If I phrase the message as a question, 'Would you close the door please?', the language implies a relationship based on equality. The structure of the clause here indicates the selection of the *interrogative* mood. But this is not the most straightforward (or congruent) way of communicating a directive or command to close the door. The interrogative is usually used to demand information (question), not to demand some kind of service (like shutting the door). A further Mood structure – the *declarative* mood, is most frequently used for expressing information in the form of a statement as in 'The door is closed'. Note however, that declarative mood can also be used incongruently to realize a command:

You should close the door.
The door needs to be closed.

The way language is organized as an interactive event involving speaker/writer and listener/reader reflects the role adopted by the speaker/writer and the role that is therefore assigned to the listener/reader. There are two fundamental roles in linguistic exchanges: giving and demanding. There are two commodities that can be exchanged: information, and goods and services. These variables, taken together, define the four primary forms of linguistic exchange: offer, command, statement, question. These and congruently realized examples are shown in Figure 2.6. As noted, incongruent realizations of demands for goods and services (commands) and demands for information (questions) can also occur.

Structure of Mood in English

Mood is a clause constituent that consists of the Subject together with the Finite element of the verbal group. As we have noted already, the Subject can be recognized

Role	Commodity exchanged	
	GOODS AND SERVICES	INFORMATION
giving	*offer* (declarative mood)	*statement* (declarative mood)
	Here's some juice.	Spiders have eight legs.
demanding	*command* (imperative mood)	*question* (interrogative mood)
	Give me that pen!	Are you ready to go?

Figure 2.6 Primary forms of linguistic exchange

because it is the element 'picked up' by a tag question. In the following sentence: 'Some members of your class want to join the society', the subject is 'Some members of your class' because this is the element that would be picked up in the tag question 'don't they?' The subjects in the following sentences appear in upper case:

One day ALFIE AND MUM AND ANNIE ROSE were coming home. (Weren't they?)

At school A LOT OF ILL FEELING AND DISRUPTION was caused by the dress code. (Wasn't it?)

SHE must go to the ball. (Mustn't she?)

The Finite can be recognized because it is one of a small number of verbal operators or 'auxiliaries' which express tense or modality.

Tense is expressed by the verbal operators in Figure 2.7. Note that in some cases in the simple present or simple past tense the Finite is 'fused' with the lexical verb. We say 'loves' and not 'does love' unless we are wanting to emphasize a contrast. Similarly we say 'gave' and not 'did give' unless we are wanting to be contrastive. In cases where the Finite is fused with the lexical verb, it does not appear explicitly in the clause, so conventionally we indicate the first letter of the lexical verb as signifying the presence of the Finite.

She	loves	her work.
Subject	F	
Mood		Residue

She	does	love	her work.
Subject	Finite		
Mood		Residue	

Modality is expressed by the verbal operators in Figure 2.8. Modality can be thought of as 'the distance between yes and no'. It represents degrees of inclination, obligation,

Past	Present	Future
did, was had, used to should	does, is has	will, shall would

Figure 2.7   Verbal operators indicating tense

Low	Median	High
can, may	will	must, ought to
could, might	would, should is to, was to	need to has to, had to

Figure 2.8   Modal operators

probability or usuality. Polarity is also part of the Finite element of the verbal group. It is expressed by 'not' in the case of negative polarity and is unmarked in the case of positive polarity. It is the elements of the Mood that make the proposition arguable. You can argue about who/what the Subject is. You can argue about the polarity – yes/no. The Finite gives the proposition a reference point in the here and now, so that it is also something that can be argued about. Temporal operators make it arguable with reference to the time of speaking. Modal operators make the proposition arguable by being presented as likely, unlikely, desirable or undesirable, for example by reference to the speaker/writer's judgement of the probabilities or obligations involved.

Mood Adjuncts relate specifically to the meaning of the finite verbal operators, expressing probability, usuality, obligation, inclination or time. Examples of commonly occurring Mood Adjuncts are listed in Figure 2.9. Mood Adjuncts are part of the mood element of the clause and are analysed as indicated in the following examples:

Pollution	is	always	a problem	near coal fired stations.
Mood			Residue	
Subject	Finite	Mood Adjunct	Complement	Adjunct (circumstantial)

Certainly	pollution	is	a problem	near coal fired stations.
Mood			Residue	
Mood Adjunct	Subject	F	Complement	Adjunct (circumstantial)

Comment Adjuncts are an additional element in the Mood structure of the clause. These are items like 'unfortunately', 'frankly', 'honestly', 'luckily', 'understandably', 'objectively' etc. They express the speaker's/writer's comment or judgement on what s/he is saying/writing.

The following text shows the deployment of the resources of Mood and Modality in a discussion on the future of suburban estuaries (Butt *et al*. 1995: 80). Finite modals are in bold; Mood Adjuncts are in bold and italics and Comment Adjuncts are in bold and underlined.

Probability/obligation	certainly, surely, probably, perhaps, maybe, possibly, definitely, positively
Usuality	always, often, usually, regularly, typically, occasionally, seldom, rarely, ever, never, once
Presumption	evidently, apparently, presumably, clearly, no doubt, obvious, of course
Inclination	gladly, willingly, readily
Time	yet, still, already, once, soon, just
Degree	quite, almost, nearly, totally, entirely, utterly, completely, literally, absolutely, scarcely, hardly
Intensity	just, simply ever, only, really, actually

Figure 2.9 Commonly occurring mood adjuncts

In conclusion, estuarine waterways within an urban environment **could** add a special dimension to daily life. An expanse of safe water **would** provide additional opportunities for recreation. These are values which **ought to** be preserved. <u>Unfortunately</u>, our social and community life is *sometimes* hostile to these values. While urban subdivision, traffic, refuse disposal and industry **may** all be essential parts of our daily life, we **must** pursue these activities without unnecessary environmental degradation. Different conflicting interests **must** be resolved so that our many, proper aspirations **may** be accompanied both now and in the future.

Structure of the Residue

The *Predicator* is the verbal group minus the temporal or modal operator. The verbal groups in the following clauses are underlined. The Predicators are shown in upper case.

More and more machines <u>are CONTROLLED</u> by computers.

You <u>can SWITCH ON</u> the electric light at any time.

Most of the electricity we use at home <u>is MADE</u> at a power station.

The machines <u>have BEEN WORKING</u> 24 hours a day for many years.

Coal burning power stations <u>may BE GOING TO BE REPLACED</u> by nuclear power plants.

The Predicator itself is non-finite (because it is the verbal group minus the temporal or modal operator). Some clauses are non-finite, containing a Predicator but no Finite element. The non-finite clauses are shown in italics and the Predicator is shown in upper case:

The rain fell day after day *FLOODING local creeks.*

TO GET the prize she put his name on the form.

The little boy became lost *while SHOPPING with his mother.*

You have to walk for five kilometres *TO SEE another house.*

There are two verbs in English which, in simple present and simple past tense, appear as Finite only. These are the verbs *be* and *have* (in the sense of possess):

A light bulb is a very common thing in our lives.

Electricity substations are very dangerous places.

Nearly every dwelling in Australia has electric power.

A *Complement* is an element within the Residue that has the potential of being Subject but is not. It is typically realized by a nominal group.

The whole country is criss-crossed by a network of cables

Mood		Residue	
Subject	|F		Predicator	Complement

A network of cables criss-crosses the whole country.

Mood		Residue	
Subject	|F|	Predicator	Complement

Some power stations burn coal or oil.

Mood	|Residue	
Subject	|F|Pr	|Complement

Coal or oil is burned   by some power stations.

Mood		Residue	
Subject	|F|	Predicator	|Complement

There is one exception to this principle. That is an attributive Complement:

Hydro-electricity is very cheap.

Subject	IF	Complement

An *Adjunct* is an element that has not got the potential to become Subject.

The wires go into your home at the electricity meter.

Mood	|Residue	
Subject	I FIPr Adjunct	Adjunct

We   use electricity   for many things.

Mood	|Residue	
Sub	FIP Complement	Adjunct

HOW DOES THE SELECTION OF THEME CONSTRUCT TEXTUAL MEANING?

Theme refers to the way a text is organized as a message by the speaker/writer. Theme represents the point of departure, the angle, or what the clause will be about. There are three possible components of Theme: Textual Theme, Interpersonal Theme and Topical Theme. To begin with, we will consider Topical Theme.

Topical Theme

In the clause in English, Theme is signalled by the element in first position. The Topical Theme is the Participant or Circumstance (or sometimes Process) that comes first in the clause. In the following text the Topical Themes are in small capitals. Note that in this text the Topical Themes are the first Participants in each clause:

> THE LION is another big cat. || LIONS live in Africa in groups [[called prides]]. || THE LION is the only cat [[that likes to live with others of its kind]]. || LION CUBS like these have spots || when THEY are small.
>
> (Hoffman 1986: 3)

If a Circumstance comes before any of the Participants in a clause then the Circumstance is the Topical Theme. In the following clause the Topical Theme is 'On a hot day':

> **On a hot day** in the garden you might see little black ants.
>
> (Butterworth 1988: 3)

'On a hot day' is the first Circumstance (telling when) so it is the Topical Theme. Then next Circumstance 'in the garden' (telling where) is not Theme because it is not in first position in the clause. And the first Participant 'you' is not Theme because it is not in first position in the clause. Note the Circumstances as Topical Themes in the following clauses from the same book:

In some rooms the ants store their food.

In other rooms the ants hatch out from the eggs.

After eight days the larva is nearly as big as a worker ant.

After three weeks the young worker ants will come out of the cocoons.

(Butterworth 1988: 11–13, 25–7)

The part of the clause that is not Theme is referred to as Rheme. The analysis is displayed as follows:

After three weeks   the young worker ants will come out of the cocoons.

Theme	Rheme

All major clauses in English have a Topical Theme except some non-finite clauses, as shown in the following extract and analysis:

Penguins are brave and will attack any enemy, hitting out with their strong beaks or using their powerful flippers as clubs.

(Seventy 1984)

Penguins   are brave

Theme (Topical)	Rheme

and   will attack any enemy

Theme		Rheme
Textual	Topical	

hitting out with their strong beaks

Theme	Rheme

or   using their powerful flippers as clubs.

Theme		Rheme
Textual		

Non-finite clauses – no Topical Theme selected

In the second clause the Topical Theme has been ellipsed. It could be analysed as follows:

and	[they]	will attack any enemy
Theme		Rheme
Textual	Topical	

Marked Topical Themes

The Topical Theme occurs most commonly as a Participant in the clause. More specifically the Topical Theme occurs most commonly as the Particpant in the clause which is the Subject of the clause (for identification of the subject see Figure 2.7). This is the case for all Topical Themes in the lion text above. In this text the Topical Themes are all Subjects in the clauses and this is the most common (or unmarked) case. When some element other than the Subject is in Theme position, this is not as common, and is referred to as a Marked Topical Theme. All Circumstances that are Themes are Marked, since Circumstances can never be Subjects (Figure 2.10). Hence the examples from the ants text above are all Marked Topical Themes.

The following are some further examples where the Participants in first position are not Subjects and are therefore Marked Topical Themes:

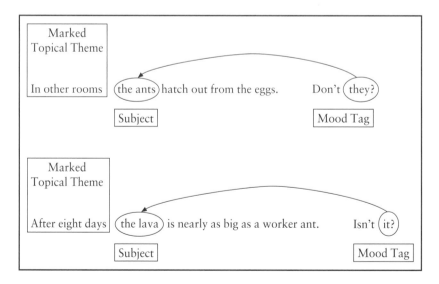

Figure 2.10 Circumstances as Marked Themes

This they expect me to finish by lunchtime. (Don't they?)
Untidiness my mother just can't tolerate.
The newest member of staff they always give the worst class to.
All remains of police corruption the government is determined to stamp out.

Textual Themes

So far we have examined Topical Themes and they have been realized by one element – a Participant or a Circumstance. However, as speakers and writers develop a text they try to give it texture, to weave meanings together in a coherent form. This frequently involves linking clauses by using conjunctions (like 'after', 'because', 'so', 'although', 'until' etc.). Since these particularly work to signal relationships between clauses, they most often occur at the beginning of clauses and when they do, a multiple Theme structure is formed. In the following sentence the conjunctions are displayed in bold italics:

My brother was shocked *when* I walked deep *and* I was only up to my ankles in water.

Both these conjunctions occur at clause boundaries. The Theme of the second and third clauses therefore comprises two elements, the conjunction and the next element.

MY BROTHER was shocked WHEN I walked deep AND I was only up to my ankles in water.

The conjunctive element forms the Textual Theme and the following element in these examples forms the Topical Theme. The convention for formally displaying the analysis is thus:

when	I	walked deep
Theme		Rheme
Textual	Topical	

The system of conjunction also provides resources for relating sentences that are not joined structurally in clause complexes. In the following text, for example we have two separate sentences, each consisting of a single clause:

She did not hand in all of the assignments.
Consequently she failed the course.

In the second clause 'Consequently' constructs the cause/effect relationship between the two clauses. It is not a Participant, Circumstance (or a Process) and hence is not a Topical Theme, but since it does occupy first position in the clause, we say it is a Textual Theme. In other words the point of departure for this clause is its logical connection to the previous clause. The Theme analysis for this clause is as follows:

Consequently	she	failed the course
Theme		Rheme
Textual	Topical	

For a list of other words like 'consequently' (conjunctive adjuncts) which function as Textual Themes when they are at the beginning of a clause, see Eggins (1994: 106).

Interpersonal Theme

Sometimes first position in the clause is occupied by an element realizing the speaker's/ writer's judgement with respect to experiential meanings of the clause. For example:

Possibly the cheapest route would be via Singapore.

The choice of 'possibly' contrasts with 'certainly' or 'probably'. These items represent a range of judgements the speaker/writer could make with respect to the likelihood of the Singapore route being the cheapest. In this case the speaker/writer is very tentative in his/her judgement. Now 'Possibly' is in first position in the clause, but it is not a Participant or Circumstance (or Process) so it is not a Topical Theme. 'Possibly' is also not a conjunction or conjunctive adjunct, so it is not a Textual Theme. Because it is concerned with judgement we call it an Interpersonal Theme. The analysis is displayed as follows:

Possibly	the cheapest route	would be via Singapore
Theme		Rheme
Interpersonal	Topical	

Here are some further examples with Interpersonal Themes in italics and Topical Themes in upper case latters.

Usually SEA PLANTS have long feathery stems that sway with the water.
Perhaps GLOBAL WARMING will bring some benefits.
Apparently NO FUNDS were provided for more staff.
Certainly HYDRO STATIONS are less polluting than coal fired stations.

As indicated in Figure 2.9, words like 'possibly', 'usually', 'perhaps', 'apparently' etc. are part of the grammatical system realizing interpersonal meanings. Specifically they are Mood Adjuncts and express probability, obligation, usuality, presumption, inclination, time, degree and intensity (see also Eggins 1994: 167, 279). Note that these Mood Adjuncts are only part of the Theme when they occur *before* the Topical Theme in a clause. In the following clause for example, 'certainly' is still a Mood Adjunct but it is not part of the Theme because it comes after the Topical Theme:

Hydro stations	are certainly less polluting than coal fired stations.
Theme	Rheme
Topical	

So the question is whether speakers/writers want to give prominence to their inter-personal judgements in orienting their listeners/readers by putting Mood Adjuncts in Theme position.

Certainly the work you do in this course is of the highest significance for your teaching.

Related to Mood Adjuncts are *Comment Adjuncts*, which function to express an assessment about the clause as a whole. Examples of these are words like 'honestly', 'understandably', 'luckily' etc. These can also function as Interpersonal Themes (see Eggins 1994: 168 for Comment Adjuncts).

Theme in interrogative clauses

So far we have examined Theme in declarative clauses, those usually associated with the speech function of making statements. Theme in interrogative clauses, those usually associated with asking questions, orients the listener to the speaker's demand for a response of a particular kind. Examples 1–8 below are all wh/ interrogatives. ('How' is also a member of the wh/ group of words.) In contrast, Example 9 is a yes/no inter-rogative, since it only requires 'yes' or 'no' in response. In wh/ interrogatives, the wh/ element occupies Theme position. The Themes in clauses 1–9 are shown in upper case:

1 WHY were Alfie's feet big?
2 WHY are they the big . . . big ones?
3 WHO 's got the biggest feet out of you and Sam?
4 WHY have you got the biggest feet?
5 OH WELL WHO 's got the biggest feet out of all the b– all the boys in our family?
6 WHAT might happen to her?
7 WHAT 's that,

8 WHAT 's happening in that picture?
9 CAN YOU do yours up?
  (In clause 5, 'who' is still the Topical Theme, and 'oh well' is the Textual Theme.)

In the case of yes/no questions, there is always a two-part Theme. The first part is the element in the verbal group, called the Finite, and the second is the Subject. In example 9, the Theme is 'Can you'. The Theme in yes/no questions is further illustrated in examples 10–12:

10 DO THEY go very fast in the fire engine?
11 DO YOU like that?
12 CAN YOU see the crashed plane?

Theme in imperative clauses

Imperative clauses are the usual realization of commands. In children's reading and writing these occur most frequently in the Procedure genre. The following procedure is used in science for children in the middle primary school:

To find out more about reflected light, try this test.

1 Cut a hole about 2.5 cm across in the bottom edge of a piece of card.
2 Fix a comb over the hole.
3 Use modelling clay to keep the card upright.
4 Use corks to hold a mirror facing the comb. Make sure the mirror is at an angle.
5 Shine a torch through the hole so the light rays hit the mirror. What happens?
(Taylor 1989: 8)

This procedure has been reproduced below with each clause on a separate line. The Topical Themes are capitalized and the Textual Themes are underlined. Notice that the first clause and clauses 3a and 4a are non-finite and do not select for Theme. In the Imperative clauses the Topical Theme is the Process. This is not the case in clauses 5a and 5b, because 5a is a declarative and 5b is an interrogative clause.

  To find out more about reflected light,
  TRY this test.
1 CUT a hole about 2.5 cm across in the bottom edge of a piece of card.
2 FIX a comb over the hole.
3 USE modelling clay
3a to keep the card upright.
4 USE corks
4a to hold a mirror facing the comb.
4b MAKE sure the mirror is at an angle.

5   SHINE a torch through the hole
5a <u>so</u> THE LIGHT RAYS hit the mirror.
5b WHAT happens?

WHAT ARE THE COHESIVE ELEMENTS IN TEXT THAT MAKE LINKS ACROSS SENTENCES?

Conjunctive relations

The types of conjunctive relations identified, the notational conventions used, and an example of each of the types of conjunctive relation are shown in Figure 2.11. These categories of conjunctive relations are based on the account in (Martin 1992) and the examples are from (Unsworth 1996).

Conjunctive relations are sometimes implicit. This occurs when the meanings unambiguously include a logical relation, of sequence or causality for example, but the writer has chosen not to make this explicit in the language. This is illustrated in the following example where the temporal relation of simultaneity between the first clause and the second clause is made explicit by the conjunction 'as', but the relation of temporal succession between clauses two and three remains implicit. It would, of course, be possible to make the temporal succession explicit by inserting 'then' at the beginning of clause three:

1 As the object moves to the right
2 it pushes or compresses the air particles next to it.
3 The compressed air particles push on the particles to their right . . .

(Chapman *et al.* 1989: 281)

One additional dimension to conjunctive relations is that they may refer to *external* (material world) logical relations, or to the writer's *internal* (rhetorical) organization of the text. You can see this is the following constructed examples:

Example 1:
Coal is formed from the remains of plant material buried for millions of years. <u>First</u> the plant material turns into peat. <u>Next</u> the peat turns into brown coal. <u>Finally</u> the brown coal turns into black coal.

Example 2:
Coal cannot be relied upon as an energy source for the future. <u>First</u> the burning of coal is highly polluting. <u>Next</u> the world's supplies are finite. <u>Finally</u> the extraction of coal is becoming more and more expensive.

In Example 1 the underlined words refer to the unfolding of the events in real time, so to the temporal sequencing of the formation of black coal. However, in Example 2, the

temporal	simultaneous successive	simul succ	*As* the prong moves outwards, it squashes or compresses the surrounding air . . . layers of dead trees and other plants built up on the forest floor *before* they could rot.
consequential	manner	man	*By* looking closely at one of the prongs, you can see that it is moving to and fro (vibrating).
	consequence	consq	Sound waves travel through gases, liquids and solids *because* they all contain particles which will carry or transmit disturbances.
	condition	cond	*If* we look at how a tuning fork produces sound, we can learn just what sound is.
	concession	conc	This is what happens in a rainforest or in the compost heap of your garden. *However*, decomposition is prevented if the plant material accumulates . . .
	purpose	purp	. . . in each case a vibration was needed *(in order) to* produce the sound.
comparative	similarity	simil	*Similarly*, the Earth's surface is most brightly lit where the sun's rays strike the surface perpendicularly.
	reformulation	i.e.	when they strike the Earth's surface perpendicularly *i.e.* when the sun is directly overhead.
	exemplification	e.g.	Normally if plant material is left on the ground surface in contact with the air (oxygen) it decomposes. *(For example)* This is what happens in a rain forest. . . .
	contrast	contr	Large vibrations cause loud sounds. *Conversely*, small vibrations cause soft sounds.
additive	addition	add	when they fall to the ground *and* become part of the soil humus.
locative	location	loc	the Earth's surface is most brightly lit *where* the sun's rays strike the surface perpendicularly.

Figure 2.11 Types of conjunctive relations, notation and examples

same underlined words refer not to temporal sequence, but to the writer's rhetorical organization of the information: 'first' is 'first in the sequence in which I choose to write', 'next' is 'what I have chosen to write next' etc. When conjunctions are used to relate sentences in this way we refer to the relation as *internal* conjunction.

Consequential relations can also be external or internal. In the following constructed example the cause/effect relationship is between events in the material world and 'so' expresses an external conjunctive relation:

The plant remains were covered with water containing very little oxygen, *so* they did not rot.

However, the nature of the cause/effect relation is quite different when the following clause occurs at the end of an explanation of how coal is formed:

Thus coal is merely carbonized plant remains.

(Chapman *et al.* 1989: 127)

Here the consequential relation is internal. The writer's use of 'thus' expresses a rhetorical cause/effect relation. This sentence could be glossed as: 'Because of the foregoing explanation of coal formation you can now accept the proposition that coal is carbonized plant remains.'

When analysing or annotating a text to show conjunctive relations, conventionally the external conjunctive relations are indicated on the right of the text representation and the internal conjunctive relations on the left. Examples of the analyses of conjunctive relations are shown in Chapter 4 in Figures 4.12 and 4.13 (for further accounts of conjunctive relations see (Martin 1992; Eggins 1994).

Lexical relations

The cohesive resource of lexical relations refers to the ways in which lexical items (nouns, verbs, adjectives and adverbs) are used to maintain the topic of the text. There are two main kinds of lexical relations – taxonomic and expectancy (Figure 2.12). Taxonomic relations refer to class/subclass or part/whole relations. These categories of relations can be further subdivided as shown in Figure 2.12. Expectancy relations refer to the predictability of the lexical items co-occurring in texts. For example, if you encounter the word 'doctor', it is highly likely that you will encounter words like 'hospital', 'surgery', 'patient' etc.

We can chart the lexical relations in texts by constructing lexical strings (Figure 2.13). These lexical strings diagram all of the lexical items (content words) in a text that can be related to an immediately preceding word through any of the kinds of relations summarized in Figure 2.12. We do not include all of the lexical items in a text – only those that can be related to others in a string (for further descriptions of lexical relations see Halliday and Hasan 1985; Martin 1992; Eggins 1994). These analyses can show not only what the principal topics are in the text and where they occur but also how they are related to each other. What is significant about the text in Figure 2.13 from the point

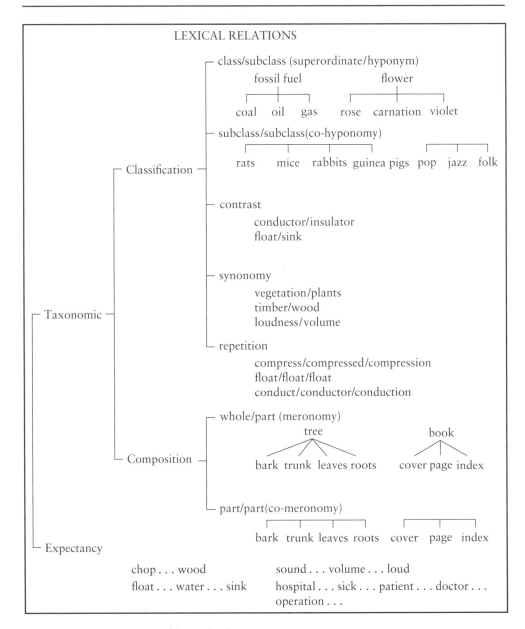

LEXICAL RELATIONS

class/subclass (superordinate/hyponym)

fossil fuel   flower

coal   oil   gas   rose   carnation   violet

subclass/subclass(co-hyponomy)

rats   mice   rabbits guinea pigs pop   jazz   folk

contrast

conductor/insulator
float/sink

synonomy

vegetation/plants
timber/wood
loudness/volume

repetition

compress/compressed/compression
float/float/float
conduct/conductor/conduction

whole/part (meronomy)

tree   book

bark trunk leaves roots   cover page index

part/part(co-meronomy)

bark trunk leaves roots   cover   page   index

Classification

Composition

Taxonomic

Expectancy

chop . . . wood   sound . . . volume . . . loud
float . . . water . . . sink   hospital . . . sick . . . patient . . . doctor . . .
                            operation . . .

Figure 2.12   Summary of lexical relations

of view of teaching young learners is that this text provides a sound basis for developing understanding of the scientific classification of dinosaurs because of its careful building of taxonomic relations. This is frequently not the case in informational texts for young children, which fail to address rudimentary scientific perspectives (Unsworth 1993a).

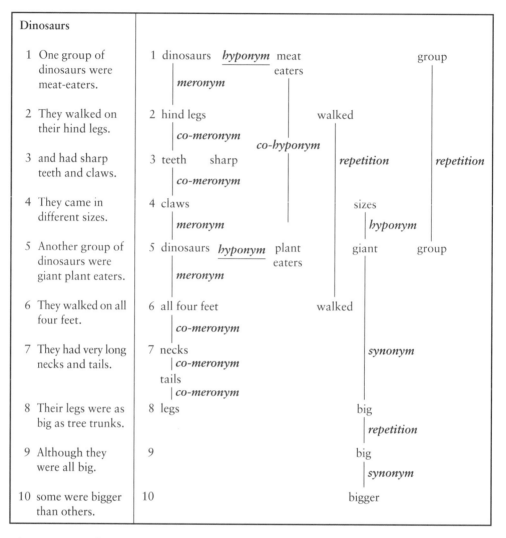

Figure 2.13   Charting lexical strings in a text
Source: Selsam and Hunt 1982.

Reference

Reference concerns the ways in which writers or speakers introduce participants into a text and then refer to them once they have been introduced. Participants may either be presented as new or presumed. If they are presumed we need to retrieve their identity from their earlier presentation in the text or from the fact that they are materially present in the context. Consider the following example:

When you dropped a solid piece of plasticine into the water it sank.

In the first clause, 'a solid piece of plasticine' is presented but in the second clause 'it' is presuming reference. We need to retrieve the identity of 'it' by reference to 'a solid piece of plasticine' in the first clause. Pronouns (it, she, he, they etc.) are among the most common presuming reference items. Other common presuming reference items are the definite article (the) and demonstrative pronouns (this, that, those). These are illustrated in the following example.

When you made the same piece of plasticine into *a boat shape*
(the) plasticine boat floated.
(This) shape pushes aside more water than the solid shape.

Another form of presuming reference is comparative reference. This presumes the identity of a participant, not because that participant has been introduced before but because a participant with which it is being compared has been introduced before. For example in the following sentence the comparative 'other' presumes the previous shape that has been mentioned.

Other shapes will float
if the plasticine has been hollowed out like the boat

These examples of presuming reference follow the presented participant (anaphoric) reference, but it is possible for the presuming reference to precede the presented participant. For example

He worked all summer on (this). *A perfect scale model of a Junkers JU88 bomber* showed the care he had taken in building it.

The presuming reference discussed to this point has concerned reference to individual participants in text. However, the referent for presuming 'whole text reference' may be all of the text up to this point, or a whole sequence of events. This can be seen in the following example:

An object's shape controls the amount of water [[it pushes out of the way]].
If the amount of water [[pushed aside, or displaced]] weighs the same or more than the object then the object will float.
If the amount of water weighs less than the object it will sink.

You can test (this) by comparing the weights of floating and overloaded boats to the weights of the water [[they displace]]

(Robson 1992b)

In some cases the identity of a presuming reference is not in the co-text at all. One such case is in oral language where the speaker is referring to something that is clearly identifiable in the material setting of the talk, for example, 'Put it down', where the identity of *it* is obvious to the observation of those involved in the communication. The other case is where the identity is retrievable from the context of culture, for example, 'The Queen Mother is 100 this year', for people in the United Kingdom (and probably a number of other countries associated with the United Kingdom), it is very clear which Queen Mother we are talking about because of shared cultural understandings.

This section has introduced some basic concepts about reference. For more detailed accounts see Halliday and Hasan (1985), Martin (1992), and Eggins (1994).

CONCLUSION

From the frequency of references to other sources, it will have become clear that this chapter has attempted only an introduction to some of the fundamental aspects of systemic functional grammar and discourse. In view of this, systemic functional descriptions may appear to be very extravagant, making use of a large number of functional differentiations and therefore, a large number of technical terms. However, this needs to be weighed up against the value of such a rich and detailed account in terms of the work it can do in providing explicit guidance to teachers and students in understanding how language is used effectively in different contexts. This is what we address in subsequent chapters, indicating the usefulness and manageability of these functional descriptions in extending what can be done to expand and enhance outcomes from traditional grammar requirements in school syllabus documents and in teaching multiliteracies across the curriculum.

NOTES

1 Geoff Williams' contribution to lecture notes to BEd (Primary) Students at the University of Sydney, 1990.
2 In the simple present tense the finite indicating tense 'is/do' is conflated with the lexical verb. We wouldn't say 'do kill' unless we wanted to indicate that the text is in response to some contestation of the proposition. Conventionally, the first letter of the lexical verb is taken to show the (conflated) presence of the finite element of the verbal group.
3 This is a constructed clause and does not appear in the *Bridge to Terabithia*.
4 This is a constructed example.
5 This is a constructed example.

CHAPTER 3

Describing visual literacies

INTRODUCTION

In the 1980s and 1990s images have come to assume more prominence relative to print in school texts and texts of popular culture (Kress 1995b, 1997; Kress and van Leeuwen 1996; Quin *et al.* 1997a). The capacity of computer-based texts to easily include and manipulate images from a variety of sources has further emphasized the significance of visual literacy in 'reading' images and text (Bolter 1998). Researchers have argued the need for a retheorization of textual communication to include the multimodal nature of contemporary texts (Goodman and Graddol 1996; Lemke 1998a, 1998b; Rassool 1999; Cope and Kalantzis 2000). However, the teaching of the 'multiliteracies' inherent in this kind of retheorizing has to date received little systematic attention in school curricula. Kress (1995b) has lamented the lack of such a 'futures' oriented perspective in the national curriculum in the United Kingdom and Lemke has reflected similar concerns about school curricula in the United States (Lemke 1998a). In Australia some state and national curriculum documents address visual literacy in the teaching of English (Curriculum Corporation 1994a, 1994b; Queensland Department of Education 1994; New South Wales Board of Studies 1998b). However, a number of studies have contrasted the attention given in such documents to student outcomes associated with visual literacy with the paucity of theoretical description (meta-language) pertaining to the nature of visual literacy (Callow 1995; Howley 1996; Luchinni 1996; Callow and Unsworth 1997). A great deal of work at the interface of theory and practice in this area remains to be done to enable all young learners to develop the critical multimodal literacies that are necessary for taking an active interpretive role in the societies of the information age.

To facilitate the integrative teaching of visual and verbal literacies necessary for the critical apprenticeship of children to the multimodal, multimedia texts of the twenty-first century, we need a theoretical account of the meaning-making resources (or visual grammar) of images that can articulate with an account of verbal grammar that similarly has a focus on describing the meaning-making resources of language. Consistent with the impact of systemic functional linguistic descriptions of language on redefining the nature and role of grammar in teaching, functional descriptions of 'visual grammar' (O'Toole 1994; Kress and van Leeuwen 1996) have begun to facilitate systematic attention by teachers to the multimodal nature of texts in developing critical literacy practices (Goodman and Graddol 1996; van Leeuwen and Humphrey 1996; Callow and Unsworth, 1997; Unsworth 1997a; Lemke 1998a, 1998b; Miller 1998; Williams 1998; Astorga 1999; Callow 1999).

The two main functions of this chapter then, parallel those of Chapter 2. The first main function is to provide an introductory description of a functionally oriented visual grammar and its relationship to functional descriptions of verbal grammar. The second main function is to indicate the usefulness of these descriptions of visual grammar in facilitating visual literacy learning and teaching. The practical significance of the functional account of visual grammar will be introduced by using curriculum area texts in conventional and electronic formats to illustrate the visual analyses and outlining the ways in which these can inform the design of learning experiences for students. Subsequent chapters will deal in more detail with visual grammar as a resource in the planning and practical implementation of teaching/learning activities.

Relating functional descriptions of visual and verbal grammar

In Chapter 2 we described the grammar of English as a resource for simultaneously making three kinds of meanings: ideational, interpersonal and textual meanings. The images we encounter, in fact the visual dimensions of all texts we encounter, also make these three kinds of meaning simultaneously. Extrapolating from the systemic functional descriptions of English grammar (Halliday 1994a; Matthiessen 1995), researchers have developed a corresponding functional account of 'visual grammar' (Kress and van Leeuwen 1990, 1996; O'Toole 1994).

This work recognizes that images, like language, realize not only representations of *material reality* but also the interpersonal interaction of *social reality* (such as relations between viewers and what is viewed). The work also recognizes that images cohere into textual compositions in different ways and so realize *semiotic reality*. More technically, functional semiotic accounts of images adopt from systemic functional linguistics the meta-functional organization of meaning-making resources:

- *representational/ideational* structures verbally and visually construct the nature of events, the objects and participants involved, and the circumstances in which they occur;
- *interactive/interpersonal* verbal and visual resources construct the nature of relationships among speakers/listeners, writers/readers, and viewers and what is viewed;
- *compositional/textual* meanings are concerned with the distribution of the information value or relative emphasis among elements of the text and image.

Here we will explore ways in which this meta-functional framework, as adopted by Kress and van Leeuwen (1996), can describe visual meaning-making in school texts in conventional and electronic formats. Although, as in language, the three meta-functions are realized simultaneously, we will initially discuss each separately. First, we will describe *representational* structures in images, which construct ideational meanings – the nature of events, the objects and participants involved, and the circumstances in which they occur. Second, we will examine the construction of *interactive* meanings in images, which include the interpersonal relationship between the viewer and the represented participants. Then we will investigate how aspects of layout construct *compositional* meanings, which are concerned with the distribution of the information value or relative emphasis among elements of the image.

REPRESENTATIONAL MEANINGS: MODELLING MATERIAL REALITY

Visual representation of material, mental and verbal events

In this section we will deal with the visual representation of participants involved in action, reaction, thinking, and speech processes. We will also consider the visual representation of the circumstances in which such processes occur.

Participants in images may represent beings of some kind like humans, animals, and mythical creatures. They may also represent artificial objects like buildings, furniture, cars and roads or natural phenomena like rivers, mountains and trees. In highly abstract images like diagrams, participants are frequently boxes or circles, as in the diagram of a biological sewage treatment plant shown in Figure 3.1.

Following Kress and van Leeuwen (1996) in their adaptation of systemic functional grammar to the visual dimension of texts, we will identify participants in images on the basis of their functional role in context of the image. Processes of action are indicated by 'action lines' or vectors. In diagrams like Figure 3.1 the lines and arrow heads indicate the direction of movement of participants like water and micro-organisms. In more naturalistic images, the vectors are usually formed by bodies or limbs or tools in action. In the image of the frog-hunting bat in Figure 3.2, the vector is formed by the oblique line from the bat's body, head and mouth towards the frog. The vector departs from the Actor and is directed to another participant called the Goal. Since the action depicted involves both an Actor and a Goal, it is referred to as a transactional structure.

In some transactional images the vectors are bi-directional so that the participants are alternatively playing the roles of Actor and Goal. You can see this in the image of magnets in Figure 3.3 showing the attraction of unlike poles and the repulsion of like poles. Another example is the picture of the brother and sister hugging in Anthony Browne's (1989) story *The Tunnel* (Figure 3.3).

Not all images involving action are transactional. In many images an Actor performs some action but there is no apparent participant to whom the action is directed – there is no Goal. In the image of the vampire bat jumping (Figure 3.4) the action is indicated

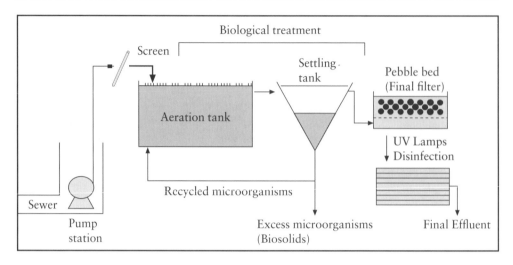

Figure 3.1   Diagram of biological sewage treatment plant
Source: http://www.yvw.com.au/schools/sewtourmain.htm (February 2000).

Figure 3.2   Actional:transactional image of frog-eating bat
Source: © Merlin D. Tuttle, Bat Conservation International, Woodside 1993: 21.

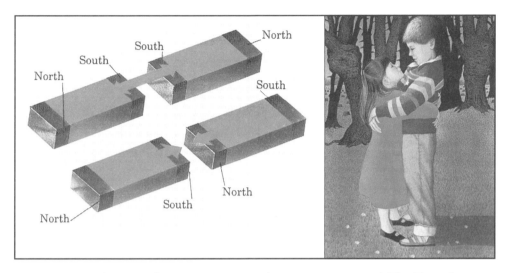

Figure 3.3   Bi-directional vectors in images from *Magnetism* and *The Tunnel*
Sources: Browne 1989; Robson 1992a: 13.

Figure 3.4   Non-transactional action (common vampire bat jumping at its prey)
Source: © Merlin D. Tuttle, Bat Conservation International, Woodside 1993: 22.

by the vectors of the head pointing forward, the downward pointing forearms and the outstretched hind legs and feet just clearing the ground surface. Although the caption states that this is a 'common vampire bat jumping at its prey', there is no visual depiction of the prey. Since there is no Goal, visually this is a non-transactional structure.

In some images there is a chain of transactions with the Goal of one transaction becoming the Actor in the next transaction and the Goal of that one becoming the Actor in the next and so on. In each case the process involves some transformation of what is being passed on. Kress and van Leeuwen (1996: 68) call these 'conversion' processes. In some cases they are linear, like representations of the formation of coal or food chains, but they can also be cyclic like the water cycle or the nitrogen cycle. An example of a conversion process representing the water cycle is shown in Figure 3.5.

When a vector is formed from the eye line of one or more of the participants so that they are looking at something, the process is a reaction rather than an action, and the participants are referred to as Reactors rather than Actors, and Phenomena rather than Goals. The image of Australian Aboriginal artist Iris Clayton looking at one of her paintings (Figure 3.6) is a reaction which is transactional because we have the Reactor and the Phenomenon depicted.

The image of the young Torres Strait Islander girl (Figure 3.7) is also a reaction, but this one is a non-transactional reaction, since the image depicts the girl as Reactor but no Phenomenon.

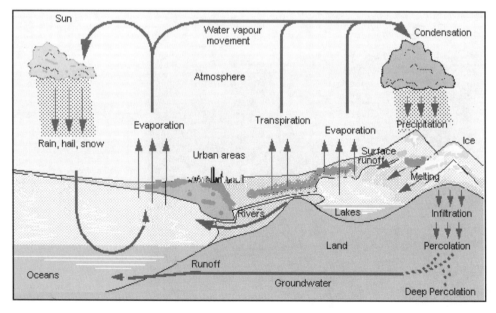

Figure 3.5 Water cycle
Source: http://www.yvw.com.au/schools/cycle 1.htm

Figure 3.6   Reactional:transactional image. Photo: M. Hill
Source: Barlow and Hill 1987b: 21.

Another kind of vector that appears in images is that connecting a speech bubble or speech balloon to a participant so that what the participant is saying is depicted visually. Of course, this has long been a feature of comic strips and cartoons, but it is now increasingly used with more naturalistic images as indicated in the image in Figure 3.8 from an informational book about bats for young readers.

The use of speech balloons in a variety of images is now very common and they often occur in images we encounter in everyday activities such as using automatic teller machines. They are very frequently used in contemporary educational materials for children, particularly in educational materials provided on the Internet websites of commercial companies and government instrumentalities. As well as speech balloons, thought 'clouds' are used to communicate what the participant is thinking. One example of the use of speech bubbles and thought clouds in the schools education section of the New South Wales Forestry Commission website is shown in Figure 3.9.

In images of course, there are frequently objects other than those which have the participant roles we have identified, like Actor, Goal, Recipient, Reactor, Phenomenon,

Figure 3.7   Reactional:non-transactional image. Photo: M. Hill
Source: Barlow and Hill 1987a: 29.

Sayer and Senser. In the image of Iris Clayton looking at her painting (Figure 3.6) we also have the bookshelf of books with vases and ornaments on top of it, as well as the wall. These are the setting. They locate the other participants. The painting is above the bookshelf and Iris is in front of the bookshelf with her arm on it. These aspects of the image correspond to circumstances of location in functional grammar. Circumstances indicating the means by which actions are performed can also be depicted visually, as can circumstances of accompaniment where there is no vector but separate participants can be distinguished – being together.

Images that classify

Images that classify organize participants into certain categories. They organize participants in terms of a 'kinds of' relation, or taxonomy. The image in Figure 3.10 is a taxonomy showing kinds of 'standard drink'. It is a covert taxonomy because the category, or superordinate, is not shown in the image. It is implicit and can be inferred

Figure 3.8   Verbal processes in images
Source: Wood and Rink 1991: 17.

Figure 3.9   Visual representation of verbal and mental processes
Source: © State Forests of NSW, http://www.forest.nsw.gov.au/Frames/f kids.htm

What's in a drink?

Some drinks contain more alcohol than others because of the way in which they are brewed or distilled. Drinks such as beer and cider are served in large glasses, while strong drinks like spirits are served in small measures. Yet each contains roughly the same amount of pure alcohol. A half pint of beer, for example, contains about the same amount of alcohol as a glass of wine or a small measure of whisky or gin.

½ pint of beer

1 measure of whisky

1 glass of wine

Figure 3.10   Covert taxonomy of standard drinks
Source: Ward 1987: 10.

from the depiction of the subordinate participants. Notice that this is a single level taxonomy with only one superordinate category and one group of subordinate participants. The classificational or taxonomic purpose of the image is reflected in the symmetrical relationship of the subordinate participants to each other, the frontal angle at eye level, and the decontextualized background. This kind of image is concerned with conceptual relations and not the presentation of events in the material world.

Covert taxonomic images that occur in informational materials for primary/ elementary age children are not always as decontextualized and symmetrical in the placement of participants as Kress and van Leeuwen (1996: 81) indicate to be the norm with this kind of image. Figure 3.11, for example, showing the different kinds of clouds, retains some elements of setting, and the placement of the cloud types shows their typical relative locations in the sky. Nevertheless, this image is clearly more concerned with conceptual relations than with presenting an actual scene in the material world. It is a covert taxonomy because the actual category or superordinate participant (cloud types) is implicit.

We could re-present the information in Figure 3.11 by drawing a more abstract tree diagram indicating the different types of clouds and make explicit the superordinate category, cloud types, as shown in Figure 3.12.

This can be a useful learning activity for students in consolidating their knowledge of the subject matter and developing explicit knowledge about the means of visual representation of taxonomic relations. Students can use implicit taxonomic information

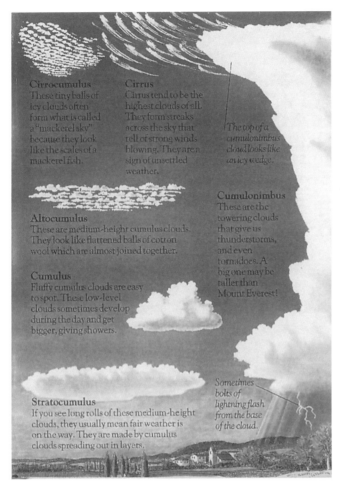

Cirrocumulus
These tiny balls of
icy clouds often
form what is called
a "mackerel sky"
because they look
like the scales of a
mackerel fish.

Cirrus
Cirrus tend to be the
highest clouds of all.
They form streaks
across the sky that
tell of strong winds
blowing. They are a
sign of unsettled
weather.

*The top of a
cumulonimbus
cloud looks like
an icy wedge.*

Altocumulus
These are medium-height cumulus clouds.
They look like flattened balls of cotton
wool which are almost joined together.

Cumulonimbus
These are the
towering clouds
that give us
thunderstorms,
and even
tornadoes. A
big one may be
taller than
Mount Everest!

Cumulus
Fluffy cumulus clouds are easy
to spot. These low-level
clouds sometimes develop
during the day and get
bigger, giving showers.

*Sometimes
bolts of
lightning flash
from the base
of the cloud.*

Stratocumulus
If you see long rolls of these medium-height
clouds, they usually mean fair weather is
on the way. They are made by cumulus
clouds spreading out in layers.

Figure 3.11   Covert taxonomy of cloud types
Source: © Dorling Kindersley, Farndon 1992.

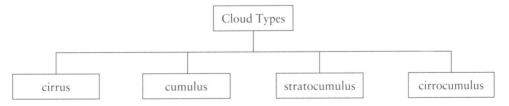

Figure 3.12   Overt single level taxonomic image of cloud types

in texts to construct more elaborated overt taxonomies than those in the source material. For example, in a book about bats for young students, fishing bats, insect eating
bats, fruit bats and bats that prey on small animals like mice are displayed pictorially
in a covert taxonomy (Wood and Rink 1991: 10–11). Students can draw, copy or find

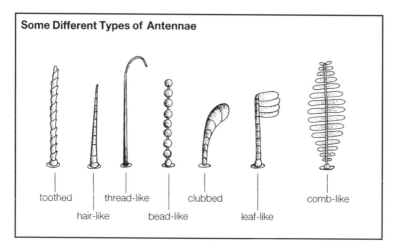

Figure 3.13   Overt single level taxonomic image
Source: Bird and Short 1998: 10. From *Insects* by Joan Short and Bettina Bird,
illustrations by Deborah Savin. Text copyright © Joan Short and Bettina Bird 1998.
Illustrations copyright © Scholastic Australia 1998. Reprinted by permission of
Scholastic Australia.

other pictures of these and other bats in the same groups and then construct an overt
pictorial taxonomy showing the superordinate, kinds of bats, and subcategories of
herbivores and carnivores. This can be done individually or collaboratively in small
groups using cut-and-paste techniques to construct charts. It can also be done using
computer-based resources, scanning images from hard copy books or downloading
images resulting from Internet searches and constructing the taxonomic display in a
word processing and/or graphics presentation software program.

   Classificatory images, which include the superordinate category, are overt taxonomies.
A further example of an overt taxonomy is shown in Figure 3.13. This is clearly
decontextualized and symmetrical, showing the superordinate category 'some different
types of antennae' and the labelled pictures of different types of antennae symmetri-
cally positioned below.

   Overt taxonomic images often take the form of tree diagrams like Figure 3.14. They
are frequently multilevel. This means that as well as the overall superordinate participant, they include one or more participants that are intermediate. These participants
are superordinate with respect to some other participants and, at the same time, are
subordinate with respect to the overall superordinate participant. This can be seen in
Figure 3.14, where the fourth category has three subparts and then subpart 'a' (insects)
itself has two further subparts – 'with wings' and 'without wings'.

   The visual construction of taxonomic relations in electronic texts makes use of
hypertext links rather than tree diagrams. In the CD ROM, *Insects – Little Creatures
in a Big World* (CSIRO 1994) viewers can explore the 'Insect Gallery'. The first screen
for the Insect Gallery is shown in Figure 3.15. This screen contains the superordinate
and part of the first level of the taxonomy. Note that the second part of this first level

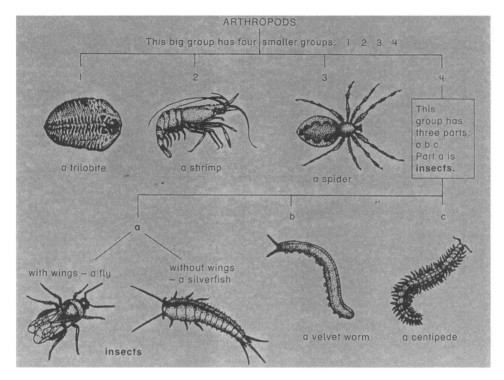

Figure 3.14   Overt multi-level taxonomic image of arthropods
Source: From *First Facts* by E. Cooper 1988: 6. Reprinted by permission of Macmillan Ltd © Macmillan Children's Books 1988. Artwork © BLA Publishing Ltd 1988.

is contained on the next screen as indicated by the 'down' arrow on the left-hand side of the screen (some young students and inexperienced users of computer-based texts will need to be alerted to these navigational devices). To get to the next level of the taxonomy, one 'clicks' on any of the first layer of subcategories like 'Ants', 'Insects and Wasps', 'Beetles' etc. The second layer of the taxonomy for Ants is shown in Figure 3.16. Students need to be able to read taxonomic relations in the traditional hard copy tree diagram formats as well as the hypertext versions of electronic texts. Again the composition by students of taxonomic representations in both modes is a useful resource not only for consolidating knowledge of the subject matter but also for gaining explicit understanding of the semiotic means by which such knowledge is constructed and communicated.

Images that show part/whole relationships

Perhaps the most commonly occurring images that show part/whole relationships, especially in texts associated with schooling, are those that depict an object with its parts labelled such as the grasshopper in Figure 3.17. Kress and van Leeuwen (1996: 89–93) refer to such images as structured analytical images, and, consistent with functional

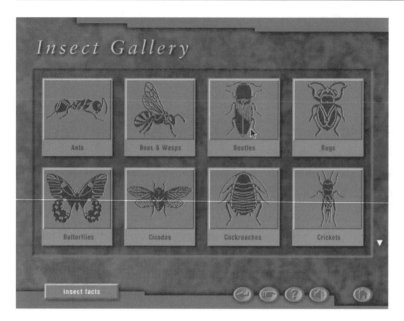

Figure 3.15   Taxonomic relations as hypertext – superordinate and first level in a CD ROM
Source: CSIRO 1994, reproduced by permission of CSIRO PUBLISHING.

grammatical descriptions of language, refer to the participant representing the whole as the Carrier and the parts as Possessive Attributes. Structured analytical images also occur as coloured drawings and photographs as well as maps.

Some images that do not include labels are nevertheless analytical, showing part/ whole relationships. These are referred to by Kress and van Leeuwen (1996: 94–5) as unstructured analytical images. Typical examples are fashion photographs of models displaying the elements of clothing that make up a particular fashion style or posed photographs of sportspersons displaying the range of personal equipment used in a particular sport. Further examples in school texts are discrete images each depicting only one part of an animal or object. This can be seen in Figure 3.18, showing the head and the stinger of a bull ant in separate images. While the head of the bull ant is perhaps readily identifiable through recognition of the eyes and jaws, identification of the stinger is problematic. The image of the stinger on the right-hand side of Figure 3.18 is magnified with respect to the scale of the image of the head on the left-hand side, but this is not acknowledged in the book at all. Nor is there any indication on this page, or elsewhere in the book, as to where the stinger is actually located on the body of the bull ant. Unstructured analytical images like this in texts for young children suggest the need for significant bridging work to be done by teachers or more experienced co-readers, if children are to understand the part–whole relationships being dealt with. One approach is first to locate examples of one common

Figure 3.16 Taxonomic relations as hypertext – second level in a CD ROM
Source: CSIRO 1994, reproduced by permission of CSIRO PUBLISHING.

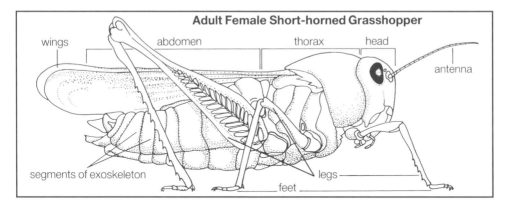

Figure 3.17 Structured analytical image of a grasshopper
Source: Bird and Short 1998: 7. From *Insects* by Joan Short and Bettina Bird,
illustrations by Deborah Savin. Text copyright © Joan Short and Bettina Bird
1998. Illustrations copyright © Scholastic Australia 1998. Reprinted by permission
of Scholastic Australia.

Other ants, such as bull ants, use their big jaws to catch small animals. Then they use their stingers to squirt acid into the animal to kill it.

Figure 3.18   Unstructured analytical image of parts of a bull ant. Photo: Kathie Atkinson
Source: MacLulich, 1998: 13.

convention for showing magnified parts of a whole, which is to show the magnified section in circle or ellipse beside a picture of the whole, so that its identity as a particular part of the whole is visually clear. These examples are used to examine and explain the visual convention to the students (see for example, Claybourne 1994: 8 for a magnified image of a bee's pollen ball). The next step is to locate an image of the bull ant which identifies the stinger or which shows the stinger so that the teacher can identify it for the students. The students and/or the teacher can then construct an image showing the bull ant and the magnified stinger in the conventional circle or ellipse alongside it. This is a visual device restricted to traditional hard copy materials. Electronic texts tend to use more dynamic approaches to dealing with part–whole relations.

Unstructured analytic images are a particular feature of some computer-based informational texts. In the CD ROM *Insects – Little Creatures in a Big World* (CSIRO 1994), the 'zoom in' feature allows the viewer to select a part of the insect and then zoom in so that a magnified version of this part of the image fills the computer screen. Figure 3.19 shows the screen depicting the termite and the hatched squares on which one can click to zoom in. Figure 3.20 shows the result of the zoom in on the square to the far left over the tip of the antennae.

Analytical images can be presented as having all of the Carrier accounted for. That is, all of the image space depicting the Carrier is taken up by Possessive Attributes.

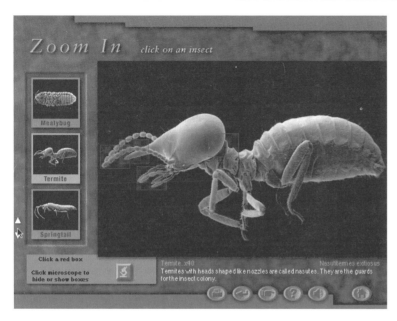

Figure 3.19 Unstructured analytical image of a termite on a CD ROM
Source: CSIRO 1994, reproduced by permission of CSIRO PUBLISHING.

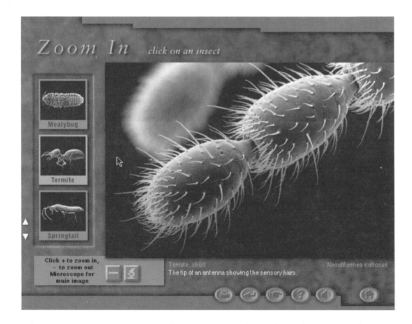

Figure 3.20 'Zoom in' of unstructured analytical image of a termite on a CD ROM
Source: CSIRO 1994, reproduced by permission of CSIRO PUBLISHING.

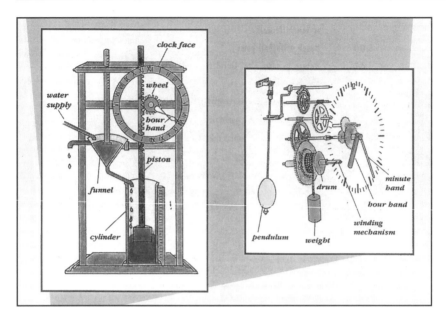

Figure 3.21   Inclusive analytic image of clockwork mechanism of a water clock
Source: New South Wales Department of Education and Training 1997.

This is the case in the drawing of the grasshopper in Figure 3.17. Kress and van Leeuwen (1996: 97–100) refer to such images as exhaustive analytical images. On the other hand, some analytical images depict some of the Possessive Attributes of a Carrier but leave much of the Carrier as blank space, not filled up by Possessive Attributes. This can be seen in Figure 3.21, where the right-hand side of the image shows some of the Possessive Attributes of the clockwork mechanism, but leaves much of the Carrier unaccounted for. Kress and van Leeuwen (1996: 97–100) refer to such images as inclusive analytic images.

Kress and van Leeuwen (1996: 99) point out that some analytical images can be simultaneously exhaustive and inclusive. Maps for example, may be exhaustive in depicting the states or provinces that comprise a country, but inclusive in depicting only some of the cities and towns, rivers, lakes, roads etc. in the states or provinces.

Types of accuracy in analytical images

If analytical images are read as accurately representing the spatial relations and the relative location of the Possessive Attributes, they are referred to by Kress and van Leeuwen (1996: 101–3) as having topographical accuracy. Figure 3.22 shows a photograph of a dynamo for use with a bicycle headlamp (an unstructured analytical image) and a structured analytical image of the dynamo in the form of a drawing. This structured analytical image is topographical because it is read as accurately scaling down the dimensions and relative location of the parts of the dynamo.

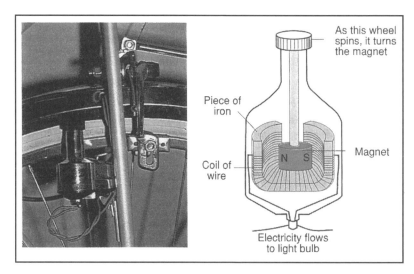

Figure 3.22 Topological accuracy in a drawing of a dynamo
Source: Stannard and Williamson 1991: 89. Reproduced by permission of Macmillan Education Australia.

Some analytical structures accurately represent the logical relations among the Possessive Attributes of a Carrier, but not their actual physical size or their distance from each other, etc. This can be seen in Figure 3.23. A photograph of a solar cell connected to power a telephone is shown on the right-hand side. On the left-hand side this is represented as a diagram that has topological accuracy. It represents how the components relate to each other functionally, but does not scale down the dimensions of the components or actual distances between them.

Maps that use scale to maintain accuracy in depicting the relative location and distance between the representations of the attributes of an actual physical context are clearly topographical images. But some maps like those representing urban railway systems like the London Underground or the Sydney Metropolitan system are topological. They depict the routes and the train stations accurately in terms of sequence, linkages and destinations, but do not indicate the relative distances of the stations from each other or the actual geographical location of stations. Similarly, diagrams like those showing a company's computer network with the number of computer terminals and their connection to 'servers' etc. may well be topologically accurate but not topographically accurate.

Concrete and abstract representation in images

Although Kress and van Leeuwen (1996: 107) include the dimensions 'concrete' and 'abstract' in their diagram of analytic image structures, they don't actually discuss the nature of this distinction nor do they refer to examples of images with these features.

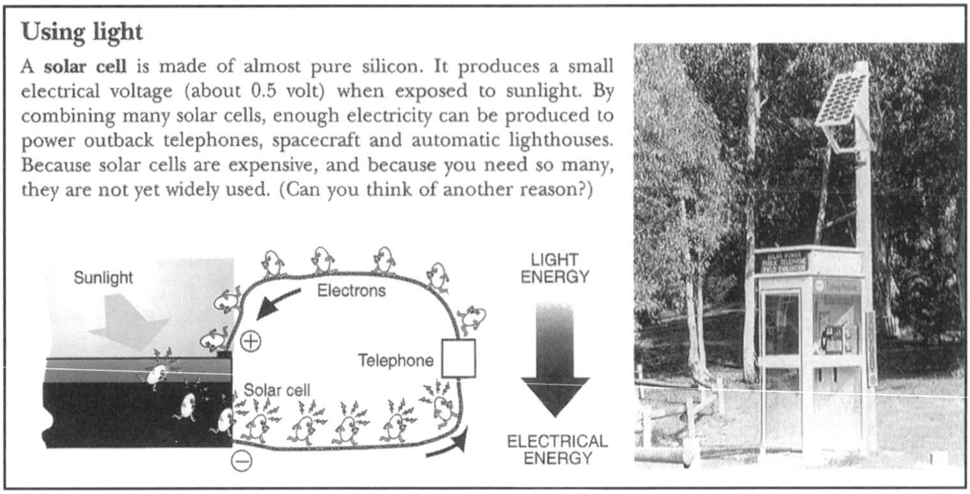
Using light
A solar cell is made of almost pure silicon. It produces a small electrical voltage (about 0.5 volt) when exposed to sunlight. By combining many solar cells, enough electricity can be produced to power outback telephones, spacecraft and automatic lighthouses. Because solar cells are expensive, and because you need so many, they are not yet widely used. (Can you think of another reason?)
Sunlight
Electrons
Telephone
Solar cell
LIGHT ENERGY
ELECTRICAL ENERGY

Figure 3.23 Topological accuracy in diagram of a solar cell powered telephone
Source: Stannard and Williamson 1991: 87. Reproduced by permission of Macmillan Education Australia.

We will make a working distinction here and note that this issue is related to the issues of modality and coding orientation in images, which will be taken up later (see p. 101).

The participants in concrete images are imitative representations of the corresponding objects in the material world, while the representations of participants in abstract images are related in an arbitrary, albeit conventionally familiar, way to corresponding objects in the material world. This can be seen in Figures 3.24 and 3.25. Both are images representing a simple electric circuit. Figure 3.25 uses representations of a cell and a switch, which are established conventions in science, but which are arbitrarily related to the actual material objects.

Time lines

Although time lines are concerned with the sequence in which events occur over time, they are more like images that represent part–whole relationships rather than narrative images that depict actual material events. Time lines depict fixed stages of a sequence as things, which are attributes of the sequence as a whole. In some cases the time intervals are drawn to scale and such time lines have topographical accuracy.

In some time lines the participants are assembled in the right sequence but the time intervals are not drawn to scale. This can be seen in Figure 3.26, where the sequence of stages in the growth of a sunflower plant are shown but the time intervals between each stage and the next are not represented to scale.

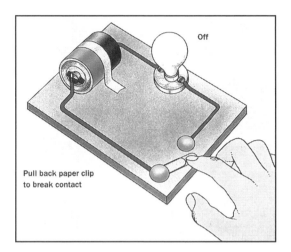

Figure 3.24 Concrete image of a simple electric circuit
Source: Whyman 1989: 11.

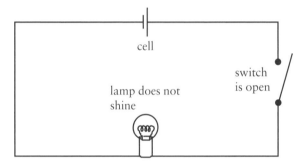

Figure 3.25 Abstract image of a simple electric circuit
Source: DeVreeze *et al*. 1992: 140, reproduced by permission of John Wiley &
Sons, Australia.

Time lines may be horizontal or vertical and are not necessarily straight at all.
Figure 3.27 shows a time line of life on earth, which was included in the 1999 form of
the literacy test taken by all students in the first year of high school in New South
Wales government schools. In this time line the colour coding seems to divide the time
into eras indicated on the right-hand side, and these are further subdivided into periods,
shown in upper case labels on the coloured time line. Close reading will indicate that
the time intervals are marked but are not drawn to scale. As one reads the time line,
one must alternately read from left to right and right to left.

Recommendations for teaching students about time lines often include individual
and collaborative construction of time lines based on recording personal experience,
logging results of classroom observational studies, or collecting information about

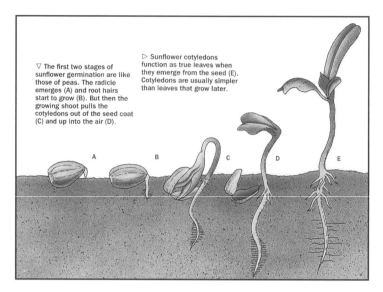

The first two stages of sunflower germination are like those of peas. The radicle emerges (A) and root hairs start to grow (B). But then the growing shoot pulls the cotyledons out of the seed coat (C) and up into the air (D).

▷ Sunflower cotyledons function as true leaves when they emerge from the seed (E). Cotyledons are usually simpler than leaves that grow later.

A   B   C   D   E

Figure 3.26   Time line of the growth of a sunflower plant
Source: Bates 1990: 11.

the emergence of natural or social phenomena over time (Moline 1995). In learning to critically interpret complex time lines such as Figure 3.27, it is important that students have opportunities to 'talk out' both the information they believe the time line is conveying, as well as their understanding of how the semiotic resources of the image are constructing this understanding.

Symbolic images

Two symbolic processes in images are referred to by Kress and van Leeuwen (1996: 108–12). The first of these is where some attribute of a participant in the image is in fact a Symbolic Attribute. Beyond its ostensive meaning, this attribute symbolizes a further implicit meaning. In Figure 3.28 the spots of blood appear to be splashed on the camera lens and symbolize the fate of the white seal. The blood appearing to be on the camera lens rather than being part of the scene to be photographed, makes this attribute salient in the image (in combination with the stark colour contrast). This 'unexpectedness' or 'out of place' quality is typical of Symbolic Attributes. Kress and van Leeuwen (1996: 108) note that Symbolic Attributes can also achieve salience by being placed in the foreground, through exaggerated size, through being especially well lit, being represented in especially fine detail or sharp focus, or through conspicuous colour or tone.

The second kind of symbolic process in images described by Kress and van Leeuwen is where the symbolic meaning derives from within the Carrier. It is the qualities of the

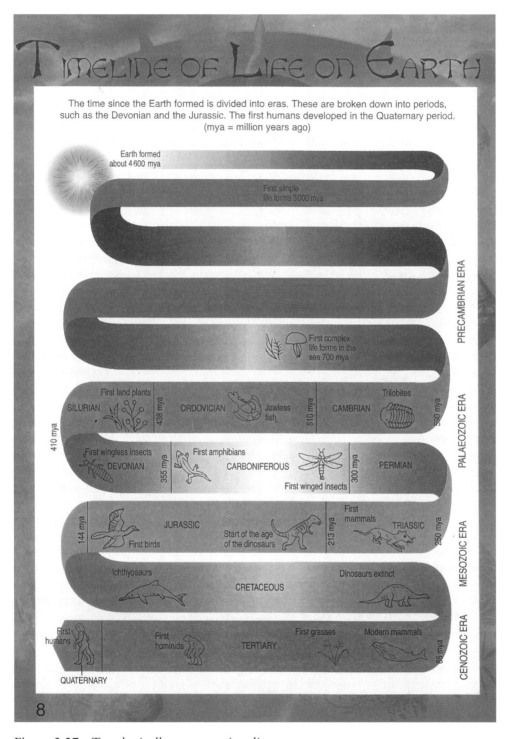

The time since the Earth formed is divided into eras. These are broken down into periods, such as the Devonian and the Jurassic. The first humans developed in the Quaternary period. (mya = million years ago)

Earth formed about 4 600 mya

First simple life forms 3000 mya

First complex life forms in the sea 700 mya

PRECAMBRIAN ERA

First land plants

SILURIAN 438 mya ORDOVICIAN Jawless fish 510 mya CAMBRIAN Trilobites 590 mya

410 mya

PALAEOZOIC ERA

First wingless insects

DEVONIAN 355 mya First amphibians CARBONIFEROUS First winged insects 300 mya PERMIAN

First mammals

144 mya JURASSIC First birds Start of the age of the dinosaurs 213 mya TRIASSIC 250 mya

MESOZOIC ERA

Ichthyosaurs CRETACEOUS Dinosaurs extinct

First humans First hominids TERTIARY First grasses Modern mammals 65 mya

CENOZOIC ERA

QUATERNARY

8

Figure 3.27 Topologically accurate time line
Source: New South Wales Department of Education and Training 1999. Image by courtesy of Hodder Wayland Picture Library.

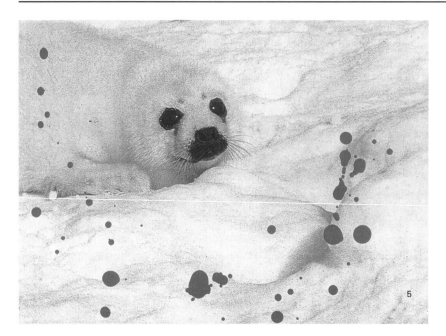

Figure 3.28   Symbolic attribute
Source: Bright 1988: 4.

Carrier that construct the symbolic meaning. Kress and van Leeuwen (1996: 112) refer to this kind of symbolic image as a Symbolic Suggestive image and exemplify this type with an image of an oil drilling installation in the Sahara. The extreme lighting conditions brought about by the setting sun acting like a kind of low backlight, de-emphasizes the detail and creates a 'mood' symbolizing the disappearance of the old Bedouin lifestyle. The accompanying text refers to this disappearing lifestyle.

INTERACTIVE MEANINGS: CONSTRUCTING VIEWER/ IMAGE RELATIONS

Interaction: visual demands and offers

When images contain human, human-like or animal participants whose gaze is directed straight at the viewer, then the viewer necessarily engages interpersonally with that represented participant. It is as if by looking straight at the viewer, the represented participant is demanding attention. Such images are referred to as 'Demands'. The image of the seal (through the blood-splashed lens) in Figure 3.28 is a Demand, and, of

Figure 3.29 Demand – sharing the joy of the catch
Source: Lockwood 1996 edition.

course, this is part of the reason that the image has such a strong impact. In Demands then, the viewer enters into some kind of imaginary interpersonal relationship with the represented participant(s) gazing directly at him or her. The nature of this relationship is influenced by other factors such as facial expression. In Figure 3.29 the smiling face of the young boy invites the viewer to share his joy in his catch of fish.

On the other hand the image in Figure 3.30 of the three girls playing in a street in Sydney in about the 1920s presents looks of unwelcoming or aloof curiosity. A scowl may suggest a disapproval of the viewer while a flirtatious smirk may suggest desire. In constructing this kind of pseudo-social bond with the viewer, images also tend to define the implied viewer. For example, a seductive pout from a young woman tends to exclude young children as implied viewers.

Where there are no human, human-like or animal participants, or these participants do not gaze at the viewer, there is no imaginary interpersonal relationship between the viewer and the represented participants. Such images are referred to as 'Offers'. What is depicted is offered to the viewer quite impersonally for his or her information and contemplation. The viewer is an invisible onlooker. Figures 3.6 and 3.7 are Offers. In these images the human participants are not gazing directly at the viewer.

Figure 3.30   Demand – unwelcoming observation
Source: Fitzgerald 1990, City of Sydney Archives.

Social distance: close-up, medium and long shots

The distances people keep from each other depend on the nature of their social relations. People with whom we are interpersonally very close, we are also likely to be physically very close to. In very intimate situations we may be so close that our field of vision includes only the other person's face. At a less intimate, but very personal distance, we may see the person's head and shoulders. People we relate to socially, but not at an intimate or very personal level, we tend to interact with at distances where our field of vision includes the other person from about the waist up. People who are strangers we are more likely to encounter at a distance where our field of vision would include the person's whole body. These tendencies form the basis of definitions of close-up, medium and long-shots, and intermediate positions along this continuum, in describing the social distance between the viewer and the represented participants in images.

Figure 3.31 Close personal distance
Source: Browne 1989.

The choice of close-up, medium or long shot or some intermediate position, is part of the construction of an imaginary relation between the viewer and the represented participants. Participants can be portrayed as if they are personally very close to the viewer or as though they are strangers. The final image in Anthony Browne's *The Tunnel* (1989) shown in Figure 3.31 constructs a relation of very close personal distance, while Figures 3.6 and 3.7 depict the participants at a far personal distance, typical of transitory social, rather than personal, relationships. Figure 3.30 of the girls playing in the street is a longer shot where the public social distance constructs the relationship between the viewer and the represented participants at that of strangers.

Although social distance has been discussed in terms of representations of human participants, it also applies to representations of buildings, landscapes and other non-human participants. For example, the telephone box in Figure 3.23 is a long shot, with all of the telephone box and the solar panel visible, indicating remote social distance. It could have been photographed from the distance of someone about to enter it. In this case we would not see all of the telephone box and the social distance would be closer to the personal.

Attitude: perspective and involvement or detachment

As well as selecting either Offer or Demand and deciding on the social distance, image makers need to determine the point of view from which the image will be depicted.

They have to decide the angle from which the photograph, painting or drawing will portray the represented participants. If the image is constructed as if the image maker, and therefore the viewer, is facing the represented participants, then the frontal plane of the represented participants and the frontal plane of the image maker are aligned or parallel. This frontal point of view suggests maximal 'involvement' between the image-maker (and the viewer) and the represented participants. What is in the image is part of what the viewer sees himself or herself as being involved in. The frontal point of view in Figure 3.29 indicates that the viewer is aligned with or part of the world of the young lad with his catch of fish.

On the other hand with the image of the young girls in the street in Figure 3.30, the frontal plane of the photographer and the viewer is not parallel to the frontal plane of the girls. The angle between the frontal plane of the viewer and the frontal plane of the represented participants is oblique. Taking the photograph from this oblique angle indicates that the world of the girls in the street is not one that the photographer sees himself or herself as part of or involved with. The oblique angle indicates detachment.

The telephone box in Figure 3.23 has been photographed from an oblique angle. This indicates detachment from the viewer. This is a telephone box that is part of someone else's world. It is not a telephone box with which the viewer has any involvement in his or her world.

Power: high angle, low angle and eye-level views

If the represented participants are seen from a high angle with the viewer looking down on them then they are depicted as if the viewer has power over them. In Figure 3.7 the young Torres Strait Islander girl is viewed from a high angle and in Figure 3.30 the girls playing in the street have been photographed from a high angle so that they are depicted as if the viewer has power over them. On the other hand the image in Figure 3.29 of the boy holding his fish portrays him at eye level, so there is a sense of equality between the represented participant and the viewer. In Figure 3.32 the whaling ship and the sailors have been photographed from a low angle. The viewer is positioned below them, perhaps on the water with the rest of the dead whale. In this image the represented participants are depicted as having power over the viewer. This might suggest the powerful position of the whalers with respect to the whales or those who oppose the the whaling industry.

The significance for critical pedagogy of knowledge about offers and demands, social distance and perspective is highlighted in the discussion by Kress and van Leeuwen (1996: 124–5, 132–3) of the portrayal of Aboriginal people in a primary/elementary school social studies text. In the chapter on Aborigines hardly any of the participants are depicted in visual demands. The exception to this is the close-up, eye-level, demand image of the Aboriginal poet, Oodgeroo Noonuccal. Other images of Aboriginal people in the text are clearly depicted as 'other'. In their earlier publication discussing this textbook Kress and van Leeuwen (1990) included a photograph from the book of three Aboriginal boys shown in a long shot, where they occupy about one quarter of

Figure 3.32   Low angle view affording power to the represented participants
Source: Cochrane 1987: 37 with permission from Glass Onion Pictures.

the height of the frame. The vertical angle is high, indicating viewer power and the horizontal angle is oblique, indicating viewer detachment. Although the boys do look at the viewer, the social distance is so great that it is difficult to distinguish their facial features. In other publications about Aboriginal people, including those from which images have been quoted in the present text, quite different viewer/image relations are constructed as indicated in Figures 3.6, 3.7 and 3.29. It is very useful to study which kinds of represented participants are, in a given context, depicted as having particular interactive relations with viewers and which are not. This will be explored further in relation to reading children's picture books in Chapter 5.

Realism: colour, context, detail, depth and light

The extent to which an image depicts the realism of the aspects of the material world it represents is determined by the benchmark of the high quality colour photograph. People judge an image to be 'naturalistic' if it approximates this level of representation. This concept of realism or credibility is referred to as modality. Colour is a major influence on naturalistic modality. Naturalistic images have high colour saturation rather than black and white. Their colours are diversified rather than monochrome, and they are modulated, using many shades of the various colours. Commonly used computer graphics and word processing software now enables easy manipulation of the colour of scanned images.

Naturalistic modality is also influenced by the contextualization of the image. In Figure 3.33 the bat is contextualized with a background showing the tree trunk and

Figure 3.33 Background contextualizing image
Source: Sloan and Latham 1985.

Bats that catch
large insects
often take them
to a perch where they
clip off their heads, legs,
and hard wing covers be-
fore eating the soft, tasty
body. In just one night, a
single bat can eat up to
half its body weight in
insects!

Figure 3.34 Image with no background contextualization
Source: Wood and Rink 1991: 20.

leaves and branches of the tree against the night sky. But in Figure 3.34 the picture of the insect-eating bat has no such background to contextualize it, and this contributes to a somewhat lower modality from a naturalistic perspective.

Modality also varies along a scale from maximum delineation of detail features of participants to the schematization of detail. In highly schematic images a head may be represented by a circle, the eyes by two dots, and the mouth by a curved line.

Objective images: cut-aways, cross-sections and explosions

Perspective resulting from the vertical and horizontal angle of an image construct viewer positions with respect to the image, and imply particular attitudes toward it. If the angle is directly frontal or perpendicular top down, this still suggests viewer positions, but such angles tend to reduce the 'attitudinizing' effect of perspective and afford some objectivity to the image (Kress and van Leeuwen 1996: 149). This is evident in Figure 3.22 showing the dynamo and Figure 3.26 showing the growth stages of a sunflower plant. In contrast Figure 3.24 from a science book for primary/elementary school students, showing the simple electric circuit, retains the perspectival effects of high vertical angle and oblique horizontal angle. This perhaps indicates the transition to more objective images in texts for the later years of schooling.

Cut-away images are objective in the sense that they show more than what is observable on the surface from any of the usual subjective positions of a viewer. Surfaces of represented participants are removed to reveal what is hidden. This can be seen in Figure 3.35 showing the internal organs of a spider.

Figure 3.35 is shown from a high vertical angle and a somewhat oblique horizontal angle, so perspective has not been completely neutralized in this image. On the other hand, Figure 3.36 shows a cross-section of a tapeworm. Cross-sections like this one are not only objective in showing what is normally hidden from observation, but they also adopt a perpendicular vertical angle (as in this case) or a direct frontal angle, neutralizing the attitudinizing effect of perspective.

Another version of the kind of objective image that reveals what is normally hidden from observation is the 'explosion', where components of a represented participant are presented as separated or 'exploded' as if ready for assembly. A popular example is *Stephen Biesty's Incredible Explosions* (Biesty and Platt 1996).

Coding orientation: what counts as real

The most common coding orientation is that of naturalism. Most people, most of the time, make judgements about the realism of an image on the basis of how 'naturally' it depicts the aspects of the material world it represents. Kress and van Leeuwen (1996: 168–71) point out that in other coding orientations, the standards of naturalism are not always the benchmarks for judging realism. They indicate that in a technological or scientific coding orientation what counts as real is what can be established

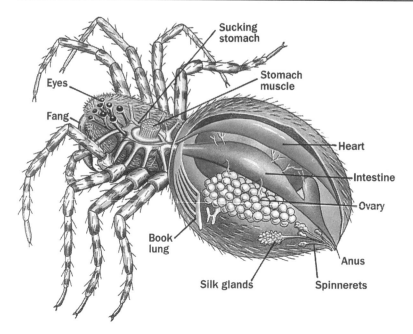

Figure 3.35   Cut-away image of a spider
Source: Hemsley 1990: 22.

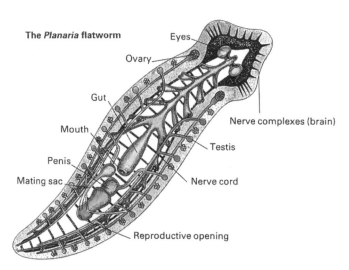

Figure 3.36   Cross-section of a tapeworm
Source: Bender 1988: 8.

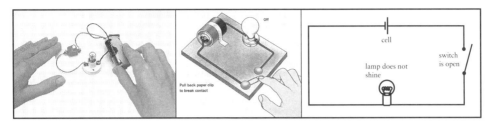

Figure 3.37   From naturalistic to scientific coding orientation
Sources: Whyman 1989: 11; Charman 1992: 28; DeVreeze *et al*. 1992: 140.

by the methods of science, so a technical line drawing without colour, perspective or context can have higher modality than a photograph. As students move through the school system, they gradually encounter a change in coding orientation in the textual representations of science they encounter. In the primary/elementary school the images are predominantly naturalistic, but they gradually change to the highly schematized images of a scientific coding orientation as students progress to the senior secondary school. The images of a simple circuit in Figure 3.37 indicate this transition. The shift from naturalism begins with truncation of human participants and reduction in contextualiza-tion and eventually reaches the highly schematized abstract representation.

Sometimes the transition in coding orientation is not well managed. Figure 3.38 shows the pages of a text exploring concepts related to Bernoulli's principle. These concern the relationship between the high speed of the air passing over the top of an airfoil and the lower speed of air passing underneath causing lower pressure on the top of the airfoil, which results in lift. The images are predominantly narrative, transactional images with high naturalistic modality. The one highly abstract image in the bottom right corner is very small and an abrupt change in coding orientation from the other images. The written text does relate the practical activity to an understanding of the technical concepts involved. It would have been possible to support this visually by including images of a transitional kind, which bridged from the naturalistic to the scientific coding orientation.

Transitional images retain some features of the naturalistic coding orientation such as more concrete rather than completely abstract participants, perspective and contextual background, albeit often somewhat truncated. In dealing with Bernoulli's principle for young students, transitional images often include a perspectival drawing of the wing of an aeroplane with superimposed horizontal vectors differentiated in width to show lower air pressure above the wing surface, and a vertical vector showing lift (see for example Lafferty 1989: 21). In the CD ROM format, *Encarta* (Microsoft 1992–94) provides this kind of transitional image in animated form. It shows the image of a person blowing on the top surface of a piece of paper and then the relevant vectors appear to indicate the relative air pressure and the lift. This is accompanied by an

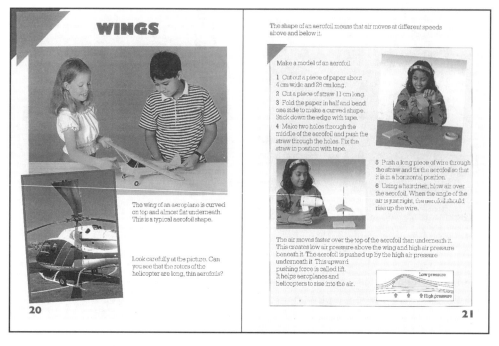

Figure 3.38   An abrupt shift in visual coding orientation
Source: Taylor 1991: 20–1.

animation of a light aircraft in flight, in which vectors representing the airflow, air pressure and lift, then appear.

COMPOSITIONAL MEANINGS: INFORMATION VALUE, FRAMING AND SALIENCE

Given and New: the information value of left and right

When we are considering the layout of texts on a page, within a page or over a double page spread, Kress and van Leeuwen (1996: 186–92) have pointed out that what is placed on the left-hand side is usually what is likely to be more familiar to the readership, and what is likely to be new is placed on the right-hand side. This reflects systemic functional linguistic descriptions of language in which the 'Given' is conflated with 'Theme' which refers to the initial units of meaning in the clause – those that occur at the left of the clause, while new information occurs at the end of the clause. Kress and van Leeuwen (1996: 186–92) have shown how this pattern of distribution of information value occurs in popular magazines, works of art and school textbooks. Within images that are part of a page layout, it is also frequently the case

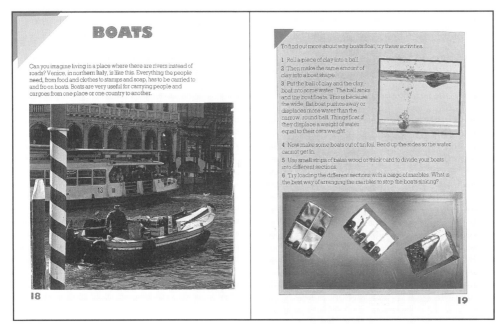

Figure 3.39   Given and New on a double page layout
Source: Taylor 1990: 18–19.

that more familiar information occurs on the left and the new information on the right. This can be seen in Figure 3.26, where the photograph of the dynamo is placed on the left and the diagram showing its internal components is on the left. Similarly, with double page spreads, what is Given is on the left-hand side and the new information is on the right-hand side. In Figure 3.39, everyday observational information and the image of boats floating is shown on the left, while the images concerning the investigation of the principles of buoyancy are shown on the right.

The Given and New structuring is quite functional in scaffolding readers' negotiation of new subject matter. It suggests that students might realistically be asked to attempt to deal independently with the left-hand side of the layout relating it to their experience and establishing a basis for progression to the right-hand side. This is where teacher-supported interactive work with the text is likely to be necessary.

Ideal and Real: the information value of top and bottom

Kress and van Leeuwen (1996: 193–203) point out that many images are structured along the vertical axis into top and bottom segments. Sometimes the dividing line is quite sharp; sometimes it is more subtle and there may be elements of the image that seem to connect the top and bottom. In advertisements the top part indicates the

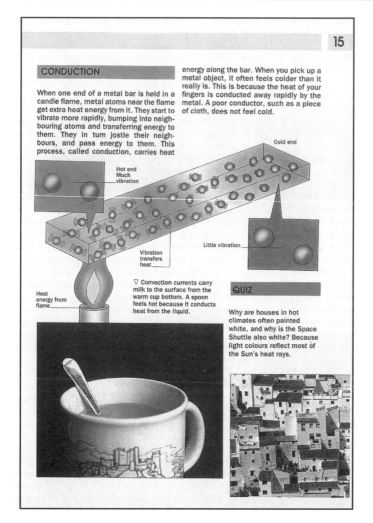

Figure 3.40   Real/Ideal – Concrete/Abstract structuring on the vertical axis
Source: Lafferty 1990: 15.

promise of the product – its imagined or ideal effects, while the bottom part of the layout indicates more concrete information about the product itself. In textbooks the top part of the layout deals with the more generalized, abstract conceptual information, while the bottom part deals with the specific, concrete observable information. The top is the realm of the ideal and the bottom is the realm of the real. In Figure 3.40 concrete, everyday, observable exemplars of the conduction of heat are provided, while the top part of the page provides the technical images and the generalized theoretical understandings. If the layout contains images only, the bottom image will be the more concrete and the top the more abstract.

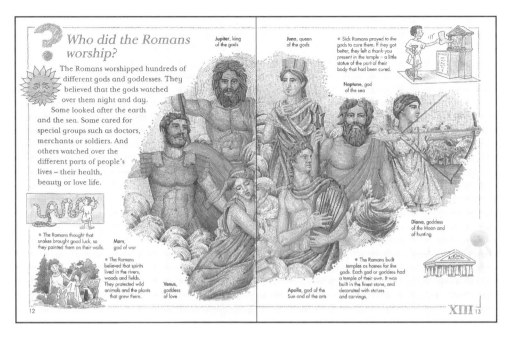

Figure 3.41   Circular Centre–margin layout
Source: Macdonald 1997: 12–13.

While the Given/New structures are consistent with the usual left to right progression in reading, the Ideal/Real structures in school curriculum texts do not necessarily map strategically onto our practice of working from the top to the bottom of the text. Students might be advised to examine the specific, concrete images at the bottom of the page before addressing the more abstract and generalized text and images usually located towards the top of the page. Often the salience of the concrete images will influence them to adopt just such a reading path.

Centre–margin layouts

Some layouts make more use of the centre, placing one element in the middle and the other elements around it, sometimes creating a kind of circular structure. This seems to be relatively uncommon in contemporary western visualization (Kress and van Leeuwen 1996: 203). It does occur, albeit infrequently, in information books for primary/elementary school students. Figure 3.41 shows the layout used throughout the book, *I Wonder Why Romans Wore Togas and Other Questions About Ancient Rome* (Macdonald 1997). The central element, called the Centre, is the nucleus of the information and the surrounding elements, the Margins, are subordinate to or

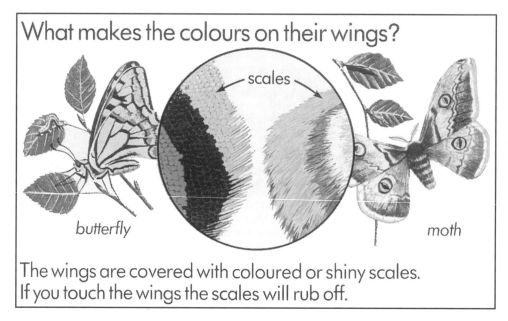

Figure 3.42 A triptych from a science book for young children
Source: Kidman Cox and Cork 1980: 5, reproduced from *Butterflies and Moths* by permission of Usborne Publishing, 83–85 Saffron Hill, London EC 1N 8RT. Copyright © 1980 Usborne Publishing Ltd.

dependent on (or sometimes peripheral to) the Centre. In these images the Margins tend to be similar in terms of information value, so there is no sense of Given and New along the horizontal dimension and no sense of Real and Ideal along the vertical dimension.

Another type of Centre and Margin layout does tend to combine with the Given and New distinction. This is the triptych, which consists of three distinct image elements in a row. Several examples from newspapers and from art are discussed by Kress and van Leeuwen (1996: 207–11, 216–18), however, these also seem to be quite rare in school curriculum texts. Figure 3.42 is a triptych illustrating the Centre–Margin structure. Here there is no sense of polarization of Given and New. The Centre is the nucleus of the information and the Margins provide the contextualizing information.

Figure 3.37 is an example of a triptych in which there is polarization of the images into a Given and New structure. The left-hand image is the Given, in the sense that it is the most familiar coding orientation, retaining many features of naturalistic modality. The image on the right-hand side is the New, in that it is the least familiar, most abstract, scientific coding orientation. The central image is like a mediator or transition element, still retaining perspective and some aspects of naturalism but with lowered modality.

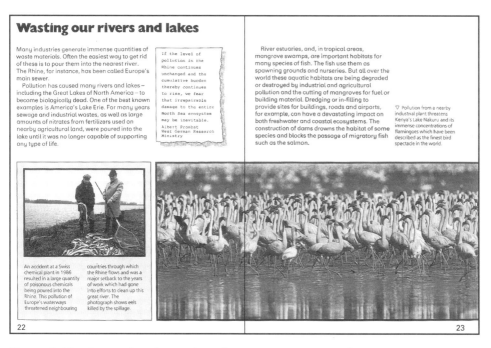

Figure 3.43   Strong framing and weak connection among elements
Source: Simon 1987: 22–3.

Framing

Elements or groups of elements within a layout may be disconnected and marked off from each other or connected, joined together. This is known as framing. Where elements are completely disconnected and marked off, they are strongly framed. Where the elements are more integrated, they are weakly framed. Framing can be achieved by the use of frame lines or borders around elements, by discontinuities of colour or shape, or by white space. Connectedness can be achieved by vectors from within images and by devices such as overlapping or superimposition of images. The more strongly framed an element is, the more it is emphasized as a separate piece of information. The double page spread entitled 'Wasting our rivers and lakes' in Figure 3.43 is strongly framed. The image of the flamingos extending from about one third of the bottom half of the left-hand page to the full extent of the bottom half of the right-hand page, clearly links the two pages. However, apart from this, the elements of the double page spread are not visually connected.

On the other hand, the double page spread entitled 'The whalers', shown in Figure 3.44, is not as strongly framed and is integrally connected. First we note the photograph of the man preparing the harpoon has no framing and is linked to the

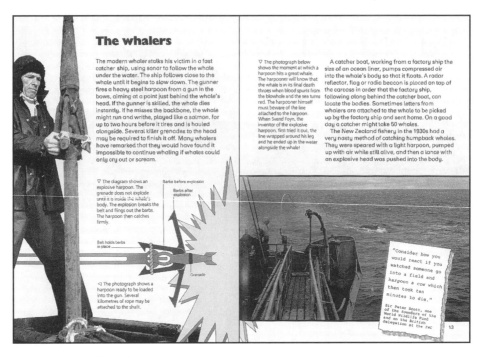

Figure 3.44   Weak framing and strong connection among elements
Source: Bright 1987: 12–13.

diagram showing how the harpoon explodes, which also has no frame. The shaft of
the harpoon in the diagram passes behind the man's legs in the photograph, but the blast
of the explosion extends over the front of the deck on which the man in the photograph is standing, so the images are intertwined. The next thing to notice is that the
star blast of the harpoon exploding extends to the right-hand page. Here the end of the
photograph of the front deck of the whaling boat firing a harpoon at a whale, is
superimposed on the star blast of the diagram, powerfully linking the diagram to both
photographs. Then the typed quotation from Sir Peter Scott is superimposed on the
photograph showing the whaling boat. Finally, the fact that the photo of the man
preparing the harpoon extends to the top of the left-hand page, and the image of the
whaling boat extends to the full width of the bottom of the right-hand page, provides
a kind of 'encompassing' frame for the print at the top of the pages. The elements of
this spatial composition are closely connected, indicating that they are part of the one
unit of information, as belonging together. What is very effectively linked here is the
individual work of the man preparing the harpoon, the violence of the harpoon blast,
the distant whale about to be shot and the personal involvement of the reader provoked by the superimposed quoted challenge. The importance of framing in constructing particular forms of cohesion among images in picture books for children will be
discussed further in Chapter 5.

Salience

Some elements in images have salience because of the effect of some or all of the factors such as the elements' relative size, their colour, their sharpness of contrast, location in the foreground, and/or distinctive framing. Human, human-like and animal participants also tend to be viewed as salient. In Figure 3.41 the central image of the Roman gods is salient because of its relative size in the layout, its centrality and its human figures, as well as strong colour contrast with the rest of the page, so this is the element that the eye is drawn to first. This is the beginning of the reading path. In Figure 3.43 about wasting our rivers and lakes, the size of the image of the flamingos, its extension across part of the left-hand page, and its colour, draw our attention. But the human figures in the image on the left-hand side, with the strongly framed border on the background, also compete for salience here, so the reading path may be from the flamingos to the left-hand side image and thence to the rest of the layout. In Figure 3.44 showing images of whaling, we have the strong contrast of the blast at the bottom centre of the layout, the strong vectors of the harpoon leading to the relatively large human figure on the left and the proportionately large space occupied by the photo of he whaling ship on the ocean. We also have the oblique angle and the highly contrasting white colour of the quotation superimposed on the photograph. The reading path here then, seems to be quite complex, but clearly encompassing the linked visual elements. In the case of Figures 3.43 and 3.44, it would seem that the reading path would first traverse the images and then proceed to the print. From that point on it would also seem that both of these layouts imply a fairly linear progression through the text. But the layouts of many contemporary texts are much less clear in suggesting this kind of linear progression. If we look at the page layout in Figure 3.45, the 'main' text is indicated by the larger font, but the framing of the central piece of text and its superimposition on the image, seems to draw the reader to this element of the layout first. In fact, the framed text is a more technical account of what is contained in the 'main' text. Does the reader progress linearly and read the simpler main text as a kind of 'advance organizer' to the framed text, or does one respond first to the framed prominence of the central text, with its link to the image, and then return to the 'main' text only if the framed text presents difficulty? As Kress and van Leeuwen point out (1996: 220–1) the layout of contemporary school texts construct quite complex choices about how to traverse the textual space and it is up the reader to choose from a range of possible reading paths. This is also obviously the case with many computer-based texts, where there are many possible pathways for navigating hypertext links.

CONCLUSION

This chapter provides a basis for a meta-language dealing with the meaning-making systems deployed in images. The work of Kress and van Leeuwen (1996), from which this work has been derived, deals with static images, although van Leeuwen has

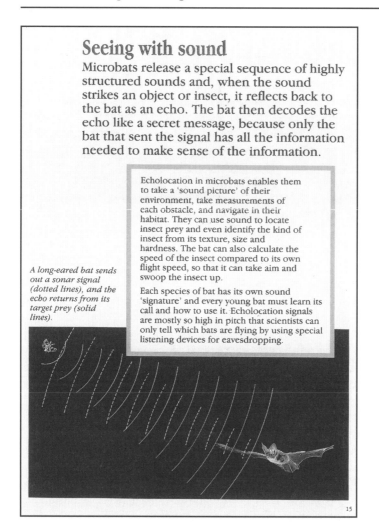

Seeing with sound

Microbats release a special sequence of highly structured sounds and, when the sound strikes an object or insect, it reflects back to the bat as an echo. The bat then decodes the echo like a secret message, because only the bat that sent the signal has all the information needed to make sense of the information.

Echolocation in microbats enables them to take a 'sound picture' of their environment, take measurements of each obstacle, and navigate in their habitat. They can use sound to locate insect prey and even identify the kind of insect from its texture, size and hardness. The bat can also calculate the speed of the insect compared to its own flight speed, so that it can take aim and swoop the insect up.

Each species of bat has its own sound 'signature' and every young bat must learn its call and how to use it. Echolocation signals are mostly so high in pitch that scientists can only tell which bats are flying by using special listening devices for eavesdropping.

A long-eared bat sends out a sonar signal (dotted lines), and the echo returns from its target prey (solid lines).

Figure 3.45   Multiple reading paths
Source: Woodside 1993: 15.

extended some aspects to descriptions of dynamic images (van Leeuwen 1996). Many contemporary practical publications for teachers, describing different forms of images (Moline 1995; Quin *et al.* 1995, 1996, 1997a, 1997b; Travers and Hancock 1996) can be subsumed by the functional semiotic systems of Kress and van Leeuwen (1996). The extrapolation of these systems from systemic functional linguistics means that teachers and students can use compatible meta-language as they interpret and construct visual and verbal texts. The practical application of this resource can be seen in the exploration of multimodal meaning-making in literature for children in Chapter 5 and then in curriculum area teaching of children from the early school years to the beginning of the secondary school years in the final three chapters of the book.

CHAPTER 4

Distinguishing the literacies of school science and humanities

THE INTERDEPENDENCE OF LITERACIES AND LEARNING IN CURRICULUM AREAS

Developing the range of literacies needed by students from diverse backgrounds to effectively negotiate school learning is a complex task. One aspect of current endeavours to resource teachers for this task is addressing the complete interconnectedness of learning in content areas and learning to control the grammatical forms and text types that construct and communicate knowledge in those content areas. This entails developing knowledge of the linguistic form of curriculum area texts. We can clearly recognize the following texts as being located in different curriculum areas:

> Billy is calm in the face of adult outrage, quietly transforming himself into his ideal of a punk ...
> (New South Wales Department of Education and Training 1997)

> *Some* of the other things the liver does include:
> 1 controlling the concentrations of digested food products in the blood. Blood from the intestines has many different concentrations of glucose and amino acids, depending on the type of meal eaten. By the time the blood leaves the liver, the concentration of these chemicals is kept constant.
> (Heffernan and Learmonth 1990: 110)

> All over the world wetlands are threatened by drainage and conversion to arable land.
> (Simon 1987: 21)

> In 1971, which part of Australia had the lowest average age of people?
> (New South Wales Department of Education and Training 1997)

Although the league sought cooperation between classes, its determination to re-establish the integrity and prosperity of Australia marked it as largely representing business and professional groups.

(Tudball 1991: 404)

We can also recognize that the language of these texts is not the everyday language we use to deal with day to day matters. It is highly unlikely that you would ever 'say' these things using these forms of language in face to face interaction. What might you say instead of 'Billy is calm in the face of adult outrage'? Perhaps you would say something like:

Billy is calm even though an adult is shouting angrily at him.

Instead of 'All over the world wetlands are threatened by drainage and conversion to arable land', you might say something like

All over the world people are draining more and more of the wetlands and con-verting them to farming land, so it is likely that a lot of wetlands will disappear altogether.

What makes the written texts above different from the more familiar oral language versions we have 'talked out' is not simply a matter of subject-specific, technical or specialized vocabulary. There are no 'technical' terms in the text about 'Billy the Punk' and only the technical term 'arable' in the wetlands text. What is different is the grammatical structure – reflecting well documented differences between the grammar of spoken and written language (Perera 1984; Halliday and Hasan 1985; Hammond 1990; Unsworth 1997b, 1999c).

The oral language we have 'talked out' of the written texts above contains more clauses per sentence than the written versions. This is very typical of spoken language – a lot of clauses inside the one sentence. We can see this pattern in classroom talk. In the following example, taken from Hammond (1990: 36), a student is talking about the novel *Z for Zachariah* (O'Brien 1975):

Like I reckon he would have been really nice || **but** now that he's been to all the towns || **and** seen like there's no life or anything || **and** he comes into the valley || **and** sees Ann || **and** sees life || **and** he just wanted power over her || **because** he's never had power or anything before.

Here we have one sentence with eight clauses – all joined by conjunctions, which are in bold type above.

Another example (from Hammond 1990: 48) is shown below where the student is talking about aboriginal studies:

When we were in Queensland ‖ my dad had some friends up there ‖ **and** he asked ‖ **if** we could borrow some guns for hunting and everything ‖ **and** as we were all going there ‖ we could see their paintings like rocks and things got patterns on them and everything.

In this case we have one sentence and six clauses and some different conjunctions.

We find this kind of grammatical structure in our own talk as well. The following is an example of the classroom talk of a secondary school science teacher (Ogborn *et al.* 1996: 41).

The *liver's part* of the *digestive system*,‖ I *guess*,‖ because *eventually food* is *taken* from the – from the *gut*, via the *blood*, to the *liver*,‖ and *stored* in the *liver* ‖ till it's *needed*, okay?,‖ so, for example, if you *have* for *lunch* four *Mars bars* and you . . . four *Mars bars* – ‖ then the *stuff* would *go* to the, to your *gut*,‖ all the *sugar* in those *Mars bars*, ‖which would be a *lot*,‖ would *come straight back* to your *gut*, and into your *blood*,‖ and your *blood* would be like *treacle*, ‖ because it's *full* of *sugar*,‖ so in fact, it's *taken straight* to the *liver*, ‖ and it's *stored* in the *liver* ‖ and *small amounts* are *let* out, uh, through the *course* of the *day*, okay?, ‖ so that's the, that's a *kind* of *storehouse* ‖ where *things* are *stored*, ‖ so the *liver stores food*,‖ it does a *whole load* of other *jobs*, ‖ but it *stores food*.

Here we have 19 clauses in the one sentence. In this extract the lexical items (content words) are italicized to distinguish them from the grammatical items (structure words). If we work out the proportion of lexical items or content words per clause, then it gives us a measure of lexical density and this indicates the density of content being communicated. In this piece of talk by the science teacher there are 57 lexical items underlined in 19 clauses so the lexical density is 3 (57/19). That is a bit higher than the usual lexical density of everyday talk which is about 2. In the example above of the student talking about *Z for Zachariah*, for example, there are 14 lexical items distributed over 10 clauses, thus the text has a lexical density of 1.4 and this is fairly typical of spoken medium.

Now if we look at a textbook segment on the same topic as the science teacher's talk about the liver, we will notice how the grammar of written science texts differs from the grammar of talk:

The *liver* has been *called* the *body's chemical factory*. It is a *large, red coloured organ* – the *largest gland* in the *body*. We have *already seen* that the *liver produces bile*, which is *stored* in the *gall bladder*, before being *used* to *help digest fats* (*see* Chapter 3). *Some* of the other *things* the *liver does include*:

1 *controlling* the *concentrations* of *digested food products* in the *blood*. *Blood* from the *intestines has* many *different concentrations* of *glucose* and *amino acids*,

depending on the *type* of *meal eaten*. By the *time* the *blood leaves* the *liver*, the *concentration* of these *chemicals* is *kept constant*.
2 *converting* the *excess glucose* into *glycogen* with the *help* of the *hormone insulin*.

(Heffernan and Learmonth 1990: 110)

This passage has six sentences, 13 clauses and 62 lexical items. So the number of clauses per sentence is much less than the classroom talk, but the lexical density is 4.8 (62/13) – appreciably higher than the lexical density of the talk at 3. The density of content to be comprehended is much greater in the written text.

Lexical densities of this order or higher are common in curriculum area texts. The following is from a book intended for upper primary and junior secondary school students:

The vanishing forests
The largest stretch of coniferous forest in the world – the taiga – encircles the earth in the northern hemisphere. The taiga supplies the bulk of the world's commercial softwood timber. The dominant tree species is larch, but fir, spruce and others are common.

(Simon 1987: 7)

In this extract there are three sentences, four clauses and 24 lexical items – a lexical density of 6.

In the forms of English used in specialized subject areas then, written medium tends to pack information more densely than spoken medium. This is achieved through greater use of lexical items (content words) in comparison with grammatical items (structure words). How is this achieved? In the student talk about 'Zachariah' or 'aboriginal studies' the lexical items occur as single words identifying single entities like:

towns, valley, guns, rocks, patterns.

However, many of the lexical items in curriculum area texts occur within groups of words that construct single entities:

'concentrations of digested food products',
'the concentration of these chemicals',
'the largest stretch of coniferous forest in the world',
'the world's commerical softwood timber'.

These groups of words that constitute single entities are known as *noun groups*. By expanding the noun groups to include more lexical items (content words), a greater amount of information is able to be included within each clause.

As students progress through the education system they need to learn to deal with the distinctive grammar of written texts with their proportionately lower number of clauses and greater complexity within the clause. Consider for example this single sentence, single clause extract from an information book for primary children:

> Many of the *wild animals traded* in the *luxury market* have been so *reduced* in *numbers* that they are in *danger* of *extinction*.
>
> (Bright 1988: 5)

In this single clause sentence we have nine content words (or lexical items) so the lexical density is 9/1 = 9. If you were telling someone this information, how many clauses would you need to use? The following is one attempt at 'talking out' this segment:

> Hunters kill some wild animals ‖so that they can sell them to traders ‖who then sell them to manufacturers ‖ who make luxury products out of parts of the animals bodies.‖ The hunters have killed so many of these wild animals that there are hardly any of them left ‖and there is a danger that they will die out completely.

This 'talking out' used two sentences and a total of six clauses. There are 23 content words (lexical items) in the text so the lexical density is 23/6 = 3.8 – less than half the lexical density of the written version. But you will notice that it is not just a matter of using more clauses and spreading out the lexical items. A significant aspect of this 'talking out' is turning single (nominalized) noun groups into noun + verb structures. We can see how these (nominalized) noun groups are built into texts by looking at the first two clauses in the introduction to *Killing for Luxury* (Bright 1988: 4)

> Man has always killed animals. The killing was traditionally for food and clothing.

In the first clause the noun groups (Man, animals) are indeed things, but in the second clause, the first noun group is a nominalization – 'The killing'. It is a simple noun group structure:

The	killing
Article	Thing

But the Thing is actually realizing an event, which implies an action. This is a very common resource in English, where we turn verbs into nouns. This 'nominalization' is a form of what Halliday (1994a) calls grammatical metaphor, and refers to

> a substitution of one grammatical class, or one grammatical structure by another; for example, *his departure* instead of *he departed*. Here the words (lexical items) are the same; what has changed is their place in the grammar. Instead of the

pronoun *he* + verb *departed*, functioning as Actor + Process in a clause, we have determiner *his* + noun *departure*, functioning as Deictic + Thing in a nominal group.

(Halliday 1993a: 79)

We can see this in our earlier example about wetlands from the book for upper primary students called *Vanishing Habitats* (Simon 1987: 21):

All over *the world wetlands* are threatened by *drainage* and *conversion to arable land*.

The noun groups are italicized. The first two (the world, wetlands) are clearly 'things' in the everyday sense, but 'drainage' and 'conversion' are 'things' only in language – they are abstract or pseudo things. In our more 'spoken' explanation of this phenomenon the events are realized as action verbs:

All over the world people *are draining* more and more of the wetlands and *converting* them to arable (farming) lands so there is a danger that the wetlands will disappear.

Grammatical metaphor is essential to the construction of specialized knowledge in language and this has been well established in the literature (Halliday 1993b; Martin 1993a, 1993c). Martin (1993a) for example, shows how nominalization is a key resource in constructing technicality:

The production of rock waste by mechanical processes   is called   weathering and chemical changes

In this example the meanings to be compacted and distilled as the technical term 'weathering' must be in a nominalized form ('The production of . . .') so that they can be grammatically equated with the nominal form of the single technical term.

The active role of language in constructing scientific understanding via the resources of grammatical metaphor is illustrated by Martin's analysis of a segment from a secondary school science textbook dealing with electricity (Martin 1993d).

As far as the ability to carry electricity is concerned, we can place most substances into one of two groups. The first group contains materials with many electrons that are free to move. These materials are called conductors . . .

The second group contains materials with very few electrons that are free to move. These materials are called non-conductors . . .

There are a few materials, such as germanium and silicon, called semiconductors. Their ability to conduct electricity is intermediate between conductors and insulators.

(Heffernan and Learmonth 1983: 212)

Martin draws attention to the role of grammatical metaphor in the realization of the criterion used to classify substances – 'the *ability* to carry electricity'.

> This kind of coding involves the nominalisation of potentiality, which in the spoken language would typically be coded as the modal verb (as in substances can/can't carry electricity).
>   . . . the nominalised rendering of the criterion, 'the ability to conduct electricity', opens up a semantic space for substances which are *partially* able to conduct electricity. This space is not available in the more spoken coding since one of the peculiarities of potentiality, as far as modality is concerned, is the fact that it is not gradable. With potentiality realised as a modal verb, substances either can or can't conduct electricity; there's nothing in between. Potentiality contrasts in this respect with other modalities, like those of probability or obligation (following Halliday 1985: 334–40).
>
>   (Martin 1993d: 95)

Martin goes on to point out that once nominalized, potentiality becomes gradable ('A low/medium/high ability to conduct electricity'). This expanded meaning potential is used to establish a category of substances whose 'ability to conduct electricity is intermediate between conductors and insulators'. In other words the construction of this uncommonsense, scientific knowledge

> depends on the grammar of writing – on a process of nominalisation which makes available meanings that are not readily available in the spoken form.
>
>   (Martin 1993d: 95)

As well as its functionality in construing the taxonomic structure of scientific knowledge through the linguistic realization of definition and classification, grammatical metaphor is also a crucial resource in explanatory texts, facilitating the development of a chain of reasoning. In order to lead on to the next step you have to be able to summarize what has gone before as 'the springboard for the next move' (Halliday 1993b: 131). By expressing a series of events as a Thing, those summarized events can then assume a participant role in the next part of the explanation. You can see this in the short extracts from both science and history texts shown in Figure 4.1.

We have noted that oral language uses many clauses in sentences and joins these clauses with conjunctions. The conjunctions are the typical grammatical means in oral language of constructing logical relations of cause, time sequence, comparison etc. using conjunctions such as 'because, therefore, then, and then, like' etc. In written language these meanings are often not realized by conjunctions but by nouns and verbs – another form of grammatical metaphor. This can be seen in the following comparisons:

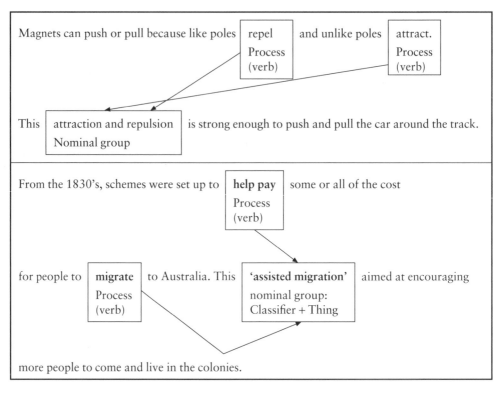

Figure 4.1   Grammatical metaphor as a resource in explanatory texts
Sources: Robson 1992a: 13; Anderson and Ashton 1993: 135.

Written mode	Spoken mode
Land use conflict is the **result** of the numerous competing demands placed on land in urban areas by various land uses. (Humphrey 1996: 19)	People argue about how they should use the land **because** different groups of people want to use the land in urban areas in different ways.
A red blood cell is circular in shape when seen from above and concave or dough-nut in shape when seen from the side. The circular shape **leads to** easy and fast transportation of oxygen to all parts of the body. The doughnut shape **results in** a large surface area to each red blood cell. **The effect of the shape** is that a lot of oxygen is absorbed by each cell. (Polias 1998: 106)	A red blood cell is circular in shape when seen from above and concave or dough-nut in shape when seen from the side. **Because** the red blood cells have a cir-cular shape, oxygen moves quickly and easily to all parts of the body. The doughnut shape gives a large surface area to each red blood cell. **Therefore** a lot of oxygen is absorbed by each cell.

You will notice that the use of nouns and verbs instead of conjunctions to realize logical relations is related to the use of nominalization. For example, in the written mode version of the second example the verb 'leads to' is associated with the nominalization 'transportation', while in the spoken version the conjunction 'because' is associated with the verb 'moves'.

The use of grammatical metaphor in written language enables the texturing of familiar or given information in Theme position at the beginning of the clause and the location of new information at the end of the clause, as is typical in English. This is illustrated using the 'blood cell' text in Figure 4.2. The information about shape, introduced as new information in the first few clauses, becomes the given information in Theme position in the subsequent clauses. Furthermore, the nominalization of the logical relation of cause ('The effect of shape') enables this compacted cumulation of the new information of the previous two clauses to be placed as what is now given information in the Theme position of the final clause.

We could, of course, provide many other kinds of examples of the functionality of the grammar of written language in constructing specialized knowledge (see for example Martin 1993d). What is clear even from this abbreviated account is that effective access to knowledge and understanding in curriculum areas entails access to the grammatical resources characteristic of the written mode. As Wells has pointed out:

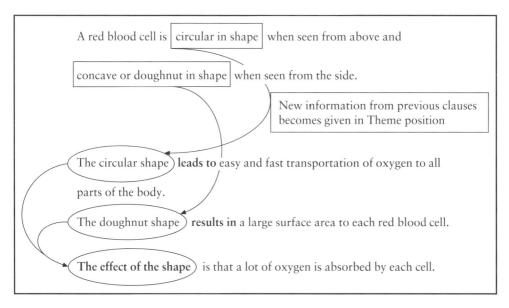

Figure 4.2 Grammatical metaphor as a resource in the texturing of given and new information
Source: Polias 1998: 106.

Through engaging with written texts in relation to the topics that they study in school, therefore, children gradually reconstitute their lexicogrammar in the more abstract written mode . . .

Thus, in learning to reconstrue experience in terms of the semantic structures of written language, children construct what Vygotsky refers to as 'scientific concepts'. That is to say, it is written texts – and the talk about them – that provide the discursive means for the development of the 'higher mental functions'.

(Wells 1994: 81–2)

SUBJECT-SPECIFIC LITERACIES IN SCHOOL LEARNING

Differentiating the genres or text types in school science and humanities

Research from a variety of theoretical perspectives (Richards 1978; Davies and Greene 1984; Street 1984; Gee 1990; Martin 1993b; Unsworth 1999a) has shown that subject areas have their own characteristic language forms and hence entail distinctive literate practices. The distinctive use of language in different school subject areas extends from word level (vocabulary) to grammar and to the organization of whole texts (genres or text types). In this section we will focus on genre variation.

Early work describing the written genres of school subject areas delineated a relatively small range of these text types (Martin 1984; Macken *et al.* 1989; Derewianka 1990a). Some of these genres are indicated in Figure 4.3.

Subsequent work has expanded the range of genres described both by identifying additional distinctive genres and by developing more delicate accounts of genre, distinguishing subtypes within families of genres (Rothery 1996; Coffin 1997; Veel 1997; Feez and Joyce 1998). Figure 4.4 summarizes the principal genres identified in the writing of school history.

If we compare the history genres in Figure 4.4 with the summary of principal genres identified in school science as shown in Figure 4.5, we will notice that there are some genres that are common and some that are distinctive to one or the other subject area.

Both taxonomic and descriptive reports and consequential and factorial explanations are common. Examples of factorial explanations in science and history are shown in Figure 4.6. Genres like Procedure and Procedural Recount are prominent in science but don't appear to be so relevant in history. Similarly, the recount genres do not seem to be so significant in science. This is not to say that such genres never occur in science texts and, in fact, historical recounts also appear in maths texts.

The principal genres of different school subject areas are distinguished by the relative frequency of their occurrence and use as well as by their differential valuing within the discipline area. For example, although historical recounts occur in science, much

Genre	Examples (abbreviated)	Stages
Recount	On Friday 25th May year four went on an excursion to the old Quarantine Station. We took the train and then the bus. The first thing we did was sketch the view we could see from the Quarantine Station. Then we went on a tour of the old buildings . . . After lunch we saw a film and then we took the bus and train back to school.	Orientation Record of Events Re-orientation
Procedure	Try making a rain detector that will set off an alarm when it starts to rain. You will need a plastic bottle or tube, sticky tape, glue, sugar cubes and some marbles. 1 Rest a tray on a board on a brick to make a slope. • Glue a row of sugar lumps near the top of the board. • Put some marbles in the container, seal the end with sticky tape and rest it on the sugar lumps . . . (Taylor 1992: 23)	Goal Materials Steps
Report	There are three main cloud groups. The highest, called cirrus, are usually made of ice crystals because the air is so cold. White fluffy piles of clouds are called cumulus, meaning 'heap'. Sometimes they join together to form huge, towering storm clouds, called cumulonimbus. Flat clouds are called stratus, meaning 'layer' . . . (Taylor 1992: 20)	General Classification Description
Explanation	Cloudy Skies Clouds are formed when warm air rises or when warm and cold air meet. Clouds are made up of billions of tiny droplets of water or ice. All air contains some water. Near the ground, this is usually in the form of an invisible gas called water vapour. But when air rises, it cools down. Cool air cannot hold as much water vapour as warm air, so some of the water vapour turns into drops of liquid water. This liquid then collects to form clouds. The process of water turning from a gas into a liquid is called condensation. (Taylor 1992: 20)	Phenomenon Identification Explanation Sequence
Exposition	Changing Attitudes Attitudes to animals have changed in the last 100 years, and today many societies have a greater respect for animal welfare. For example, concern about experiments with live animals has led to changes in the law. In the UK, since 1987, each scientific project using animals has to be registered to ensure . . . Other important changes in animal welfare have been achieved by economic means . . . the decline of the Canadian baby seal cull . . . brought about by the refusal of individuals and governments to buy . . . As individuals we can all improve the lives of animals by becoming more concerned about the way we treat them. (Barton 1987: 28)	Thesis Argument 1 Evidence Argument 2 Evidence Reinforcement of Thesis
Discussion	Economic Effects of World War I World War I had a basically stimulating effect on most aspects of the Australian economy . . . But there were forces that both encouraged and retarded growth during the war. The war offered many new opportunities through increased demand. Local wartime contracts were placed for food, clothing . . . However, the war also limited economic opportunities through disruption to trade patterns. For example, the wheat industry lost . . . The war, therefore, a mixed blessing. The net general effect was to encourage Australia's manufacturing base . . . But this was offset by a significant growth in national debt . . . (Tudball 1991: 335)	Issue Arguments for Arguments against Position

Figure 4.3   Prominent genres in school literacy identified in early research

	Genre	Social purpose	Stages
Chronicling history	Autobiographical Recount	to retell the events of your own life	Orientation Record of Events (Reorientation)
	Biographical Recount	to retell the events of a person's life	Background Record of Events (Evaluation of person)
	Historical Recount	to retell events in the past	Background Record of Events (Deduction)
Reporting history	Descriptive Report	to give information about the way things are or were	Identification Description (Deduction)
	Taxonomic Report	to organize knowledge taxonomically	Classification Description of types or parts
Explaining history	Historical Account	to account for why events happened in a particular sequence	Background Account of Events (Deduction)
	Factorial Explanation	to explain the reasons or factors that contribute to a particular outcome	Outcome Factors Reinforcement of Factors
	Consequential Explanation	to explain the effects or consequences of a situation	Input Consequences Reinforcement of consequences
Arguing history	Analytical Exposition	to put forward a point of view or argument	(Background) Thesis Arguments Reinforcement of Thesis
	Analytical Discussion	to argue the case for two or more points of view about an issue	(Background) Issue Arguments Position
	Challenge	to argue against a view	(Background) Arguments Anti-Thesis

Figure 4.4   Principal genres in school history

	Genre	Social purpose	Stages
Doing science	Procedure	To enable scientific activity, such as experiments and observations, to occur	Aim Materials needed Steps
	Procedural Recount	To recount in order and with accuracy the aim, steps, results and conclusion of a scientific activity	Aim Record of Events Conclusion
Explaining events scientifically	Sequential Explanation	To explain how something occurs or is produced – usually observable sequences of activities which take place on a regular basis	Phenomenon identification Explanation sequence (consisting of a number of phases)
	Causal Explanation	To explain why an abstract and/or not readily observable process occurs	Phenomenon identification Explanation sequence (consisting of a number of phases)
	Theoretical Explanation	To introduce and illustrate a theoretical principle and/or to explain events which are counter-intuitive	Phenomenon identification/Statement of theory Elaboration [1→n]*
	Factorial Explanation	To explain events for which there are a number of simultaneously occurring causes	Phenomenon identification Factor [1→n]
	Consequential Explanation	To explain events which have a number of simultaneously occurring effects	Phenomenon identification Effect [1→n]
	Exploration	To account for events for which there are two or more viable explanations	Issue Explanation Explanation [2→n]
Organizing scientific information	Descriptive Report	To describe the attributes, properties, behaviour etc. of a single class of object	General statement Description
	Taxonomic Report	To describe a number of classes of thing in a system of classification	General statement Description
Challenging science	Exposition	To persuade the reader to think or act in particular ways	Thesis Arguments 1→n Reinforcement of Thesis
	Discussion	To persuade the reader to accept a particular position on an issue by presenting arguments for and against the issue	Issue Dismissal of opponent's position Arguments for

Figure 4.5   Principal genres in school science
*1→n = one (or any number) of the instances of the stage named

Why did America lose?	Physical Weathering
America was the most powerful military nation in the world, yet it lost the war in Vietnam to an army of straw-hatted peasants. There are a number of reason for this:	This process is the cause of the breaking up of large rocks into smaller pieces. Physical processes can cause changes in rocks. The two most important methods are changes in *temperature* and the *freeze-thaw changes* of water.

Why did America lose?

America was the most powerful military nation in the world, yet it lost the war in Vietnam to an army of straw-hatted peasants. There are a number of reason for this:

- The South Vietnamese government was widely unpopular because of its corruption and failure to introduce land reforms. This meant the Vietcong had widespread support amongst the ordinary peasants, and the brutal methods used by the Americans to fight the war actually increased that support – they lost the battle for the 'hearts and minds' of the Vietnamese people.
- The Americans severely underestimated the Vietcong. The derogatory names such as 'dink' and 'gook' show this attitude. The Americans were overconfident and didn't take the Vietcong seriously until it was too late.
- The American army was trained to fight a conventional war of 'set-piece' battles against large armies where it could bring its superior fire-power to bear. It had difficulty adapting to the low-scale guerrilla tactics adopted by the Vietcong, which were perfectly suited to the difficult jungle terrain in Vietnam.
- Vietnam was the first media war – widespread television coverage showing the bloody reality of war undermined support for the war in America, leading to massive anti-war demonstrations and unrest at home. Deaths of student protesters like those at Ohio University in 1970 sickened many Americans and eventually forced the government to make peace.
- The Vietnamese cleverly exploited opposition to the war in America. The Tet Offensive of 1968 was considered a victory by the Vietnamese, even though they were actually defeated in battle. The television coverage of the massive American casualties convinced many Americans that the war could not be won, and Nixon was elected President on the promise to end the war.

(http://www.thehistorychannel.co.uk/classroom/frames/vietf.htm)

Physical Weathering

This process is the cause of the breaking up of large rocks into smaller pieces. Physical processes can cause changes in rocks. The two most important methods are changes in *temperature* and the *freeze-thaw changes* of water.

Changes in temperature cause the rock to expand and shrink. Different parts of the rock expand and shrink by different amounts and so the rock is made weaker. You have probably seen the effect of freeze-thaw changes of water: the size of ice cubes is always larger than the amount of water put into the ice cube trays to make them. If water is trapped in a crack in a rock and then freezes, it can force that crack to widen.

There are also four other processes that are important to the breakdown of rocks. Firstly, rocks may be shattered by *lightning* as it strikes high peaks during thunderstorms. Only very few people have been on hand to see how much change this action causes.

Secondly, *plants* assist the breakdown of rocks by their roots growing into cracks. These cracks may have first formed by temperature changes, then widened by ice freezing. The growing roots can widen cracks further.

Thirdly, *animals'* burrows often loosen and mix soil and rock pieces. This exposes fresh rock pieces to air, wind and water.

Finally, the actions of people cannot be forgotten. We can and do cause changes in rocks much more quickly than any of the natural forces. What natural forces can match bulldozers and dynamite?

(Heffernan and Learmonth 1988: 29)

Figure 4.6   Factorial explanations in school science and history
Source: Heffernan and Learmonth 1988: 29, reproduced with permission of Pearson Education, Australia.

more prominence tends to be given to scientific report and explanation genres. It appears that the use of particular genres also tends to vary across fields within subject areas. Genres like exposition and discussion that challenge science, for example, tend to occur more in less well established areas of the discipline like eco-science (Veel 1998). It does seem that there are some genres that occur in some subject areas but would be highly unlikely to occur in others. Procedural Recounts for example, seem unlikely to occur in history and English. Similarly, there are several genres that are important in English classes that do not occur in other curriculum areas. A summary of some of the principal genres appearing in the teaching of English is shown in Figure 4.7.

The story genres of English would be most infrequent in other subject areas as would the response genres. The review genre, exemplified in Figure 4.8, is characteristic of the particular association of these genres with English teaching.

The discrete genres we have been discussing are readily identifiable and account for much of what students need to read and/or write in studying particular content areas. However, it is also the case that sometimes judicious mixing or embedding of one genre inside another is used as a very effective means of achieving the purpose of the text. For example, Procedure and Explanation are mixed in the example from a primary school information book shown in Figure 4.9. This mixing (along with the illustrations) seems quite functional as a 'transitional' text, preparatory to students negotiating a greater frequency of stand-alone explanation texts as they progress through the secondary school.

Some genres function as stages in other genres. In Figure 4.10 the Evidence stage in an Analytical Exposition takes the form of an embedded Descriptive Report and an Explanation, so these two genres in fact form one stage (evidence) in the main genre of which they are a part (Humphrey 1996). Figure 4.11 shows how a Historical Recount is embedded as an argument stage in the Discussion genre (Coffin 1996: 174).

The genres charted to date in the work reported and illustrated here are not exhaustive nor does the charting of genres imply prescriptive teaching. Genres are not fixed and invariant. They identify classes of texts with particular characteristics in common, rather like the word 'chair' identifies a range of often different looking pieces of furniture with similar social purposes and certain common characteristics – and 'table' identifies another range of furniture, etc. Genres, as integral features of subject area learning and teaching then, should not be seen as straitjackets but as starting points. Students will be in a better position to both understand and critically interpret texts and to create and manipulate texts and combine elements in a purposeful way, when they understand that:

- different genres or text types exist;
- these various genres are a means of achieving different social purposes;
- genres are typically structured in particular ways; and
- genres have characteristic grammatical features.

The ways in which grammatical resources are deployed also distinguishes the language of different content areas.

	Genre	Social purpose	Stages
Persuasion	Exposition	Arguing for a particular point of view on an issue	(Background) Thesis Arguments Reinforcement of Thesis
	Disscussion	Arguing the case for one or more points of view on an issue	(Background) Issue Arguments Position
Story	Observation	Personal observations on things or events	Orientation Event Description Comment
	Recount	Reconstructing a temporal succession of events	Orientation Record of Events Reorientation
	Narrative	Dealing with unusual or problematic events and their outcomes	Orientation Complication Evaluation Resolution
	Moral tale/Fable	Telling a story with an explicit moral point	
	Exemplum	Dealing with events and giving them significance in cultural terms	Orientation Incident and Interpretation Coda
	News Story	Dealing with daily newsworthy events	Headline Lead Lead Development
Response	Personal Response	Making a personal response to a culturally significant work	Orientation Text Description Comment
	Review	Assessing the appeal and value of a culturally significant work	Context Text Description Judgement
	Interpretation	Interpreting the 'message' of a culturally significant work	Text Evaluation Text Synopsis Reaffirmation of Text Evaluation
	Critical Response	Analysing a culturally significant work for its meaning and denaturalizing the cultural values of the message.	Text Evaluation Text Deconstruction Challenge to Text Evaluation

Figure 4.7   Principal genres in school English

REVIEW	SCHEMATIC STRUCTURE
A Look at. . . . J. K. Rowling. *Harry Potter and the Philospher's Stone*	
Harry Potter is fast becoming a publishing phenomenon. The first two books about this appealing young boy have sold in record numbers around the world and made the adult best seller lists. Film rights for the first two books have been sold for a large amount. No, they are not written by John Grisham, nor are they newly discovered manuscripts by Roald Dahl. Harry Potter is the creation of J. K Rowling, a single mother of 34, who wrote the first book over four years, snatching time to write when her daughter was asleep – usually in cafes after a mad dash to lull the infant off to sleep, or late at night. **Harry Potter and the Philosopher's Stone** is her first published book.	Context
Harry Potter is an orphan. Both his parents died when he was a baby and Harry was brought up by his maternal aunt and her husband, *Mr and Mrs Dursley, of number four, Privet Drive, [who] were proud to say that they were perfectly normal, thank you very much.* Mrs and Mrs Dursley didn't want Harry but when they found him on their doorstep there wasn't anywhere else to send him. They were happy, thank you very much, with their perfect son Dudley. Since that time Harry had lived in the cupboard under the stairs, attended the local school where he was bullied mercilessly, and was generally mistreated by the Dursleys.	Text Description
Harry is a small, skinny, bespectacled schoolboy – who *looked even smaller and skinnier than he really was because all he had to wear were old clothes of Dudley's . . . Harry had a thin face, knobbly knees, black hair and bright green eyes. He wore round glasses held together with a lot of sellotape because of all the times Dudley had punched him in the nose. The only thing Harry liked about his own appearance was a very thin scar on his forehead which was shaped like a bolt of lightning.*	
Harry thought he was very ordinary until he turned eleven years of age and received a letter. Not that he was allowed to read it, but it sent Mr Dursley into a rage that became more and more irrational as more and more letters arrived. Finally a letter got through and Harry learned that he had been invited to attend Hogwart's School of Wizardry. Harry's parents had been wizards. Harry was a wizard.	
Harry Potter and the Philospher's Stone is a ripping yarn. High adventure. Good versus evil. A school story with a twist. Lessons are on Potions, Herbology, History of Magic, Charms, Defense Against the Dark Arts, Transfiguration. The school sport is quidditch, an aerial football game played on broomsticks with three goal hoops, bludgers, a quaffle and a golden snitch – it's very simple really. Harry, like his father before him, is a natural at the game and becomes the seeker for his house team riding on a Nimbus Two Thousand. Strong friendships (and enmities) are formed, and Harry comes into his own. It's magical stuff in every sense of the word. The language is witty, the plot tight, the imagination soars. It's fun.	Judgement

Figure 4.8   Example of the review genre in school English
Source: Thurton 1999: 41 (Magpies: talking about books for children).

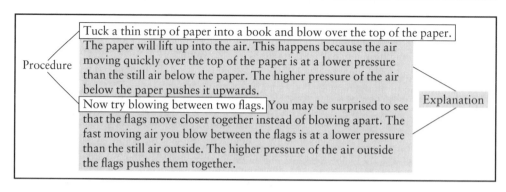

Figure 4.9   Mixed Procedure and Explanation genre
Source: Taylor 1991: 18–19.

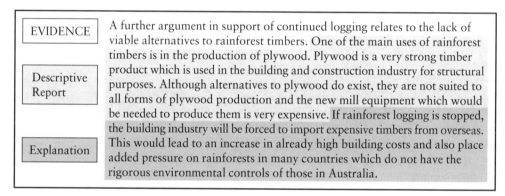

Figure 4.10   Descriptive Report and Explanation embedded as the Evidence Stage in an Analytical Exposition
Source: Humphrey 1996: 123.

Distinguishing the language of science and the language of the humanities

The language of subjects like science and geography are characterized by the development of technicality. That is, science reinterprets experience technically by defining elements of experience using technical terms (for example ecosystem, biome). These technical terms are ordered taxonomically and the logical relations among them (like temporal sequence, causality, condition, comparison etc.) are used to explain how things happen to come or be. The language of the humanities, on the other hand, is characterized by a shift to what is referred to as abstraction. As Martin (1993b: 226) points out, the discourse of history is not essentially a technical one:

Stage	Genre: Discussion	
Issue	**To what extent was the 1920s a decade of hope?** The 1920s has been called a decade of hope – by the end of the decade the anti-war feeling was very high in most countries and many treaties had been signed to ensure that there would not be another war. However, it can also be argued that the twenties had a pessimistic dimension in that they prepared the world for depression. Evidence which supports both views will, therefore, need to be examined in order to state the degree to which the 1920s can be viewed as a period of hope. This evidence will include an examination of anti-war feeling, the signing of various treaties and pacts and the economic climate.	
Argument for	One of the main forms of evidence that indicates that the 1920s was a period of hope was the strength of anti-war feeling. Soon after World War I people around the world realised just how much a disaster the war had really been. They had witnessed the millions of men who had died innocently and they were affected by the millions of dollars that had been spent on the war. As a result, anti-war feeling increased in most countries around the world.	
Argument for [Historical Recount]	Partly as an outcome of anti-war feelings many treaties were signed so that the same mistake would not be made again. In 1925 the Locarno Pact was signed at Locarno. It was a pact between Germany, France, Belgium, Great Britain and Italy. In it Germany agreed to accept her western frontier with France and Belgium as final and settled.	Record of Events Event 1
	In 1926 Germany joined the League of Nations.	Event 2
	This was very significant because firstly it showed that the other nations accepted Germany as a country and secondly it showed that Germany was prepared to forget about the past and cooperate with the other nations. Generally Germany's behaviour was a signal for the world to have hope of a peaceful future.	Deduction
Argument for	Further evidence for a peaceful future were the Dawes and Young plans . . .	
Argument against	Having looked at the recovery of World War I and the way in which the 1920s gave hope to people, the Depression, and the pessimism that arose out of this, will now be considered . . .	

Figure 4.11 Embedding of a Historical Recount as an argument in a Discussion genre
Source: Coffin 1996: 165. The text *To what extent was the 1920s a decade of hope* is reprinted with the permission of the NSW Department of Education and Training.

Aside from a small set of terms referring to periods of time (the Middle Ages, the Dark Ages, the Renaissance etc.) and possibly some distinctive -*isms* (e.g. colonialism, imperialism, jingoism etc.), relatively few technical terms are used; and where they are used they tend to be borrowed from other disciplines rather than established by the historical discourse itself (e.g. socialism, capitalism, market forces, etc.).

However, as Martin goes on to explain, the fact that the discourse of history is not technical does not make it any easier to negotiate. This is because the language of history can be very abstract. In history initially we might find individual people doing things in time and space, but the language of history then involves a move to generic classes of people participating in general classes of activities set in time. Next there is a shift away from the people and a focus on the events, but events nominalized as pseudo things (for example the Industrial Revolution; the Boxer Rebellion). As Veel and Coffin (1996) show, as students move from the genres that chronicle history (biographical recount, historical recount) to genres that explain and interpret history (historical account, factorial explanation, consequential explanation, analytical exposition etc.) the presence of people as participants is effaced. Instead of people involved in processes, these event sequences are nominalized and, as abstract participants, are related to other abstract participants.

Science and the grammar of technicality

A variety of grammatical resources are used to construct technicality. Some of these operate within the clause at the group level. They might be considered the most grammatically accessible to those less experienced with the language of science. Technical terms are sometimes defined through elaboration of the nominal group containing the technical terms. This is frequently achieved by the use of parentheses:

Snakes are reptiles (cold blooded creatures).

(Derewianka 1990a: 54)

Magnetic ferrites (metals containing iron) can be used to make hard magnets . . .

(Robson 1992a: 6)

It is also achieved by appositional structures:

When *molten rock, magma,* from the Earth's mantle bursts from the mouth of a volcano . . .

(Clark 1992: 6)

Another very common means of constructing technicality is through embedded clauses:

A direct current is passed through this solution via conducting plates *called electrodes*.

(Clark 1992: 21)

The electricity travels from the power station along thick wires. These are either buried below the ground so that they cannot be damaged, or they are held high in the air by tall metal towers *called pylons*.

(Clemence and Clemence 1987: 10)

At the clause level, however, it is the relational identifying clause that defines a technical term by equating it as Token with a meaning as Value:

The coloured ring in your eye	is called	the iris.
Value	Process: Relational:Identifying	Token

(Thomson 1988: 14)

The ends of a magnet	are called	the poles.
Value	Process: Relational:Identifying	Token

(Fitzpatrick 1984: 8)

These examples might also be considered quite grammatically accessible, but once the Value includes an embedded clause, there is the beginning of a shift to greater lexical density and the distinctive 'written' grammar of specialized knowledge:

The space around a magnet *in which its effects can be felt*	is called	its magnetic field.
Value	Process: Relational:Identifying	Token

(Robson 1992a: 10)

Materials *that allow electrons to pass through them.*	are called	conductors.
Value	Process: Relational:Identifying	Token

(Pople and Williams 1990: 212)

There is a further shift to the grammar of written language with the technical definition of processes. This necessarily entails the use of grammatical metaphor as pointed out on page 118. This is because the technical term for a process is a virtual or pseudo Thing, realized grammatically as a noun or noun group. In order for the relational identifying clause to equate this technical Thing as Token with its meaning or Value, the latter also needs to be in nominal form. Hence nominalizations are used as grammatical metaphors to realize events in the grammatical form of Things. This can be seen in the following definition of electrolysis where 'breaking down' and 'recombining' are grammaticalized as if they were things:

Electrolysis	is	the breaking down and recombining of a substance in its pure form by electricity.
Token	Process: Relational:Identifying	Value

The role of nominalization in the definition of technical terms becomes more significant in explaining science. Processes are explained by an implication sequence of causally and/or temporally related events. This event sequence is then defined using a technical term.

> As its speed slows, the river can no longer carry such a heavy load and so it starts to drop sand and mud on the river bed. This process is called deposition.
>
> (Bramwell 1986: 9)

These technical terms, like 'deposition' in this text, are then used subsequently in the text to establish an extended explanation.

> The channel is usually kept open by the scouring effect of the river and tides, but some deposition does occur.
>
> (Bramwell 1986: 9)

The explanation of some phenomena involves the use of nominalization to define a number of implication sequences in turn, which are then related to each other. In the following explanation of how sound travels, the technical term 'compression' compacts and defines the implication sequence explained in clauses 1–5. A further nominalization, 'the stretching apart of air particles' (avoiding the technical term 'rarefaction'), similarly compacts the meaning of the implication sequence in clauses 7–10. The recursive nature of these related implication sequences is then realized grammatically as a Thing ('a series of compressions and stretchings of air particles'). In this nominalized form the recursion of related event sequences becomes a participant functioning as Goal of the material process 'is sent' in clause 14 and is equated with the technical term sound wave in clause 15.

1 As the object moves to the right
2 it pushes or compresses the air particles next to it.
3 The compressed air particles then push on the particles to their right
4 and compress them.

5 As each air particle pushes on the next one to its right
6 *the compression* travels through the air.
7 When the vibrating object moves back to its left
8 the air particles next to it are no longer being pushed.
9 They spread out
10 or are stretched apart.
11 As a compression travels through the air
12 it is followed by *the stretching apart of air particles*.
13 Because the vibrating object continually moves back and forth
14 *a series of compressions and stretchings of air particles* is sent out from the object.
15 These compressions and stretchings make up a sound wave.

(Chapman *et al.* 1989: 281)

The extent of the shift toward the characteristically 'written' grammar of specialized knowledge becomes greater as we move from sequential explanation to consequential explanation to theoretical explanation (Veel 1997). We have seen on page 115 that lexical density is an index of the extent to which texts are more 'spoken-like' or more 'written-like'. In illustrating this increase in lexical density in relation to different explanation types Veel (1997) provides a comparison of text segments from procedural and theoretical explanations:

Sequential explanation:
As the **sugar cane comes** from the **farms** ‖ it is **washed** of **dirt** ‖ and **shredded** into many **small pieces**.

Theoretical explanation:
If, on the other hand, the **density** of the **fluid** is **greater** than the **average density** of the **object**, ‖ the **weight** of the **displaced fluid** will **exceed** the **weight** of the **object**.

(The lexical items are in bold and the clause boundaries are indicated by vertical parallel lines [‖].) The difference in lexical density can be seen immediately, but if one were to calculate it for these two segments, that of the Procedural Explanation is 2.7 (eight lexical items divided by three clauses) and that of the Theoretical Explanation is 6 (twelve lexical items divided by two clauses).

The relative use of grammatical metaphor in Sequential and Consequential Explanations can be seen by comparing the explanation of sound waves above with the following explanation of coal formation. In the coal text below nominalizations are italicized and logical metaphor is circled.

1 Coal was formed from *the remains* of plants buried by sediments.
2 In ancient forests, <<.2.1>> layers of dead trees and other plants built up on the forest floor
2.1 <<which were warm and humid>>

3   before they could rot.
4   As the land sank
5   these layers of vegetation were covered with water
6   which deposited sediments of gravel, sand, mud and silt.
7   Over millions of years the weight of the sediments and high temperatures removed much of the water from *the plant remains*.
8   *These plant remains* are known as peat.
9   As the peat was compressed
10   and became warmer
11   moisture was driven out
12   and it became brown coal, or lignite.
13   In some places, more layers of sediment built up on top of the brown coal.
14   This (caused) more and more moisture to be driven out
15   and black coal was formed.
16   Anthracite has *the lowest moisture content* of all types
17   but it is rarely found in Australia.

(DeVreeze *et al.* 1992: 131)

These texts were compared as part of a study of 18 science explanations (Unsworth 1996). The main categories of grammatical metaphor were those involving the formation of noun structures from verb structures (i.e. nominalization: compress→compression) and those where a noun or a verb is used instead of a conjunction (i.e. logical metaphor: so/the effect). The density of grammatical metaphor as a whole in the sound text was more than one instance per clause, whereas in the coal text the density was less than half of this. Consistent with research by Veel (1997), these texts reflect the trend for consequential explanations of phenomena like 'sound waves' to make significantly more use of grammatical metaphor and hence to differ much more from the grammar of everyday talk than do sequential explanations like those dealing with coal formation. This is not a critique of the language of consequential explanation and on page 119 and elsewhere (Unsworth 1997a) the functionality of grammatical metaphor in such explanations has been pointed out.

Consequential and theoretical explanations obviously entail greater use of conjunctions indicating cause while the conjunctions in Sequential Explanations are predominantly those of temporal relations. We have also noted that in Consequential Explanations conjunctive relations are more likely to be realized metaphorically as nouns or verbs. Consequential Explanations also make more use of internal conjunctive relations (see Chapter 2, pages 64–6).

The coal and sound texts used here to illustrate the analyses of conjunctive relations in science explanation texts are from a study by Unsworth (1996). The internal and external conjunctive relations for the coal text are shown in Figure 4.12. Internal conjunction is indicated on the left-hand side of the text and external conjunction on the right-hand side. It can be seen in Figure 4.12 that internal conjunction in the coal explanation is minimal. The only occurrence is internal reformulation linking the

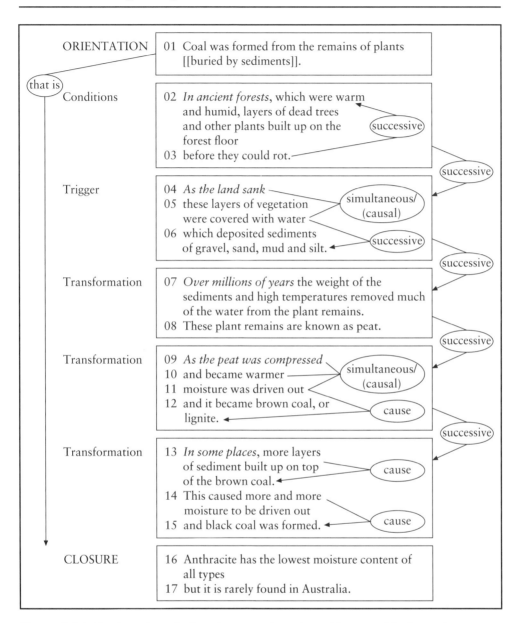

Figure 4.12 Conjunctive relations in an explanation of how coal is formed
Source: DeVreeze *et al.* 1992: 131–40, reproduced by permission of John Wiley &
Sons, Australia.

Explanation Summary to the implication sequences. The text is then organized by external temporal:successive relations linking each stage of schematic structure (Conditions, Trigger and Transformations). This reflects the simple serial structure of the sequential explanation.

The deployment of conjunctive relations in the explanation of how sound travels is shown in Figure 4.13. In contrast to the coal text (Figure 4.12), it can be seen in Figure 4.13 that internal conjunction is a major feature in the explanation of sound waves. Here there is a kind of 'sandwich' structure of internal reformulation (i.e.) and internal consequence (Thus) relating the implication sequences as simultaneously the reformulation of the Phenomenon Exemplification and the rhetorical means for the Conclusion. Internal consequence is also used both in linking elements within the implication sequences and linking events within those elements. These internal conjunctive relations have a major role because the explanation of sound waves is concerned with progressively reconstruing the component technical events of sound transmission as more abstract macrotechnical events, i.e. air particles pushing on the particles next to them → a compression travels through the air. The reasoning required for this kind of reconstrual is not concerned with the external relations among material events but the internal logic of rhetoric which allows a conclusion to be drawn from the account of material evidence. This can be seen in Figure 4.13 within both the compression and rarefaction elements. Then, in the same way, at the next level of abstraction, the successive relations among the compression and rarefaction elements are the rhetorical means for progression to the seriation element. Hence we have a 'nested' serial structure essential to this kind of causal explanation involving the progressive reconstrual of events at higher levels of abstraction.

The differences in the conjunctive relations reflect the different reasoning required in the explanation of coal formation and of how sound travels. The organization of the coal texts reflects mainly the unfolding of events over time, as is typical of sequential explanations. The organization of the sound texts involves the interrelationship of the sequencing of events and rhetorical relations among events at different levels of abstraction, as is more typical of consequential explanations.

School science texts provide a basis for apprenticing students to the technical nature of scientific English. We have briefly considered how the grammatical resources of English are characteristically deployed in pedagogic texts to construct the technical language of school science. As students progress in their science learning and engage with the nature of scientific explanation, they need to extend their grammatical repertoire to include the use of grammatical metaphor for both the construction of technicality and construction of reasoning in scientific texts.

The humanities and the grammar of abstraction

While autobiographical and biographical recounts are about particular individuals and the historically significant events in their lives, historical recounts focus on groups of

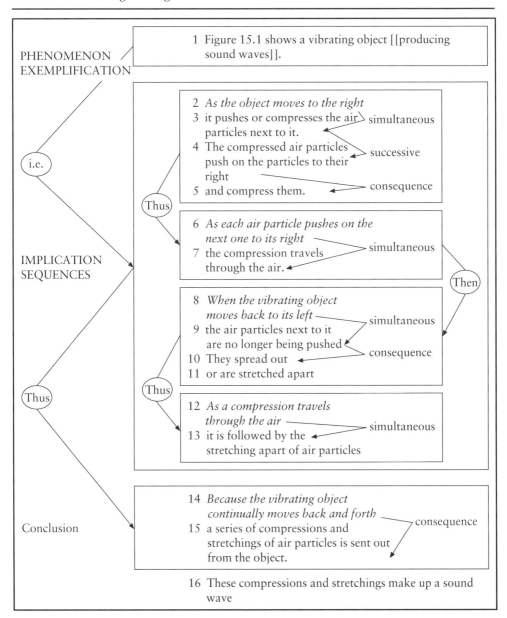

PHENOMENON
EXEMPLIFICATION

1 Figure 15.1 shows a vibrating object [[producing sound waves]].

i.e.

IMPLICATION
SEQUENCES

Thus

Thus

2 *As the object moves to the right*
3 it pushes or compresses the air — simultaneous
  particles next to it.
4 The compressed air particles — successive
  push on the particles to their
  right
5 and compress them. — consequence

6 *As each air particle pushes on the*
  next one to its right — simultaneous
7 the compression travels
  through the air.

8 *When the vibrating object*
  moves back to its left — simultaneous
9 the air particles next to it
  are no longer being pushed — consequence
10 They spread out
11 or are stretched apart

12 *As a compression travels*
  through the air — simultaneous
13 it is followed by the
  stretching apart of air particles

Then

Thus

Conclusion

14 *Because the vibrating object*
  continually moves back and forth — consequence
15 a series of compressions and
  stretchings of air particles is sent out
  from the object.

16 These compressions and stretchings make up a sound wave

Figure 4.13 Conjunctive relations in an explanation of how sound travels
Source: Chapman *et al.* 1989: 281, reproduced by permission of John Wiley & Sons, Australia.

people and the kinds of events in which they were engaged. This move towards general-
ization is realized grammatically by the use of generic human and non-human participants but relatively little use of grammatical metaphor, as can be seen in the following
segment of a historical recount about the Australian response in the Second World War:

> The Australian Government called up every fit man to join the Armed Forces.
> Women also joined. They didn't fire guns or fight in war areas. Instead they
> worked in offices at the bases. They drove cars, sent signals, coded messages, and
> did all kinds of work that set men free to do the fighting.
>   The Government ordered workers to factories making goods for the war: every-
> thing from boots to bandages, from bombs to battleships, from aircraft to barbed
> wire, and pots and pans for the army cooks.
>
> (Pownall 1982: 104)

In genres that explain and interpret history (historical account, factorial explanation, consequential explanation, analytical exposition etc.) human participants tend
to be effaced. Instead of people involved in events, we find that event sequences are
nominalized and as abstract participants are related to other abstract participants.
This can be seen in the following excerpt from a secondary school history text analysed by Martin (1993b):

> The enlargement of Australia's steel-making capacity, and of chemicals, rubber,
> metal goods and motor vehicles all owed something to the demands of war.
>
> (Simmelhaig and Spenceley 1984: 172)

Notice that the nominalizations here ('The enlargement of Australia's steel-making
capacity' and 'the demands of war') are not technical terms, but in realizing events
metaphorically as pseudo Things, they remove any mention of human involvement
and hence construct a very abstract version of what occurred. This can be easily seen
if you try to 'talk out' this text into the grammar of spoken language.

> Australians made more steel, chemicals, rubber, metal goods and motor vehicles than
> they had before partly because they needed more of these goods to fight the war.

To get this back to the concrete, lived experience of the time, you would have to add
in more of the subsumed events like 'built more factories', 'employed more women',
'worked longer hours'. But Martin points out that the abstraction of the written version also involves what he calls 'buried reasoning', or the metaphorical realization of
cause–effect relations. In spoken medium logico-semantic relations such as cause–
effect are most commonly realized by conjunctions. In the 'talked out' version of the
text above, the reasoning is realized by the conjunction 'because'. In the written version this is 'buried' in the process 'owed'. This metaphorical realization of conjunctive
relations by processes like 'results in' and 'depends on', and nominal groups like 'the

effect', 'the reason' and 'the result' are more frequent in written medium and characteristic of genres that explain and challenge in history.

The use of grammatical metaphor, enabling events to be 'frozen' and packaged as virtual things in the form of nominal groups, makes it possible to locate them at the beginning of the clause (in Theme position) as the 'given' or point of departure for the clause. It also enables them to be located at the end of the clause in the position associated with new information. Nominalization is therefore a grammatical resource for appropriately texturing the flow of given and new information (Martin 1993b; Coffin 1997) as we have indicated on page 119. We can also see this in the account of the reasons for the explosion of the US Space Shuttle Challenger in 1986 in the following text:

> The precise cause of the explosion was a combination of bad design and bad management. A component failed because there was a leak of gases through an imperfect joint. The decision to launch was taken against expert engineering advice.
> (Wright 1986: 23)

The fact of the explosion is established in the images and captions in the prior text, so the appropriate point of departure, the shared orientation for further exploration, is 'the precise cause of the explosion'. To get 'cause' into this first position, and to be able to modify it with 'precise', the nominalization of the logical relation, because → cause, as well as the nominalization of explosion is necessary. A similar explanation can be offered for the nominalization which occurs as Theme in the final clause – 'The decision to launch'. The 'decision to launch' is what is known. It is the 'given' orientation for exploring further. What is new is 'against expert engineering advice' and hence appropriately occurs at the end of the clause. If non-metaphorical constructions using the verbs 'decided' and 'advised' were used, this kind of texturing would not be possible. But, as well as facilitating the management of the information flow in the text, the effacing of human participants also avoids the need to indicate the participants who 'decided' to launch the spacecraft and those who advised against it.

As with the shift in science texts from sequential to consequential explanation, so as history texts move from chronicling history in recounts to explaining in historical accounts, there is a shift to greater use of 'internal' conjunction. We can see this in the use of 'firstly' and 'second' temporally ordering rhetorical arguments rather than sequencing events in the following text about women and technology in the 1920s:

> Most of the new forms of technology associated with the 'Roaring Twenties' relied on electricity and it is easy to assume that the new appliances made life easier for women. This theory needs critical examination.
>
> Firstly, not all the new forms of technology were electric. Those that used gas – stoves and some fires – were available earlier in the 1900s. Moreover, these gas appliances saved mainly men's labour rather than women's. There was no longer the need for the wood to be cut for the daily fire required for normal cooking and heating purposes.
>
> Second, not all the devices saved much labour. The electric iron, for example, only made the task of ironing slightly quicker. Vacuum cleaners produced only

small gain, being of real use only with wall-to-wall carpet which was much less common than bare wooden floors and carpet squares.

(Tudball 1991: 348)

The use of internal consequential conjunctive relations setting up reasoning based on the causal relations among rhetorical arguments rather than causal relations among material events can be seen in the following text about industrial expansion in Australia after World War II (Figure 4.14). Internal conjunctive relations are indicated on the left-hand side and external relations on the right-hand side.

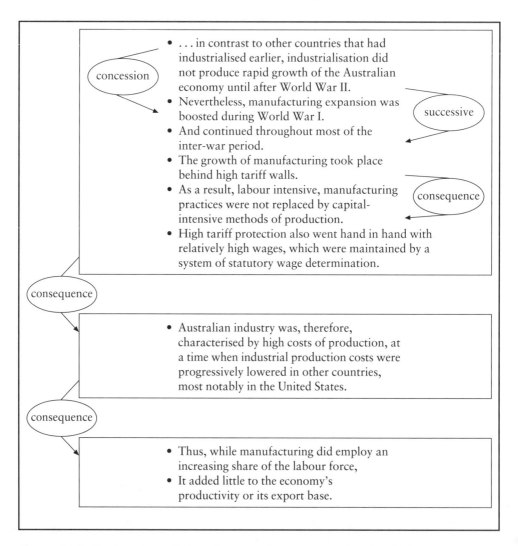

Figure 4.14 Conjunctive relations in an explanatory text in school history
Source: Tudball 1991: 95, reproduced by permission of John Wiley & Sons, Australia.

In both history and in science, more complex genres whose purpose is to explain and interpret the field make greater use of internal conjunction. They are also more lexically dense, making greater use of grammatical metaphor. While the explanatory genres of history include more metaphorical forms of logical relations, where conjunctive relations are realized by nouns and verbs, this appears to be less so in science. For the most part these resources of written medium are functional in constructing the specialized knowledge of these discipline areas, but they also construct particular interpretive biases within the form of the texts.

THE GRAMMATICAL 'COLOURING' OF MEANING IN SCIENCE AND HISTORY TEXTS

In the 19th century Protection Stations were set up where Aborigines were encouraged to replace their traditional lifestyles with European ones.

(Coffin 1996: 92)

This text, like all texts, is not an innocent statement of fact. Like all texts, it deploys a variety of grammatical means of colouring its argument to position the reader to see it from the writer's viewpoint. By teaching students these colouring techniques, we can help them to see the constructedness of the texts, so that they are less likely to simply take the text at face value but may be more aware of its deliberate positioning of them as readers.

One familiar aspect of colouring in the above text is the use of words with positive effect like 'encouraged' instead of say 'required' or 'coerced'. But notice also how whoever is doing the encouraging is not mentioned, so grammatically speaking the agentless passive voice is used to obviate or diminish the possibility of those directly responsible being subject to critique.

Grammatical metaphor is also central to the construction of particular interpretive perspectives. Once events are grammaticalized as things, they are constructed as 'givens', which are less susceptible to argument. We can see this in the following text where nominalization establishes as accepted 'squandering of the earth's natural resources'.

Squandering of the earth's natural resources is creating an increasingly ravaged world.

(Simon 1987: 5)

Nominalization also facilitates the use of the extensive resources for qualification within the nominal group. In the following text 'impact' is a highly metaphorical form of the logical relations of cause, congruently realized by conjunctions like 'so' and 'because'. These relations can also be realized metaphorically as verbs like 'cause' and 'affect' etc., but the nominal form enables the inclusion within the nominal group structure of the epithet 'devastating'.

Dredging or in-filling to provide sites for buildings, roads and airports, for example, can have a devastating impact on both freshwater and coastal ecosystems.

(Simon 1987: 23)

The nominalizing tendency of written medium in the construction of specialized knowledge then, also entails the 'naturalizing' of particular interpretive perspectives.

History deals with the accumulation of events over long periods of time, so it tends to bundle such sequences of events together and package them as if they were a 'thing'. Hence we have the use of nominalization realizing periods of time like 'the Depression', 'the Gold Rushes', 'the Chinese Revolution' etc.

This makes it possible for a whole series of separate events, for example, attacking, burning, destroying, fighting, and resisting to be condensed into a single Nominal Group such as 'this period of Black resistance'.

(Coffin 1996: 91)

The particular nominalization selected to do this condensing of events is strongly linked to the ideological and cultural perspective of the writer of the history. Compare the following possible nominalizations all condensing events over the same time span:

this period of peasant unrest,
this period of rural conflict,
this period of peasant lawlessness,
this period of peasant violence,
this period of violent suppression of peasants.

As nominalizations these periods of time can participate in a process as in the following example:

The period of violent suppression provided a catalyst for organized resistance.

Periods of time as noun groups can become the Appraiser – time and events themselves are responsible for proving, demonstrating and showing. In this way the role of the historian/writer as interpreter is obscured and what is really an interpretation becomes naturalized as fact and hence unquestionable. For example:

The period of peasant resistance *showed* how strongly rural workers opposed the new requirements.

Deductions of this kind can be further abstracted from the writer responsible for them by choosing a grammatical structure which avoids verbs like 'showed', 'demonstrated' or 'proved'. Instead a less straightforward way of grammaticalizing deduction is to use a noun like 'sign', which can then be qualified by 'good'. The deductive process has been nominalized in this way in the following example:

Joining the League of Nations was a clear *sign* that the country wanted to be part of the rest of the world.

By effacing the writer as interpreter of events and disguising deductions as facts, grammatical choices are made to position the reader to accept an interpretation as unproblematic and indisputable.

The advocacy position in the following text about the greenhouse effect is obviously partly constructed by the use of vocabulary like 'dramatically' and 'disastrous', but again, as Veel points out, grammatical metaphor is also a central resource.

Carbon dioxide levels have increased dramatically over the past two hundred years. Increased burning of fossil fuels and deforestation are the main contributors to this increase. If such trends continue the climatic changes due to the 'Greenhouse Effect' may have disastrous consequences.

(quoted in Veel 1998: 139)

Instead of saying 'There is more carbon dioxide in the air now than there was 200 years ago', by making 'carbon dioxide levels' a participant in the process 'have increased', the writer is able to pass interpersonal comment on it – 'dramatically'. The event in the first clause is then nominalized as 'this increase' caused by the nominalized realizations of human activities: 'increased burning of fossil fuels' and 'deforestation'. These meanings are then abstracted in the nominal group 'such trends', which is made the condition for the final clause. In this final clause we have not only the compacting of meaning in the nominalization, 'the climatic changes due to the Greenhouse Effect', but also 'consequences', the metaphorical form of logical relations realized non-metaphorically by conjunctions like 'because' and 'so' etc. In this nominal form the logical relation can also be qualified by 'disastrous'. There is, of course, the 'low' modal verb 'may', indicating some tentativeness in the argument. However, as Veel (1998) emphasizes, it is the distinctive grammatical resources of written medium which allow the writer to combine persuasion with specialized technical knowledge to take up the role of 'informed advocate'.

The grammar of interpersonal meaning is integral to the construction of interpretive perspectives in texts. As in the case of the greenhouse text above, the use of modal verbs like 'may', for example, indicates the uncertain state of knowledge in the field. Mood adjuncts can also indicate the probability or usuality inherent in accounts of certain phenomena. In the following texts, for example, modalization seems to be essential to the explanation of the initiating conditions in coal formation, as indicated by the Thematic Modal Adjuncts:

Usually dead plant leaves and stems, when they fall to the ground, are broken down and become part of the soil humus.

(Heffernan and Learmonth 1988: 70)

Normally, if plant material is left on the ground surface in contact with the air (oxygen), it decomposes.

(Chapman *et al.* 1989: 27)

On the other hand, the use of modal verbs in some texts has more to do with differences in the interpersonal positioning of the reader. The following texts deal with similar ideational meanings but the direct address to the reader and the inclusion of the modal verb may in the first text construct a different interpersonal relationship from that in the second text.

You may have seen (Figure 2.6) that the Earth is drawn with its axis 'tipped over' or tilted.

(Heffernan and Learmonth 1989: 21)

As seen in Figure 10.9, the Earth's axis remains tilted in the same direction throughout its orbit.

(DeVreeze *et al.* 1992: 149–50)

The same kind of variation is found in the following texts. In this case it is achieved by the inclusive 'we' and the high modal 'must' in the first text:

To discover the cause of the seasons, we must look again at the Earth in its orbit around the sun.

(Bramwell 1987: 9)

The seasons are caused by the Earth's orbit around the sun.

(Pettigrew 1986b: 20)

The resources of Mood and Modality can be used to construct a very patronizing relationship between the writer and the reader of textbooks, as indicated by the italicized mood adjuncts in the following texts:

You can *even* hear sound travelling through wood.

(Pettigrew 1986a: 12)

Thus coal is *merely* carbonized plant remains.

(Chapman *et al.* 1989: 127)

The grammatical form of texts in school science and humanities positions readers to interpret as natural the colouring of meanings that is inevitably part of the construction of specialized knowledge in these fields. The grammatical form of these texts also positions readers interpersonally in relation to the authority of the text. By alerting students to these techniques, we make it possible for them to recognize and resist such positioning. To do this we need the kind of functional grammatical knowledge that can be deployed as a tool for critical reading (for functional grammar as a tool for critical literacy see Martin 1989, 1995b, 1996, 1997, 2000; Macken and Rothery 1991; Fairclough 1992, 1995).

CONCLUSION

This chapter has shown how knowledge about language from a functional semiotic perspective facilitates understanding of the distinctive literacies of different school curriculum areas and the development of critical, reflective literacies. Space has limited the coverage in a number of respects. The discussion here has been limited to the aspects of functional descriptions of language introduced in Chapter 2. However a good deal of work on critical literacies has drawn on Martin's recently developed description of appraisal systems in English (Martin 1995a, 1996, 1997). These systems augment functional linguistic descriptions of resources for realizing interpersonal meaning, indicating how choice of lexis can colour representations of experience with particular forms of affect, judgement and valuation as well as grades of personal perspective and degrees of amplification. Appraisal systems have provided a further tool for the teaching of critical literacy practices (Martin 2000; Rothery and Stenglin 2000). The range of curriculum areas addressed here has also been necessarily restricted, but further work like this is being done across a number of curriculum areas including mathematics (Miller *et al.* 1999; O'Halloran 1999; Veel 1999). The growing work on functional semiotic accounts of images in distinguishing curriculum area literacies (Humphrey 1996; Lemke 1998b; Miller 1998; Veel 1998) will be taken up in the practical classroom focus on teaching multiliteracies in Chapters 6, 7 and 8.

CHAPTER 5

Exploring multimodal meaning-making in literature for children

CHILDREN'S LITERATURE IN AN AGE OF MULTILITERACIES

Children's literature continues to exist in an ever more complex environment of literacies. Contemporary children's novels and picture books continue to enjoy publishing success in book formats while some contemporary and traditional stories for children appear on CD ROMs, on the Internet and as movie adaptations. Children's literature is seen as a crucial resource in nurturing the child's progress from basic literacy to a level of critical and cultural literacy necessary for effective adult life (Hollindale 1995). The visual and verbal forms of contemporary literature for children construct an active role for the reader as she or he fills in the possibilities left by interpretive gaps or ambiguities within the text, images or the interaction between them (Williams 1987b; Meek 1988; Lonsdale 1993; Stephens and Watson 1994; Watson 1997; Prain 1998). But the extent to which such orientations to active interpretive reading are taken up by young readers is also influenced by the kinds of talk around texts in which they participate. Experienced readers who are able to interact with children and their books in ways that celebrate story as well as visual and verbal means by which it is constructed, not only encourage pleasure in reading, but also encourage the analytic satisfaction of understanding the ways in which the text is producing pleasure and how it is positioning the reader as an interpretive agent (Chambers 1985; Meek 1988; Misson 1998). In order to enhance such interactions, the next section of this chapter addresses the role of knowledge about language in furthering enjoyment of literary texts through reading grammatically. The third section examines the parallel role of knowledge about visual grammar and then the fourth section explores the construction of meaning at the intersection of language and image. The recontextualization of literary texts for children in computer-based formats is briefly discussed in the fifth section.

READING GRAMMATICALLY: ENGAGING WITH THE CONSTRUCTEDNESS OF LITERARY TEXTS

Despite the impact of 'back to basics' influences on literacy curricula and pedagogy, children's literature continues, to a significant extent, to enjoy a privileged position over the banality of purpose-written texts for literacy instruction. This privileging of children's literature as a resource for English teaching continues to extend from the early to the final years of schooling. Support for this position is most frequently based on the capacity of literary texts to engage children's interests and their concern with significant issues in children's lives. While such arguments perhaps assume that the language of literary texts provides appropriate, useful and even 'natural' examples of language for classroom work, attention in classrooms, and in the professional literature, to the role of grammatical form in constructing literary experience is rare. Nevertheless, some educators have been able to provide convincing evidence that in classroom work with children's literature there is no necessary dichotomy between enjoyment and engagement with story and exploration of the textual construction of story. Literary texts can be sources of enjoyment for children both because of their 'what' – their characters, plots and themes – and also their 'how' – the linguistic (and visual) forms through which the meanings are made.

If we are to help children understand some of the ways in which literary texts achieve their effects, it is clear that we need to have access to the kind of grammatical description that will enable us to talk explicitly about language form and its use in constructing the various kinds of meanings at stake in children's literary texts. This does not mean that we necessarily need to teach children all, or even the same grammatical descriptions that we use. Rather, if we can use more explicit grammatical resources in planning work for children, we can more easily and effectively structure learning activities that enable children to understand how grammatical choices construct particular types of meanings. In such contexts we can adjust the nature and extent of our explicit teaching of grammatical description in accordance with what is appropriate for children at a particular stage. The case to be made here is that, in this kind of mediation, systemic functional grammar provides the kind of resource that teachers, and ultimately children (Williams 1998, 2000), can use to enhance their understanding of the relationship between the 'what' and the 'how' of literary texts. To advance the case we will draw on some established British and Australian work, applying systemic functional linguistics to the study of children's literature as well as some related emerging work by students at the University of Sydney.

Systemic functional linguistics proposes that all clauses in all texts simultaneously construct three types of meanings:

- ideational meanings involve the representation of objects, events and the circumstances of their relations in the material world;
- interpersonal meanings involve the nature of the relationships among the interactive participants;

- textual meanings deal with the ways in which linguistic signs can cohere to form texts.

Ideational meanings are realized by the grammatical structures of the transitivity system involving Participants, Processes and Circumstances of various kinds. Interpersonal meanings are realized by the mood and modality systems in the grammar and textual meanings are realized in part by the Theme/Rheme system (see Chapter 2 for details of these grammatical systems).

Although the three major grammatical systems realize the three main types of meaning simultaneously, in order to show how they can be used as a resource for understanding the patterned construction of literary texts, the construction of ideational, interpersonal and textual meanings will be discussed separately in the following three subsections. In each case analyses of selections from picture books and children's novels will indicate the contribution of the particular grammatical features to the interpretive possibilities of the texts. Finally, the three analyses will be applied to the one text to show how co-patterning of grammatical choices across the three systems simultaneously construe ideational, interpersonal and textual meanings.

Constructing textual meaning: the functional grammatical concept of Theme

One of the favourite books for 4-year-old George was *The Tale of Peter Rabbit* (Potter 1987). This story had been read to him many times and there were several copies of the book in different formats in the household. Below is a partial transcript of George engaging in some 'reading-like' behaviour with his mother. He maintained the meaning and the pace of the reading, but his reproduction is not word perfect, nor is it likely he could have read these words outside the context of this story. The original words of the text are given first and then George's reading is shown in italics with his mother's encouragement in normal type:

> But round the end of the cucumber frame, whom should he meet but Mr McGregor.
>
> (Potter 1987: 24–5)

> *But round the end of the cucumber frame who did she . . . who did he meet?*
> Ahh, let's see what happens. That's right, but . . . Oh no!
> *Mr McGregor.*

George's control of the form of language in this segment of the story is very interesting. It can partly be explained because it is a climactic part of the story and George's excitement and engagement with the story had led him to attend very closely to the language at this point. But it is also interesting that the form of the language here is quite different from the forms of oral language with which George would have been more familiar. In ordinary conversation it would be more likely to take the form:

But he met Mr McGregor just as he got to the end of the cucumber frame.

In both versions the adversative 'But' carries the anticipation that something is amiss. However, in the written version, this is emphasized by the choice of the locative ('round the end of the cucumber frame') to occupy first position, or Theme in the clause – usually occupied by the subject. In the spoken version the subject and Theme of the first clause is 'he' (Peter) and the subject and Theme of the second clause is 'he' (Mr McGregor). In the written version the locative is a 'marked' Theme, since it is not the subject. The effect of this selection of a marked Theme is to keep the 'given' information in Theme position, and to delay the revelation of the subject, allowing the focus to fall appropriately on Mr McGregor at the end of the clause. The effect is to set the stage and to have the action burst onto it when Mr McGregor is announced. Not only is George negotiating the recoding of the print, at the same time he is learning how linguistic resources are deployed differently in written language to make the meanings that engage us in stories.

As children enjoy stories at school they can be alerted to various effects of the pattern of Theme selection as one aspect of gaining an explicit understanding of how grammatical choices construct meanings. The fact that marked Themes – that is, where, apart from conjunctive devices or modal adverbs like 'probably' etc., some other element like a complement or circumstantial adjunct (adverb or adverbial phrase) precedes the subject and is thus in the topical Theme position in the clause – occur much less frequently than unmarked Themes – where the subject precedes all other elements except conjunctives and modal adverbs – makes a marked Theme a signal that the reader's attention is being drawn to what is being dealt with at this point in the text. In some picture books marked Themes signal the episodic development of the story. This can be seen in *Drac and the Gremlin* (Baillie 1991). There are 67 clauses in the text of this story and only five clauses have marked Themes. As shown in Figure 5.1, all five of these marked Themes are positioned at the boundaries of the four episodes in the story: Drac's subduing of the Gremlin; the encounter with General Min; the encounter with the Terrible Tongued Dragon; and finally Drac and the Gremlin receiving their reward.

Similarly, marked Topical Themes occur in only five clauses in *Zoo* (Browne 1994) and they are all located at the boundaries of episodes in the story as indicated in Figure 5.2. In addition, in *Zoo* there is only one instance of a dependent (hypotactic) clause preceding the main clause in a sentence:

When we finally got there Dad *had* to have a row with the man in the ticket booth.

This can be understood as a clause functioning as a marked Theme (Martin 1992: 435).

Episode	Clause	Marked Themes
Gremlin	12	<u>At last</u> Drac traps the Gremlin in the misty valleys of Melachon.
General Min	13	<u>At that moment</u>, an emerald eaglon slips from the sky.
	42	<u>With a howl of despair</u> she flees deep into the jungle.
Terrible Tongued Dragon	43	But the white wizard hovers near Drac. (no marked theme to begin episode)
	61	<u>Together</u> they drive the Terrible Tongued Dragon from the Mountain.
Reward	62	<u>Later</u> they return to the palace.

Figure 5.1   Marked Themes reflect episodic boundaries in *Drac and the Gremlin* (Baillie 1991)

Episode	Marked Themes
Orientation	<u>Last Sunday</u> we all went to the zoo.
In transit to the zoo	<u>After a while</u> Harry and I got really bored.
Events before lunch	<u>When we finally got there</u> Dad had to have a row with the man in the ticket booth.
Events after lunch	<u>After that</u> we went to the gift shop to spend our pocket money.
Conclusion	<u>In the car</u> Mum asked us what was the best bit of the day.
Coda	<u>That night</u> I had a very strange dream.

Figure 5.2   Marked Themes reflect episodic boundaries in *Zoo* (Browne 1994)

The patterning of Theme selection can, of course, draw attention to other aspects of the story apart from episodic structure. In *Gorilla* (Browne 1983) we know that time is very problematic, both in the sense of what is lacked between Hannah and her father, and in the sense that the events that seem to transform their relationship take place within a very condensed time frame. Williams has discussed the textual means by which an inexperienced reader's attention might be drawn to time as a problematic (Williams 1987a). At one very obvious level this is achieved by the use of parallel patterns in the second paragraph:

Her father didn't have time to take her to see one at the zoo.
He didn't have time for anything.

But Williams also points out that, less obviously, the marked Themes of the first few pages of the text also work systematically to draw attention to time. The following clauses show all of the marked Themes (italicized) that occur in the text up to the arrival of the gorilla in the middle of the night:

and *in the evening* he worked at home
But *the next day* he was always too busy
But *at the weekend* he was always too tired
The night before her birthday, Hannah went . . .
In the middle of the night, Hannah woke up
In the night something amazing happened.

The point is not just that these elements do occur as marked Themes, but that *wherever* there is a marked Theme in these pages, it is a Circumstance of Time. It is clear that this is a patterning that is relevant to the interpretation of the story and which assists in drawing the young readers' attention to some of the interpretive possibilities of the text.

Five Times Dizzy (Wheatley 1982) is a short novel about a Greek migrant family in Newtown, Sydney. Yaya has recently arrived from Greece and is terribly lonely and homesick. Her nostalgia for the things she cannot find in her new environment (nature, animals, particularly her goat, the village community) and the fact that, with nothing to do, she spends her days alone in her room, drain her energy and make her older and melancholic. Her granddaughter, Mareka, not prepared to see her Yaya like this, is determined to find anything for Yaya to keep her busy, preferably something she used to do back home. In Yaya's thoughts there is a constant comparison between her new environment and the old country, between the past and the present. Language choices draw attention to the significance of this difference since it is the source of Yaya's misery, which in turn, is the source of Mareka's actions and thoughts throughout the book. This is particularly clear in the third chapter which is taken up with Yaya's morning walk in the neighbourhood. It is interesting to note how often time and place are marked Themes in this chapter as the following examples illustrate:

And here there was nothing she could do about it. *At home* now, if Costa was sick, there'd be herbs on the hillside that she could gather and make a medicine from. *But here!* How can you heal someone with train soot and concrete?

In Greece, people look at their neighbours all the time. *In Greece*, you don't live behind walls and fences. . . .

At home she used to walk seven or eight kilometres a day, up and down the mountain-sides, leading Poppy to new grazing spots. *Here* she only dared walk at dawn, before the traffic.

At home the child had had lots of friends but *here* she was always serving in the shop . . . It was odd that at home she never used to notice her feet, but *here* they felt tired and heavy. Yaya sighed. She had to admit it. *These days* she felt like an old woman.

(Wheatley 1982: 15, 18, 21)

As readers become alert to this kind of patterning, its use to mark the reversal of Yaya's fortunes at the end of the book brings significant emphasis to the transformation that has taken place:

Mareka pauses and shifts uncomfortably, remembering back to that day months ago when she'd come home and thought Yaya was dead. *These days*, it's hard to keep up with her.

(Wheatley 1982: 88)

The role of the pattern of Theme selection in highlighting readers' perception of the structure of narrative and drawing attention to experiential meanings integral to interpretive possibilities of text segments, has been discussed by Knowles and Malmkjaer (1996: 75) in relation to *The Secret Garden* (Burnett 1992). They also discuss Thematization as 'a powerful tool for reinforcing a writer's explicit message'. To support this discussion they analyse part of the opening paragraph in the final chapter of *The Secret Garden* to point out how Burnett used Theme choice to pre-empt opposition to her strong claim about the effect of the mental lives of Mary and Colin on their physical condition.

Exploration of the patterning of Theme selection is an aspect of the analysis of textual meaning-making which can be introduced to very young readers to consider simple structural features of narrative. It can also introduce young readers to the ways in which writers draw attention to interpretive possibilities of story and can be extended to the investigation of quite complex issues about the textual construction of ideological positioning in narratives. However, the textual meanings realized by Theme selection also need to be seen in a complementary relation to the realization of ideational and interpersonal meanings.

Constructing ideational meaning: processes, participants and circumstances

Primary school children who had very little prior systematic knowledge of grammar were able to use functional descriptions of Process types, Participant and Circumstances, to see how different examples encode a variety of meanings relevant to the representation of character in Anthony Browne's *Piggybook* (1986). The teacher drew attention to 'said' as the most common verb used in quoting or reporting speech and then experimented with the children in choosing alternative verbal processes like 'yelled', 'whispered' etc. It was this orientation and subsequent discrimination of verbal processes (saying verbs) that enabled the children to discuss the effect of Browne's selection of verbal processes like 'squealed', 'grunted', 'snorted' and 'snuffled'. The children were also able to appreciate that in the first part of the story Mrs Piggott was the only Actor engaged in Material Processes (action verbs) which entailed a Goal. While Mr Piggott and the boys were Actors in Material Processes they didn't actually act upon anything whereas Mrs Piggott 'washed all the breakfast things . . . made all the beds . . . vacuumed all the carpets . . . and then she went to work'. At the end of the story however, all of the characters were Actors in Material Processes that had Goals, for example, 'Patrick and Simon made the beds. Mr Piggott did the ironing' (Williams 1998).

It is the introduction of the use of this meta-language as a resource that facilitates further grammatically-based interpretive work. For example, in Anthony Browne's *Zoo* Dad is the dominant Sayer (in 16 verbal processes), while Mum is the Sayer six times, as is the narrator, and Harry is the Sayer only once. But 'said' is only used three times to project/report Dad's speech. On the other occasions the verbal processes reporting/ projecting Dad's speech are 'roared', 'snorted', 'howled', 'jeered' etc. However, for Mum and the narrator only 'said' is used. But beyond verbal processes, while the narrator and Harry are sometimes Senser in mental processes of perception ('Next we saw the baboons'), the only character who is Senser in mental processes of cognition is Mum – ' "I don't think the zoo really is for animals," said Mum'. Explicit knowledge of the grammatical form of the text assists readers to see the constructedness of characterization and the bases of alignments of readers with the point of view of particular characters. In fact, mental processes are the least frequent in *Zoo*, and, although the narrative is about an excursion, there is a fairly even distribution of verbal, material and relational processes.

Most of the relational processes are attributive and the nature of the attributes reflects key concerns of the book. The first attribute of the brothers as Carrier is a positive one – 'We were really excited'. However their excitement quickly becomes frustrated as they get caught in a traffic jam. The children become tired and bored and there follows a succession of negative attributes. Some of these concern fault-finding by Dad, embarrassment and hunger. When they eventually see the gorillas, which they really wanted to see, they are pronounced as only 'quite good'. The Carriers with the most positive attributes are food and and the café. This is also the case with relational possessive processes – especially the long nominal group used by the narrator to describe his lunch – 'I had a burger with chips and beans and loads of tomato ketchup, and a chocolate ice-cream with raspberry sauce'. The only relational identifying pro- cesses occur in the clauses where Mum asks 'what was the best bit of the day'. The narrator identifies this as 'the burger and chips and the beans', and Harry 'the monkey hats', while Dad said 'the best bit was going home'.

We have already discussed the pattern of Theme selection in Nadia Wheatley's *Five Times Dizzy* (1982) and noted how it was used to emphasize the changes that Yaya had to adjust to and also how she changed from the beginning to the end of the story. As well as looking at Theme as a resource drawing attention to these aspects of the novel, we can also look at the patterns of process selection to consider more closely the nature of the changes that occurred. In the first part of the novel Yaya is mainly constructed as Carrier in relational attributive clauses. The following are some examples from the first five pages of the novel:

'She was so still and stiff';
'SHE'S DEAD' (as Mareka mistakenly thought);
'She was homesick all the time';
'Yaya was limp now, limp and tired.'

By the end of the book it is not relational processes in which Yaya is involved but mainly material processes as indicated in the following examples from pages 71–81:

'Yaya smiled but she kept on pottering around the corners swinging her incense burner and cleansing away any remains of evil';
'A few days ago Yaya had made a herbal face-wash that had completely cleared up her pimples';
'Yaya was smiling and singing the rhythm to herself as she took the lead from Mama';
'Yaya strode out of the crowd and was suddenly hugging her.'

The selection of verbs constructs Yaya's move from passivity and misery to energy and joy.

The importance as an element of narration of the writer's selection of processes for a participant to engage in has been noted by Knowles and Malmkjaer (1996). They illustrate this in their discussion of *The Secret Garden* (Burnett 1992), showing how the development of Mary Lennox from inactivity to action is traceable through a shift in the participant roles to which she is assigned. In Chapter 1 for example 37.5 per cent of the instances in which she is mentioned is as Actor in material processes; 24.3 per cent as Goal; 20.1 per cent as Senser in mental processes and 13.8 per cent as Carrier in relational attributive processes. By Chapter 8 however Mary is Actor in material processes on 62.5 per cent of occasions in which she is mentioned. The pedagogical potential of explicit attention to the grammatical construction of characterization has been picked up in school syllabus documents. The Queensland *English 1–10 Syllabus* (Queensland Department of Education 1995), for example, provides sample lessons using these ideas to teach children about characterization in Judith Wright's short story *The Ant Lion* (quoted in Queensland Department of Education 1995).

To this point we have considered only the grammatical construction of textual and ideational meaning. We will now consider how the grammatical construction of interpersonal meaning can also be seen as a resource for the interpretive reading of literary texts.

Constructing interpersonal meaning: the grammatical resources of mood and modality

An examination of the deployment of the grammatical resources of the mood and modality systems in the dialogic text and the language of the narrator can also facilitate

Character	Total Utterances	Command	Question	Statement
		Imperative	Interrogative	Declarative
Dad	14	3	4	7
Mum	7	2	0	5
Harry	4	1	1	2
I (narrator)	5	2	3	0

Figure 5.3 Speech functions of characters in *Zoo* (Browne 1994)

understanding of the construction of point of view and the differential alignment of readers with the various characters of the narrative. We will look first at the dialogic text in *Zoo*. Figure 5.3 shows the distribution of speech functions.

Dad dominates the dialogue. He issues more commands and they are qualitatively different from Mum's commands. While Dad's commands are direct and at times intimidating ('Come DOWN you little ratbag!'), Mum's command is modified by the more positive vocative, 'boys', and by the inclusive imperative 'let's' ('"Come on, boys," said Mum, "let's get something to eat"').

Dialogue is usually initiated by the questions from the boys or Dad. The boys ask yes/no questions seeking permission (usually about eating) and why questions about their father's negative response to their earlier request. In contrast, the dialogue initiated by Dad is in the form of wh questions which are riddle type jokes and one rhetorical rude remark about the boys ('Which one is the monkey?'). Although the boys are supposed to answer the riddles, the punchlines are actually supplied by Dad, which only he finds funny. So Dad does not engage in meaningful dialogue with the boys. Instead he either imposes his speech on them or answers their questions in the negative without giving reasons ('Because I say so'). On the other hand when Mum refuses the boy's request to have lunch, she does not do so with a direct 'no' but uses a declarative clause to express her negative answer. She says by way of explanation, 'But, we've only just got here'. The only time Dad addresses Mum directly is to refute her sympathetic utterance, 'Poor thing', concerning the tiger.

Examining the interpersonal grammar of the dialogue then, can contribute to an understanding of how character is constructed. But the mood and modality choices within the narration are also important in this respect. The use of modal verbs indicating a high level of obligation to describe Dad's behaviour point to the fact that Dad behaves this way habitually ('Dad had to have a row'; 'Dad had to do his King Kong impersonation'). The inclusion of mood adjuncts like 'sometimes' and 'of course' reinforce this notion of habitual behaviour ('Sometimes he can be really embarrassing'; 'Of course Dad had to do his King Kong impersonation'). And the comment adjunct 'luckily' indicates the feeling of relief in the narrator ('but luckily we were the only ones there'). The modal verbs and mood adjuncts also construct the narrator's judgements on events. For example, the unwelcome obligation to look at the polar bears and the boredom experienced in doing so is expressed not only by the negative attribute 'stupid' and repetition of the circumstance of location, 'up and down', but also in the high modal verb 'had to' and the modal adjunct 'just' ('Then we had to go and see the polar bear. It looked really stupid, just walking up and down, up and down').

Many other patterns of mood selection within dialogue can be investigated. For example, in Alan Baillie's *Drac and the Gremlin* (1991) the dialogic elements are mainly concentrated at the beginning and end of the story. At the beginning most of the dialogue is the White Wizard's commands to Drac and later Drac's commands to the Gremlin. Since the children are subordinate to the White Wizard she issues commands to Drac in the form of direct imperatives:

'Great Queen Drac, come to my aid before all is lost!'

'But beware the Terrible Tongued Dragon'

The Gremlin, however, is not so unequivocally subordinate to Drac. This is reflected in the form of Drac's commands. She employs interpersonal metaphor, using declarative mood to code her commands:

'We must unite against this awful peril. You will join me and we will save Tirnol Two!'

Similarly, various patterns of mood and modality choice within the narration can be investigated. In Anthony Browne's *Gorilla* (1983), the pattern of mood adjuncts 'maybe', 'always' and 'never' constructs Hannah's feeling of being neglected by her father:

When Hannah asked him a question, he would say, 'Not now. I'm busy. Maybe tomorrow.'
But the next day he was always too busy. 'Not now. Maybe at the weekend,' he would say.
But at the weekend he was always too tired.
They never did anything together.

The investigation of mood and modality choices can also be used to illuminate aspects of narrative technique in novels for older readers. This has been shown in work by McDonald (1999) using Libby Gleeson's novel *I am Susannah* (1987). The story begins with Susie struggling to come to terms with the departure from Sydney to Melbourne of her life-long best friend, Kim. It then turns on the forthcoming teenage party, where a kissing game is planned. Susie does not want to attend the party or participate in the game, but finds she cannot say so. The departure of her friend and her reluctance to take up schoolmates' invitations lead her to spend time alone, often in a nearby cemetery where she and Kim used to play. Here she becomes fascinated by a mysterious 'blue lady', who has taken up residence in Kim's old house. The novel then alternates between Susie secretly observing the 'blue lady'; spending time on homework; in school; talking with her mother and her mother's friend, Nina; waiting for Kim to write her letters; and shopping for clothes for the party, at her mother's insistence. These scenes all include Susie's mental commentary on the people and events occurring around her, with her commentary operating in sharp contrast to the words she speaks. The author constructs this commentary by including Susie's internal dialogue in italicized text.

When Kim announces her departure, Susie's concern about who she will now sit with is voiced only internally – to herself:

Her straight black hair fell below her shoulders. *Who will I sit with? Kim. Always Kim.* 'Do you want to go?'

(Gleeson 1987: 2)

In this case Susie is questioning herself. But sometimes she states information to herself as is the case when she is reflecting on her father who lives overseas:

He grew up in Australia. He spoke English with Mum.

(Gleeson 1987: 81)

On other occasions Susie's internal dialogue involves imperatives directed at herself. One occasion is her mental struggle with the teacher's requiring her to collect waste papers from the schoolyard:

She picked up two sandwich wrappers and an empty chip packet.
Rip them up. Tear them into tiny bits. Make fifty pieces easily and take them to him. Dump them on his desk. Here's your fifty papers. Stick them in the bin yourself.
She turned at the climbing bars and headed for the bubblers.

(Gleeson 1987: 61)

McDonald points out that there are a lot of imperatives and interrogatives in the italicized internal dialogue, and that the internal commands and questions are directed mainly to Susie herself. Furthermore the use of internal questions and commands lies in ironic contrast with Susie's actual silence and lack of action in much of the novel. All of this constructs a character struggling with herself – wanting to do, and say, more than she does. Explicit attention to the grammar of this internal dialogue enhances readers' understanding of the nature of this construction.

Reading literary texts as co-patternings of the deployment of grammatical resources

If one takes the view that verbal art works in part through the co-patterning of thematically important discourse features (Hasan 1985), then systemic functional grammar provides a means of exploring this kind of co-patterning among the grammatical features that construct ideational, interpersonal and textual meaning respectively. To illustrate this we will consider a brief passage from the early part of Katherine Paterson's *Bridge to Terabithia* (1977). One of the main characters, Jesse, has been up early – running – something he has done all summer:

> Ever since he'd been in first grade he'd been 'that crazy little kid that draws all the time'. But one day – April the twenty-second, a drizzly Monday, it had been, he ran ahead of them all, the red mud slooching up through the holes in the bottom of his sneakers. For the rest of that day, and until after lunch on the next, he had been 'the fastest kid in the third, fourth and fifth grades', and he only a fourth grader. On Tuesday, Wayne Pettis had won again as usual. But this year Wayne Pettis would be in the sixth grade. He'd play football until Christmas and baseball until June with the rest of the big guys. Anybody had a chance to be the fastest runner, and, by Miss Bessie, this year it was going to be Jesse Oliver Aarons, Jr.
>
> (Paterson 1977: 11–12)

The text is reproduced again below, divided in clauses. The marked Themes are shown in capitals. The first clause, as a whole, is shown as a marked Theme. This again follows work by (Martin 1992), indicating that where a dependent clause precedes the main clause, this is not the 'default' option in normal English usage and hence the dependent clause is in marked Theme position with respect to the second clause.

01 EVER SINCE HE'D BEEN IN FIRST GRADE

02 he'd been 'that crazy little kid [[that draws all the time]]'.

03 BUT ONE DAY – APRIL THE TWENTY-SECOND, <<05>> he ran ahead of them all

04 the red mud slooching up through the holes in the bottom of his sneakers.

05 <<A DRIZZLY MONDAY, it had been>>

06 FOR THE REST OF THAT DAY, AND UNTIL AFTER LUNCH ON THE NEXT, he had been 'the fastest kid in the third, fourth and fifth grades',

07 and he only a fourth grader.

08 ON TUESDAY, Wayne Pettis had won again as usual.

09 BUT THIS YEAR Wayne Pettis would be in the sixth grade.

10 He'd play football until Christmas and baseball until June with the rest of the big guys.

11 Anybody had a chance to be the fastest runner,

12 and, by Miss Bessie, THIS YEAR it was going to be Jesse Oliver Aarons, Jr.

Before considering the marked Themes, we should note some significant aspects of interpersonal meaning. One of these is the modal adjunct 'only' in clause 7, reflecting Jesse's view of his own rising status via his running. We need to understand that 'Miss Bessie' is the cow that observes his running every day, so that the modal adjunct 'by Miss Bessie' in the last clause constructs an interpersonal position of determination.

It is significant to notice the large proportion of marked Themes in this passage and that they are all concerned with time, so time is a key issue in this text. The marked Themes indicate progression in time from first grade (Jesse is about to enter the fifth grade), to the present day and then into the future of 'this year' and 'this year' is marked Theme twice, drawing more attention to its significance. One further point is the specificity of the time references in the marked Themes – 'April the twenty-second'; 'For the rest of that day and until after lunch on the next'; 'On Tuesday'. The fact that Jesse recalls the times so specifically emphasizes the significance of the events so recorded.

Next we need to look at the third aspect of the systemic functional grammatical analysis – the construction of ideational meaning. Here we will focus on the occurrence of relational identifying clauses. These clauses define an element uniquely: x is (equals) y, so the elements are interchangeable: y is (equals) x. There are only three such relational identifying clauses in this text. They are italicized in the passage shown below again.

01 EVER SINCE HE'D BEEN IN FIRST GRADE
02 *he'd been 'that crazy little kid [[that draws all the time]]'.*
03 BUT ONE DAY – APRIL THE TWENTY-SECOND, <<05>> he ran ahead of them all
04 the red mud slooching up through the holes in the bottom of his sneakers.
05 <<A DRIZZLY MONDAY, it had been>>
06 FOR THE REST OF THAT DAY, AND UNTIL AFTER LUNCH ON THE NEXT, *he had been 'the fastest kid in the third, fourth and fifth grades',*
07 and he only a fourth grader.
08 ON TUESDAY, Wayne Pettis had won again as usual.
09 BUT THIS YEAR Wayne Pettis would be in the sixth grade.
10 He'd play football until Christmas and baseball until June with the rest of the big guys.
11 Anybody had a chance to be the fastest runner,
12 and, by Miss Bessie, THIS YEAR *it was going to be Jesse Oliver Aarons, Jr.*

Clause 2 identifies Jesse from other people's perspective and in the past. In clause 6 Jesse is identified from his own and other people's perspective, again in the past, but there is a big difference between being known as 'that crazy little kid that draws all the time' and 'the fastest kid'. This is where the specificity of the marked Themes helps to point out how significant that identity change was to Jesse. The final clause is significant because it identifies Jess in the future, it is the second time 'this year' has been marked Theme and it is the second time that 'the fastest runner' has been part of the identification, but this time without qualification. These three identifying clauses in the text occur in combination with the marked Themes that draw attention to the times that are turning points in the way Jesse is identified and the last of these includes the interpersonal Theme 'by Miss Bessie'. Hence it is the co-patterning of the grammatical features making different kinds of meanings that construct the portrayal of Jesse in terms of its literary significance in the novel.

This kind of co-patterning has been discussed in relation to Nina Bawden's *Carrie's War* (1974) by Knowles and Malmkjaer (1996: 121). In one example they discuss the role of Carrie's imagination in the portrayal of Hepzibah:

> Her voice was pitched low and soft. Her spell-binding voice, Carrie thought, and looked up at her. She was holding a candle and her eyes shone in its light and her gleaming hair fell like silk on her shoulders. A beautiful witch, Carrie thought.
>
> (Bawden 1974: 65)

Knowles and Malmkjaer (1996: 121) as well as noting the role of the mental process, 'thought', in constructing ideational meaning, also note that the Phenomenon in each of these mental process clauses are marked Themes and that this co-patterning enables the author to give special status to the two nominal groups that carry particular significance for the reader and for Carrie.

Meek (1988) claims that 'texts teach what readers learn', thus drawing attention to the fact that children's literary development depends on their understanding of the significance of variation in semantic patterning in texts. Developing students' experience in reading grammatically from a systemic functional grammatical perspective is one way of resourcing readers' critical understanding of both how and what texts teach.

ANALYSING MEANING-MAKING WITHIN AND ACROSS IMAGES

Far from lessening children's enjoyment of literature, analysing the means by which images make meanings helps them feel they are getting closer to the texts and what it is they enjoy about them (Nodelman 1988: 37; Misson 1998: 108). An analytical approach also increases young readers' interest in critical appreciation of the texts they encounter. However, if children are to learn how to analyse the ways images make meanings, they need to gain knowledge of the visual meaning-making systems deployed in images. There is significant support for the view that systematic knowledge of this kind is essential and that it should be explicitly taught (Nodelman 1988: 37; Doonan 1993: 8). But what kind of description of visual meaning-making resources is most appropriate for analysing multimodal literary texts for children?

The prevalent view, at least until well into the 1990s, has been well summarized by Perry Nodelman:

It is unfortunately true that most discussion of children's picture books has either ignored their visual elements altogether or else treated the pictures as objects of a traditional sort of art appreciation . . . rather than narrative elements.

(1988: ix)

Nodelman argued that approaches based on art appreciation were misguided because they did not take account of the narrative role of the images. He argued that, from this perspective, we might best understand images in picture books 'in the light of some form of semiotic theory', which suggests

the possibility of a system underlying visual communication that is something like a grammar – something like the system of relationships and contexts that makes verbal communication possible.

(Nodelman 1988: ix)

Here, and in the subsequent detailed discussion of the visual construction of action, of interactive relationships between image and viewer and of the effects of variation in layout, Nodelman seemed to be anticipating the emergence of Kress and van Leeuwen's functional 'grammar of visual design' (see Chapter 3) extrapolated from systemic func-tional linguistics. Kress and van Leeuwen's visual grammar was published in its initial form in 1990 and in a revised and further developed form in 1996. Although this work has been extensively applied in other fields (Goodman and Graddol 1996; Humphrey 1996; Shirato and Yell 1996; Callow and Unsworth 1997; Unsworth 1997a), it is only now beginning to be used in work with children's literature (Williams 1998, 2000; Astorga 1999).

A significant attraction of Kress and van Leeuwen's (1996) account of visual semiosis is that it does address Nodelman's concern with the ways in which the meanings made within and across images contribute to the narrative. In addition, because this func-tional account of visual grammar is aligned with functional descriptions of language (Chapter 2), it facilitates further exploration of how interpretations based on the visual and verbal modes of picture books

depend not just on our understanding of visual competences and codes of signi-fication, not even just on those codes and the equally complex codes of language and narrative uses of language, but also on intersecting relationships of both with each other.

(Nodelman 1988: 20)

Kress and van Leeuwen's work recognizes that images, like language, can realize not only representations of *material reality* but also the interpersonal interaction of *social reality* (such as relations between viewers and what is viewed). The work also recog-nizes that images cohere into textual compositions in different ways and so realize *semiotic reality*. More technically, Kress and van Leeuwen's functional semiotic account of images adopts from systemic functional linguistics the meta-functional organization of meaning-making resources:

- the ideational meta-function involves the representation of objects and their relations in the material world;
- the interpersonal meta-function involves the nature of the relationships among the interactive participants;
- and the textual meta-function deals with the ways in which linguistic and/or visual signs can cohere to form texts.

Here we will explore ways in which this meta-functional framework adopted by Kress and van Leeuwen (see Chapter 3) can describe visual meaning-making in picture books. Although, as in language, the three meta-functions are realized simultaneously, we will initially discuss each separately. First, we will consider aspects of *representational* structures, which visually construct the nature of events, the objects and participants involved, and the circumstances in which they occur. Second, we will examine the construction of *interactive* meanings in images, which include the interpersonal relationship between the viewer and the represented participants. Then we will investigate how aspects of layout construct *compositional* meanings, which are concerned with the distribution of the information value or relative emphasis among elements of the image.

Representational meanings: from actions and reactions to the symbolic

Representational meanings in images centre upon the actions and reactions of the various participants and the circumstances in which they occur. Images may also incorporate verbal processes and mental processes, realized by the inclusion in the image of 'speech bubbles' and 'thought clouds' – and some images are symbolic.

Action is realized visually by various conventions. One of these is the blurring of an element in an image to convey the idea of movement. This occurs in the third image of *Drac and the Gremlin* (Baillie 1991) where the Gremlin is about to pounce on Drac's back. The written text of *Drac and the Gremlin* is a fantasy science fiction narrative of the 'Star Wars' type, while the illustrations undercut this by locating it in an ordinary Australian back yard with the two children, the Gremlin (a young boy) and Drac (an older girl), engaged in imaginative play with the family's pet dog and cat and with an older female, presumably the mother, occasionally intervening. As well as the blur, to indicate speed, the action in this image of the Gremlin's pounce is conveyed by what Kress and van Leeuwen (1996: 57) refer to as vectors and Nodelman (1988: 160) discusses as 'action lines'. Here the vectors are formed by the lines of the Gremlin's limbs 'in action' – his arms outstretched towards Drac's back, his left leg pointing slightly forward and his right leg bent backward from the knee as if he had just jumped. The oblique angle of his body and his hair flowing backwards add complementary vectors indicating the nature of the movement.

The vectors can also indicate action without its necessarily being at speed, however. For example, in the image of the Gremlin immediately prior to the one referred to above, we get the impression of the Gremlin advancing very gingerly, creeping up in preparation for the pounce. Here the forearms are horizontal with the right arm pointing slightly upwards and the left arm slightly downwards; the left leg is forward and the right leg is shown bent backwards at the knee, the foot off the ground and the toe pointing towards the ground. It is as if he had just carefully raised his foot to move forward.

It is not just the difference in the type of action depicted in these two images that is significant. The image of the Gremlin alone is described by Kress and van Leeuwen as 'actional' – he is not acting on anyone or anything else. On the other hand, the 'pounce' image is 'transactional' because the Gremlin is acting on Drac. In fact, nearly all of the images in this book are transactional with Drac and/or the Gremlin acting on another participant: Drac chasing and then holding the Gremlin; Drac and the Gremlin riding the tyre-swing; chasing General Min; wrestling the Terrible Tongued Dragon etc.

In *Where the Wild Things Are* (Sendak 1962) the first two images of Max are transactional, with Max driving in a nail and then pursuing the dog with a fork. However most of the remaining images are 'actional' with Max acting but not acting on anyone or anything else. Max is in his boat but doesn't act on it. There is, however, the image of him telling the Wild Things to 'BE STILL!' with the vectors of his outstretched arms directed toward the Wild Things. There is also the image of Max riding one of the Wild Things, but during much of the wild rumpus and subsequently Max is acting himself but not doing anything to anyone else.

In the third image of *Where the Wild Things Are* we see Max in his bedroom. His head is turned and his gaze is directed towards the left of the image. There is a strong, yet invisible vector realizing his line of sight, but there is no indication what he is looking at. Kress and van Leeuwen aptly refer to images of this kind as 'reactional'. This one is a 'non-transactional' reactional image since we are not shown what Max is reacting to. On the other hand in *Drac and the Gremlin* there are two images which show Drac reacting to specific elements within the image. The first shows her gaze directed toward the 'emerald eaglon', while she is holding the Gremlin. The second is the image showing Drac's gaze directed to the butterfly on her shoulder. These are 'transactional' reactions according to Kress and van Leeuwen. The final image in the book also shows Drac reacting, but her gaze seems to look beyond the Gremlin licking his ice-cream with the Terrible Tongued Dragon looking on. The depiction of Drac in reactional images corresponds to the division of the story into episodes: her reacting to the 'emerald eaglon' marks the beginning of the episode with General Min; her reacting to the butterfly marks the beginning of the episode with the Terrible Tongued Dragon; and the image of both Drac and the Gremlin reacting to their reward of the 'Twin Crimson Cones of Tirnol Two' marks the beginning of the final stage of the story, with the concluding image also showing Drac in an intriguing non-transactional reaction. The fact that it is Drac's reactions we most frequently observe is a significant influence on our interpretive response to the narrative. Similarly, in *Zoo* (Browne 1994) although Mum is depicted in only four images apart from the initial introductory image, three of these images depict Mum reacting to something, presumed to be the animals. Significantly, the first of these shows Mum peering through the wire grille while the boys are fighting. The next image shows Mum with her head on a tilt looking curiously, while the other family members gesticulate. The third image in the sequence again shows Mum looking, somewhat glumly while the other family members respond physically and verbally to what they are looking at. So the visual construction of reaction is concentrated in the image of Mum and it is at the bottom of the page containing this third image that Mum's reaction is rendered in the verbal text:

'I don't think the zoo really is for animals,' said Mum. 'I think it is for people.'

As well as actional and reactional processes, Kress and van Leeuwen drew attention to the visual construction of verbal and mental processes in the form of 'speech bubbles' and 'thought clouds' respectively. Most of the speech bubbles in *Zoo* contain Dad's utterances. They provide speech that is not included in the main text and serve to emphasize particular features of Dad's character.

It is interesting to explore the bases for the selection of dialogue that is located in speech bubbles. In Russell Hoban's *The Flight of Bembel Rudzuk* (1982) the speech bubbles repeat dialogue from the main text and are colour coded to identify the character from whom the utterance came. The dialogic segments selected for inclusion in the speech bubble are those for which the speaker is not easily identified in the main text by inexperienced readers. These include quoted speech where there is no projecting clause like 'Bembel Rudzuk said' and instances where this projecting clause follows the quoted speech (Unsworth 1993c). In Pat Hutchins' *Don't Forget the Bacon* (1978a) we find both speech bubbles and thought clouds, with the latter being central to the way the book plays with the strategy of mental rehearsing of the shopping list in order to remember all of the items.

While the actional, reactional, mental and verbal processes in which participants are involved are the central aspects of the visual narrative structures described by Kress and van Leeuwen, they occur in circumstances such as the *setting* in which the processes take place, the *means* by which the processes are effected and the *accompaniment* of other participants while such processes take place. Far from being an inert background, the settings of images can provoke active engagement of the reader in the nature of the development of the narrative. For example, changes in the common setting for the images in Pat Hutchins' *You'll Soon Grow Into Them, Titch* (1985) build up the foreshadowing of the resolution to Titch always being at the end of the hand-me-down chain. As the mother's pregnancy progresses, the knitting gradually takes shape as booties, the plants in the garden, and potplants gradually come into bloom and the bird in the tree outside completes its nest and lays its eggs. More thought provoking is the setting in *Where the Wild Things Are*, where the moon is full at the beginning, progresses through its phases during Max's encounter with the Wild Things and then is the full moon again when we see Max back in his bedroom 'where he found his supper waiting for him and it was still hot'.

Circumstances of means, dealing with the instruments by which processes are effected can be equally intriguingly provocative. For instance the second image in *Where the Wild Things Are* shows Max chasing the dog. But why is Max chasing the dog with a fork?

Finally, circumstances of accompaniment in the images of picture books are often commented upon in the context of some readers failing to notice that minor participants accompanying the main participants are involved in their own subsidiary narrative in the sequence of images. In *Don't Forget the Bacon* (Hutchins 1978a) there is the dog being tantalized/tormented by the butterfly throughout the story and it has been reported (Watson 1996: 151) that adult readers frequently do not notice the adventurous baby in *The Story of Chicken Licken* (Ormerod 1985).

The discussion of representational meanings to this point has been confined to the framework described by Kress and van Leeuwen as narrative structures. However, they also describe a framework dealing with conceptual representations. This framework has three main subsections which describe classificational, analytical and symbolic processes. The first two of these subsections are concerned with the visual construction of taxonomic and part/whole relations respectively. While these are of little interest in discussing images in literary texts, the subsection dealing with the visual construction of symbolic processes can obviously be related to the extensive exploration of symbolic images in picture books among discussants of children's literature (Nodelman 1988; Doonan 1993; Watson and Styles 1996).

Symbolism is a communicative process that involves physical objects representing abstract ideas rather than their ostensive selves. Because the objects, or representations of them, are not actually the ideas they represent, symbols always depend on specific associations derived from cultural knowledge. For example, one reading of *John Brown, Rose and the Midnight Cat* (Wagner 1977) involves the cat symbolizing death, and Stephens and Watson (1994: 4) noted that this was the reading on which the illustrator Ron Brooks based his original set of drawings for the story. However, it is interesting to speculate whether this reading would be possible if the cat were white and whether white, as the traditional colour of mourning in China until recent times, might make such a reading possible for some cultural groups (Stephens and Watson 1994: 4). Since all symbolism is inherently arcane, it might seem surprising that there is so much of it in picture books for children who presumably do not have highly sophisticated cultural knowledge. But picture books provide an effective site for cultural apprenticeship of this kind:

Children provided with both the general information that symbols exist and specific information about the meanings of particular visual symbols will have the tools to appreciate the otherwise hidden subtleties of many picture books.

(Nodelman, 1988: 107)

Perhaps most occurrences of particular visual symbols will necessitate directly teaching young readers about them, however children's knowledge of a framework for recognizing the visual construction of symbolism may help them to apply the cultural knowledge they already have and that which they acquire through this kind of teaching. Kress and van Leeuwen describe two types of visual symbolic structures. The first of these is a symbolic attribute. This is some element of the image, usually associated with cultural symbolic values, which is an unexpected, unusual or ostentatious aspect of the representational meanings of the image. Anthony Browne's work is replete with such images. In *Zoo* there is a good example in the image of Dad where he refuses to let the boys have the chocolate that Mum had brought. The shape of the clouds behind Dad's head give the impression of being a pair of horns attached to Dad's head, so the clouds are the symbolic attribute in this image. In *Hansel and Gretel* (Browne 1995) the image of the mother looking over the children in bed in the wardrobe mirror, shows that the mother's shadow appears to be wearing a witch's hat formed by the break between the curtains. In *Gorilla* the image showing Hannah with the gorilla in the hall about to depart for the zoo has the hat, overcoat and boots of Hannah's father hanging on the hall stand to mirror the attire of the gorilla directly opposite. Of course, the symmetry of these elements of the image draws attention to the comparative drabness and obvious emptiness of the father's clothes symbolizing Hannah's view of her empty, boring and essentially absent father. Once alerted to the notion of symbolic attributes within images, children are frequently quite astute at identifying the kinds of symmetries and incongruities that often signal symbolic meanings.

The second type of visual symbolic structure described by Kress and van Leeuwen is the suggestive symbolic image. In these images it is not that an element of the image is a symbolic attribute conferring an identity or symbolic meaning on a represented participant in the image. Rather, in suggestive images it is the quality of the image itself which confers a symbolic meaning beyond that which is materially represented in the image. One example of this kind of symbolic suggestive image is the empty chair at the conclusion of John Burningham's *Granpa* (1984). Such an example of this kind of symbolism is perhaps reasonably accessible to many young readers. Somewhat more complex is the penultimate image in *Zoo*, where we are looking down from a high angle on the older son, the narrator, sitting against the wall on the floor with his head down on his arms resting on his knees and parallel, vertical shadow lines extending across the image like bars in a cage or cell.

There are, of course, many other aspects of visual symbolic and related metaphorical meaning-making in images that cannot be pursued here. Doonan for example, discusses 'pictorial analogies', which are visual metaphors and similes that enable 'what is shown to appear as one thing but also carry other meanings' (1993: 42). Doonan also emphasizes how such 'readings' can be made accessible to inexperienced readers. But the realization of the various kinds of representational meanings we have considered in this section are only the first of three distinctive kinds of meaning-making. While all images construct representational meanings they also simultaneously construct interactive meanings.

Interactive meanings – viewer positioning, point of view and modality

Interactive meanings concern the ways in which the viewer is positioned interpersonally in relation to the image. Images described by Kress and van Leeuwen as 'demands' engage the viewer in a kind of direct pseudo-social interpersonal exchange. These are the images in which the gaze of a (human/animal or human/animal-like) represented participant is directed straight toward the viewer. These images occur less frequently in picture books than those that do not engage the viewer in this way (Nodelman 1988: 151). Images in which there is no direct gaze toward the viewer are called 'offers' by Kress and van Leeuwen.

When demands occur in picture books, they tend to reflect significant points at which an especially high level of personal involvement of the reader/viewer is being provoked. In *Where the Wild Things Are* (Sendak 1962) there is only one clear demand in the book. This is where Max is in his private boat and about to sail off 'through night and day'. The demand is a happy, inviting one, perhaps encouraging readers to accept this invitation as Max sails off on his adventure. The first image in *Drac and the Gremlin* (Baillie 1991) is also a demand in which the heroine, Drac, with a conspiratorial, mischievous look and smile invites the viewer to share what is to come next. Visual demands are used in this book to introduce the main characters. As well as the introduction of Drac in this way, we also first meet 'the terrible tongued dragon' (the family dog) and 'General Min' (the family cat) via demands. In the image which introduces the Gremlin (the young boy) the gaze is not as clearly directed straight toward the viewer, and we only ever see the back of the head and the hands of the adult female figure.

The introductory demand images of Drac, the terrible tongued dragon and General Min are all close shot images, as if the viewer is positioned within an intimate social distance of the represented participant, intensifying interpersonal engagement at points where new characters are introduced and new episodes begin. The intensification of personal engagement is certainly achieved by the threatening demand of an attacking dog in Libby Hathorn and Gregory Rogers' *Way Home* (Hathorn and Rogers 1994). This is a story about a boy called Shane who rescues a kitten and negotiates various encounters in inner-city streets to eventually bring the kitten safely to the place that he, as a street kid, calls home. On the other hand the demand image of Max, in *Where the Wild Things Are*, is a long shot and the social distance is public, so although interpersonal engagement is there, it is more distanced rather than intimate. In Anthony Browne's *Zoo* the demands introducing the family members are medium to close shots. The image at the most intimate social distance is that of the gorilla towards the end of the book, but this is not a demand. The demand image at the most intimate social distance is of Dad looking down from a great height above the text where he refuses to let the boys have the chocolate that Mum had brought. The combination of the demand, close social distance and the low vertical angle of the image clearly construct the power that Dad has, and which the viewer is positioned to feel.

Variation in the vertical angle (from a high shot looking down on participants to a low shot looking up at participants) is one means by which inexperienced readers can learn about the construction of different points of view within narrative. Williams (1998) draws attention to this, pointing out variation in vertical angle in *Where the Wild Things Are*. He notes that in the first images viewers are positioned in a vertical angle from which they look down on the mischievous Max. However, there is a major change at a strategic point in the plot, where Max 'sailed off through night and day'. This coincides with the introduction of the only demand image in the book. Here the viewing angle also drops quite dramatically so that now the reader looks up into Max's smiling face. There is a steep low angle where Max is king of the Wild Things, but by the final image, where Max is restored to his bedroom, the angle is again high, suggesting Max has been restored to his 'normal' state of power. Williams (1998: 29) goes on to point out

> The general significance of the vertical angle becomes obvious if we contemplate the likely effect on child readers if the text were to finish with an image of Max, or even more so an image of one of the wild things, from a low vertical angle.

Nodelman also discusses the role of changing vertical angle, noting that in *Peter Rabbit* (Potter 1987), throughout the book we see Peter from below or head on when he feels in command; but when he overeats we see him lying against the ground, from above; and the same thing happens when he is caught in the netting and nearly gives up. Nodelman further indicates that significant use of changing angles tends to emphasize the intense drama of the story depicted (1988: 151).

In *Drac and the Gremlin* there is interesting variation in the use of vertical angle. Most of the images of the children playing are from a high angle, with a few exceptions like Drac and the Gremlin aboard the Anti-Gravity Solar-Powered Planet Hopper, Drac contemplating the White Wizard and the appearance of the Terrible Tongued Dragon. There seems to be a significant drop in the vertical angle after episodes with General Min and the Terrible Tongued Dragon have been resolved and the children have received their reward of the Twin Crimson Cones of Tirnol Two. As equilibrium is established at the conclusion of the story the vertical angle is neither high nor low. In contrast to the initial demand image of Drac, the final demand image shows her looking directly at the viewer and in the same vertical plane.

The association of changes in vertical angle with variation in point of view in Anthony Browne's *Gorilla* is discussed by Williams (1998: 28–30). Initially the high angle views of Hannah position the reader as more powerful in observing 'just a little child'. However, when Hannah makes a request of her father in the fourth image, the reader takes up a vertical angle, which is much lower and is in fact, an exaggeration of Hannah's perspective: 'The reader is no longer positioned as just an observer of the girl, but literally associated with her perspective by taking on a similar power position with respect to the father' (Williams 1998: 29). Williams goes on to point out that there is no stable relationship with respect to power between the reader and the focalizing character, so the child reader cannot simply associate with Hannah's orientation, at least not in any simple sense of identification. Williams sees this aspect of the visual construction of point of view as most important for discussion of children's entry into visual practices in that young readers are simultaneously positioned as both engaged as part of the narrativized experience and somewhat detached from it as observer of Hannah's actions and responses.

In the same discussion of the visual construction of point of view in *Gorilla*, Williams draws attention to concepts of visual modality as described by Kress and van Leeuwen (1996). He compares the first and second images in which Hannah is at the kitchen table opposite her father. In the first of these images the colours of the kitchen are very desaturated and the three-dimensional objects very flattened with very regular geometric shapes. The modality is low – our judgement of the 'reality' of the image, in a naturalistic sense, is quite low. The impression is that of a cold, abstracted, perhaps clinical environment. This is in contrast with the second kitchen image in which there is a high degree of colour saturation, irregular shapes and a greater depth of field. These features suggest higher modality – a greater sense of 'reality' in the image in a naturalistic sense. But Williams points out that it is more complicated than that. In the first kitchen image not all of the elements are desaturated and abstracted. Those associated with Hannah, her clothes and the chair she is sitting on are rich in colour and detail. This suggests that 'less than real' depiction of the scene is in fact Hannah's view of it and Williams further suggests that this underlines irony in the written text, which many adults would recognize as the exaggerated point of view of the child:

> But she had never seen a real gorilla. Her father didn't have time to take her to see one at the zoo. He didn't have time for anything.
>
> (Browne 1983)

Although not discussed in terms of Kress and van Leeuwen's accounts of modality, Nodelman's (1988: 64) comparison of the different use of colour in the first and final images of Max in his bedroom in *Where the Wild Things Are* also indicates the usefulness of analysing this aspect of images. Nodelman indicates that the colours of the wall and the bed change from the first image to the second. But he also suggests that the colours in the first image are discordant, reflecting the jarring energies and tension of the context of situation. On the other hand he notes that in the second image the colours are more harmonious and 'everything is suffused with a warming yellow that brings the room together'. This unified calm within the colouring reflects the satisfying resolution of the story. It is also possible to 'read' the contrast across the two bedroom images in terms of modality. In the first the colour saturation is relatively low and the detail of the objects is less clear. The increase in colour saturation is quite obvious in the second image and can be clearly seen by comparing the sky through the window in both images. The greater detail in the second image can be seen by comparing the depiction of the green leaves on the plant and also the door knob and keyhole. The calming unifying choice of colours is also being contextualized by the somewhat higher modality of a more 'real' depiction of Max's world.

There are of course, many other aspects of interactive meanings in images that could be explored in relation to the few books mentioned here and in exploring other books. Awareness of this aspect of visual meaning-making provokes further fascination in young readers' interrogation of literary texts. But these interactive meanings and the representational meanings discussed earlier are complemented by and made simultaneously with compositional meanings.

Compositional meanings – framing, information value, reading path and intertextuality

It is very clear that the division of layout into left and right segments is the most common means of organizing the information value of the visual elements in picture books. The left–right division in images usually reflects the feature of written English where what is given information occurs in the first part of the clause and what is new comes at the end of the clause (Halliday 1994a: 296–302). Since the double page spread is the usual syntagm in picture books, what is on the left-hand page corresponds to what is given or known and what is on the right-hand page is that which is new. In John Burningham's *Come Away from the Water, Shirley* (1977), the given situation of the parents commanding Shirley from their seats on the beach always occurs on the left-hand page and the new situations of Shirley's adventure are always depicted on the right. On the other hand, somewhat unusually in Burningham's *Granpa* (1984), it is the imagined or remembered situation that is consistently depicted on the left and the given or familiar situation on the right. In Anthony Browne's *Zoo*, once the family have arrived at the zoo, the humans are consistently on the left and the animals on the right. In *Gorilla*, the image and text that both appear on the left-hand page are organized so that the image depicting what is given is to the left, and the print introducing new information is always to the right of the image. Then, when we consider the double page spread, the image on the right-hand side depicts the new situation.

One variation to this horizontal polarization of the layout is what Kress and van Leeuwen (1996) refer to as a triptych. This is the horizontal arrangement of three separately framed images in the one syntagm. One of these occurs in *Gorilla*, where we see in the first frame the toy gorilla Hannah has thrown onto the floor near her doll and doll's house. In the middle frame we see the gorilla is significantly larger and the doll is looking at him. The final frame shows the gorilla as too large to be contained within the frame and the doll's hair standing on end, mouth open and eyes stretched wide open. In this layout what is in the left-hand frame is the given and what is in the right-hand frame is the new, with the centre frame mediating the given–new information value. Another example of a triptych is in Sendak's *In the Night Kitchen* (1973) when Mickey 'skipped from the oven and into bread dough all ready to rise in the night kitchen'. A further variation to the horizontal organization of information value in layout is the circular arrangement of the image such as we see in *Drac and the Gremlin* where Drac is 'fighting' the Terrible Tongued Dragon. Rather than a polarized given–new information structure, this circular layout arrangement tends to emphasize continuity and fluidity.

The form of framing of images, or lack thereof, is a very active feature of layout in constructing the nature of the narrative. We will briefly illustrate this by considering framing in *Where the Wild Things Are* and *Zoo*. In *Where the Wild Things Are*, as Nodelman (1988: 52) points out, when we first see Max making mischief it is in framed images on the right-hand side of the page and these images do not fill all of the right-hand page. The pictures become bigger and the frames smaller as Max is sent to his room, until they fill the entire right-hand page. As Max begins his journey to the Wild Things the images creep across onto the left-hand side of the page. Upon the arrival of Max in his boat the images have extended fully across the double page spread, framed by the edges of the page and about a quarter of the page of white paper at the bottom of the double page spread where the print is contained. For the duration of the wild rumpus the images have completely taken over every bit of space on the double page spreads. Then we find that the framing changes reverse, the images gradually receding to the right-hand side of the page, but significantly the final image of Max in his bedroom fully takes up the right-hand page, in contrast to the first image of Max in his bedroom.

In *Zoo*, the framing around the images of the family is not prominent nor straight – as if the images had been cut out from somewhere else. By contrast, once the family arrive at the zoo, the images of the zoo animals are all on the right-hand side pages and they are all heavily framed with thick, black, straight border lines. This pattern is maintained until we see a much more distinct, albeit not quite straight, grey-black bordering around the image of the boys wearing their monkey hats. Then we see a distinct yellow border around the image of the family and other members of the public looking at the orang-utan. Then the second to last image of the book shows the older son, the narrator, who had a very strange dream in his room that night. This image has the same thick, black, straight border which surrounded all of the images of the animals in the zoo, so the transposition of framing is complete. There is one exception to the framing style for the images of the zoo animals. This is in the image of the gorilla. Note that, from a naturalistic point of view, this is the image of highest modality in the book and it is at a very intimate social distance. The gaps in the outside border separating the quadrants mean that the gorilla's face is actually divided into four separate pieces. Suffice it to say that the use of framing is far from incidental to the construction of the interpretive possibilities of this book.

Pamela Allen's *Black Dog* (1991) is a story, at one level, about a young girl and her pet dog. Christina gradually pays less and less attention to Black dog and their friendship until eventually he goes to desperate lengths to win back her attention. In the first part of the story what is established both visually and verbally is the close, inseparable friendship of Christina and her dog. After the first page of the story the double page spread on pages 2 and 3 contains two images, separated horizontally on page 2 and a third image on page 3. In fact, vectors within the images and reading paths influenced by birds drawn within and outside of the frames of the images, create continuity among the three images. In the image on the top of page 2 Christina and Black dog are most salient. There is a unity among the participants achieved partly by the consistency of colour of the birds and Christina's hair and dress extending beyond Black Dog to the birds again. This is supported by the complementary vectors of Christina's forward look towards Black Dog and her outstretched arms and Black Dog's looking back at Christina. In the picture at the bottom of page 2, again Christina and Black Dog are salient. Unity is suggested by the arc their bodies form together. In fact this arc complements the arc achieved by the bodies of Christina and Black Dog in the picture on the top of the page, so that we have this impression of a circle being formed by their bodies across both pictures. By the image on page 3 togetherness is complete with the tight circle formed by the intertwining of Christina and Black Dog. The autumn leaves surrounding them support the circular vector of Christina's foot, Black Dog's nose, Christina's hand, Christina's head and Christina's body. The cross hatching of the background provide further circular vectors spiralling toward the happiness of Christina and Black Dog in the balancing centre of the image. The colour of many of the autumn leaves being the same as the bird outside the left-hand border provides the link back to the images of the previous page. These images construct the inseparability, love and happiness of Christina and Black Dog, so crucial to understanding the development of the story.

Even from this brief discussion it can be seen that the patterns of compositional meanings among the images are a significant narrative resource in the construction of the interpretive possibilities of story in picture books. It is the analysis of the images in this way, and opportunities for talk around the text that it makes available, which hold the potential to expand young readers' interpretive reading practices.

INTERPRETING MEANING-MAKING AT THE INTERSECTION OF LANGUAGE AND IMAGE

In this section we will return to Pamela Allen's *Black Dog* to show how the functional analyses of language and image we have been exploring can be brought together to understand how visual and verbal resources are combined in literary meaning-making. Before doing so, however, we will briefly outline some existing work on interpreting meaning at the intersection of language and image in picture books.

Some picture books can be read without 'reading' the pictures and the essentials of the narrative can be maintained (Michaels and Walsh 1990). This does not mean the pictures are redundant. They frequently elaborate aspects of setting and cultural diversity as in books like Arlene Mosel's retelling of *Tikki Tikki Tembo* (1968), Junko Morimoto's tale of *The White Crane* (1983), or most of the Aboriginal tales of Dick Roughsey (1973), in which the illustrations draw on the traditions of Aboriginal art.

In some picture books the images clearly support the inexperienced reader's efforts in negotiating the story via the print. Pat Hutchins' *The Wind Blew* (1978b) begins with a picture and the words follow. Maintaining this pattern, the story is advanced visually on the left-hand page followed by the words. Each new character is introduced visually before the words tell us what is to happen, allowing readers to anticipate each new stage of the narrative from the images and this is then confirmed by the print. Similar techniques are used in Hutchins' *Don't Forget the Bacon* (1978a). The young protagonist tries to remember the items on his shopping list by associating them with objects that he observes, which rhyme with the list items. In the second part of the book as he returns home revisiting the observed objects and checking off the obtained rhyming items, the participation of the inexperienced reader is strongly scaffolded. For example, picture cues for the observed rhyming items like 'A pile of chairs' on one page and 'a flight of stairs' on the adjacent page cue the reader to predict what will be on the next page by remembering the association of the rhyme from the outward journey in the first part of the book. The text on the next page does show 'a pound of pears' with the illustration to confirm it. Detailed accounts have been written of this kind of scaffolding (Williams 1987b) in somewhat longer narratives in picture books like Shirley Hughes' *Alfie Gets in First* (1981). A further example of very sophisticated scaffolding occurs in Russell Hoban's *The Flight of Bembel Rudzuk* (1982). Here careful selection and colour coding of speech bubbles is used to scaffold inexperienced readers' negotiating of complex dialogic exchanges in the main text (Unsworth 1993c).

Our focus will be on the more integrative, complementary meaning-making role of visual and verbal text in picture books. Some aspects of this have been extensively documented. Michaels and Walsh (1990) draw attention to the counterpointing of visual and verbal text in 'dual narratives' like John Burningham's *Come Away from the Water, Shirley* (1977) and *Time to Get Out of the Bath, Shirley* (1978), where the images construct a different story from that constructed by the text. They also discuss more complex interweaving of visual and verbal meaning-making in Burningham's *Granpa* (1984). Rather than a single narrator we have snatches of dialogue between Granpa and his granddaughter, which does not comprise a connected whole without the images. As well as providing a setting for the dialogue, the images give some clues about preceding actions or words, which do not appear in the verbal text. Further work on complementary visual and verbal meaning-making has been done by J. Graham (1990). She discusses Edward Ardizzone's *Little Tim and the Brave Sea Captain* (1982), indicating that the text tells us Tim was sad, but the picture tells of his enormous seriousness and determination. Graham goes on to provide many examples of different kinds of complementarity. She points out for example, that in Charles Keeping's *Through the Window* (1970) the verbal text is composed of Jacob's questions and the answers have to come from reading the illustrations, and that secondary narratives in Pat Hutchins' 'Titch' books (1985) and subtle humour in Hiawyn Oram's *Angry Arthur* (1984) appear only in the images. The functional visual and verbal textual analyses we have been using enable us to extend this kind of work on integrative visual and verbal meaning-making in quite explicit and specific terms. To illustrate this we will return to the beginning of Pamela Allen's *Black Dog* (1991).

Black Dog and Christina are constructed at the very beginning of the story by means of this nominal group complex – 'Black Dog and Christina':

Black Dog and Christina lived together in a little house near a forest.
They were the best of friends.

The inclusion of the circumstance of accompaniment 'together', although ideationally redundant, is significant to the story. Notice that 'Black Dog and Christina' and 'They' are in Theme position, so attention is drawn to their togetherness as the point of departure for these clauses and for the story. The next two pages are the double page spread from which the images were analysed previously. The clauses immediately underneath each of the three images begin with marked Themes:

In the spring they ran together over the hills.
In the summer they swam together in the river.
In the autumn they played together in the fallen leaves.

Attention is drawn to the passing of the seasons by locating them in Theme position and the continuity of the togetherness of Black Dog and Christina is emphasized by the repetition of the grammatical structure across the three clauses, the use of the pronoun 'they' and the inclusion of 'together'. The final sentence on the right-hand side of this double page spread begins with a dependent clause drawing attention to the change in season:

As it got cooler,
together they collected sticks for the fire that kept them warm during the long winter evenings.

Note, however, that the second clause also has a marked Theme – 'together' – again ideationally redundant but important to the subsequent development of the story and located as marked Theme to indicate its information value. Significantly this marked Theme occurs once more just prior to the appearance of the birds that ate the crumbs Christina had scattered:

Together Black Dog and Christina watched and waited.

This is the last time Black Dog appears in Theme position until the third to last page of the book and he is only mentioned on one other occasion in the verbal text up to that third to last page. Visually he continues to appear but more and more separated from Christina, who stands alone at the window watching for her elusive blue bird.

We approach the climax in *Black Dog* at the third last double page spread. Christina has been neglecting Black Dog, staring out of the window every day in the hope of seeing the beautiful blue bird that has appeared in her dreams. In the image on the top of the left-hand page we see Christina as she hears a noise in the trees and excitedly presses her face to the glass, believing her blue bird will appear. Ideationally this a narrative image of the non-transactional reaction type. The vectors of Christina's hands, nose, hair and her eyes indicate she is reacting to something that is not in this image. Interactively it is an offer – we are not interpersonally engaged with Christina but observe her. In compositional terms this image is the given, conventionally located to the left on the double page spread in terms of the Kress and van Leeuwen (1996) account of compositional meanings in images. It is the culmination of many pages of Christina's dreaming at night and staring out of the window during the day. What is new is shown on the right-hand side of the page. Black Dog has climbed high into the enormous trees. Salience is provided by the size and direction of the tree trunks. They create a very powerful vector drawing the eye to the top of the page and beyond it. The branches of the trees point upwards and continue off the page. The tree on the far left leans inwards to provide a clue to the balancing centre of the picture – Black Dog. The height Black Dog has climbed to is shown by perspective. His size and minimal colour variation make him look vulnerable and ridiculous. This is further emphasized by his body forming an opposite arc to that of the tree branches.

The written text on the left-hand side of the page helps to develop this as one of the most powerful images in the book both by what it tells the reader and what it does not tell us. Black Dog is not mentioned in the text. We are led to look more closely at the image on the right-hand side by Themes in the clauses in the text on the left-hand page beginning with 'the tree' and 'A branch'. Expectation is further set up interpersonally by the narrator directly appealing to the reader with 'Listen! Did you hear a crack? Surely there was a flash of blue!' The mood adjunct 'surely' in interpersonal Theme position adds to the irony since the reader has already seen Black Dog. But this irony is reinforced verbally when next we are *told* that 'At last she would see her strange and precious dream bird.' But we have been *shown* Black Dog. The picture of Christina on the top of the left-hand page draws our attention to seeing what actually occurs before being told in the text. Christina forms a vector to Black Dog by her gaze. Her hair, eye and nose creates a reading path leading to Black Dog. It is the integrative deployment of visual and verbal structures constructing ideational, interpersonal/interactive and textual/compositional meanings that achieve the impact of this segment of literary art, and access to functional descriptions of visual and verbal grammar can facilitate explanations of how it is achieved.

READING LITERARY TEXTS IN COMPUTER-BASED FORMATS

Electronic media are not simply changing the way stories are told; they are changing the very nature of story, of what we understand narratives to be. However, hypertext models of narrative in electronic format and 'linear' models of narrative in conventional book format will exist in parallel for some time in the future. Consequently two quite different mindsets about narratives for children will be operating simultaneously in the education system (Hunt 2000). In this section we will note briefly the kind of radical transformation of story by electronic media described by Hunt, but the main focus will be on his second point about the co-existence of hypertextual and linear narratives. First we will look at the kinds of stories that have appeared in electronic format and then refer to ways in which hypertext has been used in stories composed specifically for computer-based presentation. Next we will look at examples of contemporary children's literature that have been very popular in book format and subsequently recontextualized in CD ROM formats. To conclude this section we will suggest that these kinds of explorations are important for both students and teachers since the kinds of cyber readers children become and the kinds of cyber literary understandings they develop will be influenced not only by the kinds of cyber texts they access but also the kinds of discussion around those texts that they experience.

As Hunt (2000) has pointed out, in written narratives there is considerable variability in the kinds of images different readers construct of characters and to some extent also settings, but the outcomes of the narrative always remain the same. In computer games, on the other hand, the characters and settings are fixed but the outcomes are determined by the players. Hypertext environments potentially enhance these possibilities for reader 'control' or choice from among optional lines of development of the narrative, as made popular at one time by the 'choose your own adventure' stories. This kind of influence is quite variable in currently available computer-based literature for children. Very few contemporary, well-established authors of children's literature publish in electronic formats. A small number of successful picture books have subsequently appeared in CD ROM format. Most electronic publishing of children's literature involves what might be called 'classics' written some time ago (like the Beatrix Potter books), traditional tales of various kinds, and purpose-written material for computer-based formats by relatively unknown authors or newly emerging, multiple but anonymous authors associated with the publishing company. Some purpose-written CD ROM 'talking books', used predominantly in some school literacy programs, have been criticized (Miller and Olsen 1998) because they result in what has been called 'truncated learning'. This seems to be because the nature of the hypertext links encourages interactivity with the electronic media but with discrete elements that are not cohesive or fundamentally related to significant aspects of the story. On the other hand, some purpose-written electronic story materials have deployed hypertext and multimodal resources in ways that enhance literary construction of point of view and meta-fictional elements, to engage readers in active, reflexive story reading in ways that would not be possible in conventional book formats.

Two such CD ROMs were used in a case study of children's exploration of electronic narratives (James 1999). One of these was *Payuta and the Ice God* (Ubisoft, n.d.). This is the story of an Eskimo boy whose sister is kidnapped by Kiadnic the Ice God to be his cook. With the help of creatures like a narwhal, a polar bear, and an eagle, he reaches the Mountain of Clouds where he finds the fallen Ice Star – famous in

Eskimo legends. Payuta picks it up, releasing Nature from the Ice God's grip. Spring returns and Kiadnic's power is destroyed. Payuta and his sister return home triumphant. James (1999) describes how a range of hypertext links enhance the story. For example, in the ice cave clicking on a number of hypertext links (hot spots) made Kiadnic's face metamorphose menacingly out of the rock, accompanied by frightening music. In other sections of the story clicking on the illustrations makes the graphics interactive. In one example the perspective changes from viewing Payuta on a rock ledge to a bird's eye view of the river below as if the viewer were poised on the ledge, aligning the viewer with the hero's point of view.

The second CD ROM, *Lulu's Enchanted Book* (Victor-Pujebet n.d.), similarly included hot spots integral to enhanced interpretive possibilities of the story. Frequently the written text entices the reader to activate hidden illustrations. For example, at one point the text states 'Lulu loved masquerading in the most outrageous outfits and posed before the mirror.' The mirror is a hot spot that makes Lulu comment aloud on her appearance as she simultaneously changes into one of three costumes. James (1999) further describes the ways in which hot spots are used to enhance the inclusion of metafictive elements. For example, a subtitle 'The Cutout' is a textual clue to the fact that if the reader clicks on the image, one character draws a frame around another character and cuts her out of the page, rolling her up like a poster. These electronic stories blend some aspects of hypertext and linear models of narrative so that we have these different mindsets Hunt (2000) referred to, to some extent co-existing in the one story.

The recontextualization of existing literary texts in book format as CD ROMs has also made quite variable use of the resources of electronic hypertext environments. Like all 'talking books' published by Discis, *The Paper Bag Princess* (Munsch 1994) appears on the screen as an open book. Clicking on the printed text activates the reading but there are no interactive images etc. *The Polar Express* (Van Allsburg 1985) in its CD ROM version includes the same images as the book but with animated elements, such as the train moving on the track and the reindeer moving in the snow. The language is the same as in the book version apart from differences in vocabulary apparently reflecting differences between American and British English like 'conductor' for 'guard' and 'dressing gown' for 'robe'.

The CD ROM version of *Stellaluna* (Cannon 1995) is very different from the original book. In this story a baby bat, Stellaluna, is separated from its mother when she was avoiding an attacking owl. Stellaluna lives in a nest with a family of young birds and adopts bird-like behaviours. Eventually Stellaluna and the mother bat are reunited but Stellaluna visits the birds she has made friends with and lived harmoniously with despite their differences. A lot of additional text is included in the CD ROM. For example 21 additional lines of text in the CD ROM are directly attributable to Stellaluna. In the original book version only 15 lines of text are spoken or thought by Stellaluna. These inclusions seem to be designed to make meanings explicit and remove the opportunity for inference, as in the additions 'I love you, Stellaluna' and 'I love you' (from Stellaluna to Mother Bat). The additions also seem to be more colloquial than the more standard forms of English in the book format *Stellaluna* ('I gotta eat something' and 'I wanna take a nap, you guys'). The effect of this is emphasized by the somewhat unfamiliar standard form of the text from the book that is omitted in the CD ROM ('"You slept at night?" gasped another. "How very strange," they all murmured.') The CD ROM includes many hot spots with animated images, which are gratuitous intrusions into the story. For example, when the text states 'They perched in silence for a long time', instead of making time for a reflective pause, the 'silence' is interrupted by squawking and inappropriate action. A number of activities of jungle animals are included which are quite unrelated to each other or to the story, like a monkey running up a tree, elephants splashing water at each other, a giraffe drinking and then gargling and a bird sliding down the giraffe's neck. These in combination with aspects of the changes in the language, very significantly change the somewhat serious tone of the book to almost a slapstick approach to frivolous humour in the CD ROM version.

The extent and type of variability within story across modes as well as the variability across stories within modes, provide a rich resource for the exploration of how multimodal resources can be deployed to shape and reshape the interpretive possibilities of narrative. This kind of exploration needs to be a central concern in developing the multiliteracies entailed in engaging with children's literature in computer-based formats.

CONCLUSION

Some classroom work with children's literature has been undertaken, drawing on both the functional linguistic and visual descriptions discussed in this chapter (Howley 1996; Williams 1998, 2000). This work suggests that children have been able to readily learn basic elements of the meta-language outlined here and have been able to use it productively and pleasurably in their exploration of literary texts. Additional classroom observations have informed the suggestions for further application of these functional semiotic accounts of multimodal meaning-making in literature for children outlined in sample programs for young children in Chapter 6 and for older children in Chapter 8.

PART III

Classroom practicalities

Developing multiliteracies in the early school years

INTRODUCTION

Literacy development is a fundamentally social process. The kinds of readers and writers children become will be crucially influenced by the kinds of texts they are given access to and the kinds of interactions around those texts that they experience. Although these influences will derive from many different contexts in children's lives, the range of home and school contexts, and the interrelationships among these, will be of particular significance. Negotiating this social construction of literacies among schools, their communities and government educational authorities, involves teachers in a complex range of activities both within classrooms and in interfacing with community and institutional expectations. In the early years of schooling the intensity of this negotiation is quite palpable to the parents and teachers of young children and to the children themselves as they gradually learn what counts as literacy practices in various social contexts. Schools may appear to have a common view that they want children not merely to be able to read and write, but to be engaged readers and writers, entailing both enjoyment and critically productive individual and social activity. However, it is in the processes of 'doing' literacy that children learn what counts as literacy. This chapter addresses the 'doing' of multiliteracies in classrooms in the early years of school. It is concerned with classroom practicalities of developing the young literacy learner's resources as a code-breaker, text comprehender/composer and critic in relation to a range of textual forms in both conventional and electronic formats. The focus is on developing children's knowledge about language and image (meta-semiotic understanding) at the same time as they are learning verbal and visual language and learning through verbal and visual language. The principal organizational framework for managing this orientation is the Literacy Development Cycle (LDC), which entails modelled, guided and independent reading and writing practice through a structured program of whole class and small group learning experiences. The principles and organization of the LDC will first be outlined, indicating its use with literary texts for children in the first or second year of school. Next a detailed program of work using the LDC with literary texts for children in the second or third year of school will be described. Further examples of lessons using the LDC with electronic texts and with factual texts in curriculum area learning will then be discussed.

THE LITERACY DEVELOPMENT CYCLE (LDC)

The LDC and approaches to early literacy pedagogy

The Literacy Development Cycle is predicated on a number of previously elaborated assumptions about early literacy pedagogy (Unsworth and O'Toole 1993), which are briefly reformulated here:

- The texts children encounter should be composed for genuine communicative purposes and not those constructed principally to include repetitions of sound/symbol relations, vocabulary items or grammatical structures.
- Children's engagement with texts should be enjoyable and functional in meeting their own social purposes.
- Literary texts for young children are provocative of children's active, interpretive orientations to the construction of meaning in texts.
- As well as literary narratives, many other texts such as rhymes, jokes, songs, traditional tales, informational texts associated with curriculum area learning, environmental texts, personal texts and texts of popular culture have an important role in early literacy development.
- Young children's literacy learning is like an apprenticeship, involving both guidance and explicit teaching from a master practitioner.
- Early literacy development is enhanced by the provision of recurrent, enjoyable and supportive contexts where the same texts are revisited over time.
- The development of children's control of the conventions of written text in their reading and writing is characterized by gradual approximation to the accepted practices of the community.

Such a list, of course, is far from exhaustive. Many other issues could be included, such as the significance for young speakers of English as a second language of learning literacy in their first language; problematic aspects of grading reading materials and matching text difficulty to learners' reading levels; and the provision for children who experience various kinds of specific difficulties in literacy learning. While space does not permit discussion of such matters, the concern here is to indicate the kind of orientation to early literacy pedagogy into which the LDC is deployed to integrate the development of multiliteracies and their meta-languages.

The challenge is to determine how to construct the kinds of classroom learning contexts which will take account of the kinds of issues we have noted. How can we provide in classrooms of 20 to 30 or more young children, the recurrent, enjoyable and supportive contexts where engaging children's books and other materials are introduced and periodically revisited, where each child reads and talks with the teacher about the texts, where there is close attention to print and sound/symbol relationships and progressive approximation to effective, independent reading and writing behaviours? Such a goal is difficult but not unrealistic. Many teachers have worked cooperatively to develop exceptional programs which have involved collaboration with parents, teacher librarians, support teachers, classes of older pupils, partner classes through Internet contact, the community library and others. The development of a facilitative classroom context involves a good deal of work on many fronts over considerable time – from establishing a dynamic classroom library, a reading corner, listening post facility, computer access etc. to organizing time for independent silent reading, times for parents or other experienced readers to read aloud to children, liaison with parents, home-reading schemes, book clubs etc. It is not possible, in the space available, for us to take this kind of comprehensive perspective on classroom organization and programming. As a starting point, however, the Literacy Development Cycle provides a systematic but flexible framework for optimizing the teaching and learning of multiliteracies in the mainstream infants classroom.

Describing the LDC and integrative reading and writing pedagogy

In its most generalized form the LDC (Figure 6.1) incorporates modelled, guided and independent practice in the comprehension/composition of multimodal texts in conventional and electronic formats. The literacy lessons based on the LDC are usually scheduled for about 90 minutes, incorporating modelled, guided and independent practice, although additional modelled reading and opportunities for independent reading and writing also occur at other times in the school day. In the first two years of schooling much of the teaching of writing will be highly integrated with the teaching of reading. The usual structuring of the LDC-based literacy lessons is outlined in Figure 6.2.

   Although it is useful to think systematically about the stages in a lesson and the kinds of learning experiences that typify these stages, it is also crucial that these do not degenerate into formulaic rituals. The organization of these sessions must be responsive to the possibilities afforded by the form of the text and the experiences and needs of the children in being able to benefit from those possibilities. After outlining the purposes of the lesson segments indicated in Figure 6.2 and the kinds of activities that may be involved in them, we will show how they have been used in planning the unit of work based on the construction of grandfathers in books for young children.

Orientation to the text

The *preparatory reading* phase of this stage makes use of material that is familiar and/or easily and confidently dealt with by the children. Initially, with younger children,

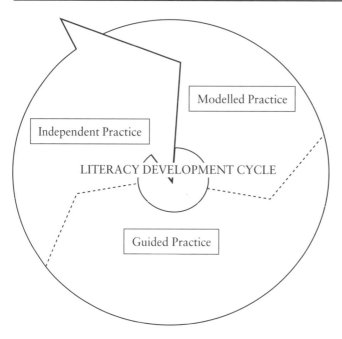

Figure 6.1   The Literacy Development Cycle

Lesson stages	Reading	Writing	Group	Time
Orientation to the text				
Preparatory reading	Independent		Class	about 5 mins
Introduction of new text	Guided		Class	about 5 mins
Reading the text				
Teacher's introductory reading	Modelled		Class	about 5 mins
Collaborative reading	Guided		Class	about 10 mins
Working with the text				
Exploration of text meanings	Guided	Guided	Class	15 mins
Consolidation of text processing	Guided	Guided	Groups	20 mins
Reviewing reading and writing				
Extension reading and writing	Independent	Independent	Groups	20 mins
Presentation, reflection and feedback	Independent	Independent	Class	10 mins

Figure 6.2   Usual structuring of LDC-based lessons in the early years of schooling

it might involve making one or two selections from a variety of chants, poems, songs, rhymes etc. – for example, 'Five little ducks went out one day' (Scales 1981: 131) or 'One, two, buckle my shoe' (Davies *et al.* 1987: 43). These are sung/read by the teacher and the class as a whole group. When the words are pretty well known by heart, they can be displayed on a chart and the teacher can informally encourage the children to 'read' as they perform, by pointing and rehearsing lines with them. The aim is for maximum participation as a group with familiar, easy material so that the children feel confident in contributing to the activity. As the children gain more experience, or with older children, the same purpose can be achieved by rereading familiar and favourite books (including those that have been introduced in previous lessons) via group readings with improvised drama etc. as well as sharing children's own writing and the results of previous class/group work. This activity occupies the first few minutes of the lessson.

The second phase in this first stage of the lesson is the *introduction of a new text*. Here the purpose is to arouse interest in the book (or CD ROM or website) by drawing attention to its external characteristics and noting features such as the cover/homepage design, the title, the name of the author and the publisher. This provides the opportunity to discuss the text as a social artefact – some children may have seen the text before, they may have heard of the author or have other 'Picture Puffins' books, 'Discus' CD ROMs, or some other such imprint or series, at home. Children may utilize cues from the cover to suggest what kind of a text it is and what it may be about etc. There is also the opportunity to attend to children's developing knowledge of sound/symbol relationships in identifying the name of the author and the title. For example, are there any children in the class whose first name is the same as that of the author? Whose names are different but start the same way as the author's? Similarly for surnames and names that begin the same as words in the title – 'Hunter' for example – or 'where have we seen that word before?' The title and author's name (and perhaps also associated names and words) can be written on the blackboard, further demonstrating and rehearsing the sound–symbol relationships. This activity also occupies a few minutes, so that the 'orientation to the text' stage takes about five minutes or so overall.

Reading the text

There are two phases in this second stage of the lesson. These are *the teacher's introductory reading* and then *collaborative reading*. The teacher's introductory reading provides a model for the children. Ideally, when reading books, the teacher should be seated to the side of the book placed on an easel or stand so that she or he can look at the book with the children as she or he reads. It is not essential that the book be a 'big book' for this to work quite satisfactorily if the children are seated on the floor, close to the teacher. If electronic texts are used with the whole class, a data projector and a large screen are desirable. If electronic texts are being dealt with in small groups around a small number of computers, the teacher should also be seated in front of a computer. Children should be encouraged to comment on what they thought about the story or information, what they noticed about the text and the illustrations, any patterns they noticed or what puzzled them etc.

In the second phase of collaborative reading the children's contribution to the reading is gradually increased. Then the teacher can suggest that she or he reads the text again so that the children can review their comments and see what else they notice. The teacher should suggest to the children that they join in the reading. By using gesture, glance and movement the teacher can demonstratively encourage the children to participate at appropriate points. The follow-up discussion should include the planning of systematic participation by the children in the third reading. This might amount to allocating groups of children to read particular parts (three different groups to read the parts of the three little pigs for example, and the whole class to join in with the Wolf's threat – 'I'll huff and I'll puff . . .'). It might also include allocating some children the task of making sound effects, for example to accompany the 'billy goats gruff' walking over the bridge. These steps might well vary according to the form of the text and the experience of the children, but the object is to engage them with the 'reading' of the text in a supporting and enjoyable context. The overall 'reading the text stage' of the lesson may take about 10 minutes.

Working with the text

The first phase of this stage of the lesson is the *exploration of text meanings*. This 'talk around text' is crucial to the development of what it means to be a reader. In literary texts for example, children can explore the patterns and puzzles, the deliberate ambiguities of the illustrations and the text and the perspectives from which the story is told. The form of literary texts frequently provokes children to initiate these important questions. Did Rosie the hen in *Rosie's Walk* (Hutchins 1968), know all the time that the fox was following her? Was there really a monster in David McKee's *Not Now, Bernard* (McKee 1987)? If Max just had a dream about the Wild Things (Sendak 1962), how come it is a full moon when he goes to his bedroom and not a full moon when the forest grew and he was with the Wild Things? Who said 'That was not a nice thing to say to Grandpa' in John Burningham's *Granpa* (1984)? This kind of whole class interactive exploration usually takes about 10 minutes.

The second phase in working with the text is the *consolidation of text processing*. This is where children interact closely with print and image to confirm and extend their meaning-making strategies based on their integrative use of cues from the semiotics of illustration, discourse structure, grammatical patternings and grapho-phonic relationships. They need structured opportunities to deal directly with print, to learn and rehearse the grammatical and grapho-phonic knowledge that is essential to the development of their facility with written language. Similarly they need to learn visual literacy strategies for interpreting not only what is conveyed in images but also how this is achieved and how the meanings realized visually are related to the verbal construction of meaning.

This phase is undertaken as small group work and occupies about 20 minutes. There is no suggestion here that children should be grouped according to any crude notions of 'reading ability', which would be quite counter-productive. Rather the groupings should be functionally organized so that some children, even if they are not very experienced readers, can undertake work with a good deal of independence from the teacher so that she or he can systematically allocate time to more intensive interaction with each child in the class (Unsworth and O'Toole 1993). Computer-based tasks, listening post tasks (where a group of up to eight children listen to a cassette tape recording of stories and respond to pre-recorded tasks, using headsets connected by a common junction box to a single cassette player), recreations of stories with flannel-board illustrations, text reconstructions or text innovations, labelling of illustrations etc. can be varied to achieve this. One group of children is targeted for more intensive teacher interaction each day.

Working with the text usually involves young children in writing activities. These range from directed short tasks to creative more extended texts. Directed tasks include vocabulary building involving location of synonyms, antonyms etc., building grammatical knowledge by selection, grouping or reworking functional elements of clauses, open-ended short answer questions, and completion tasks such as 'cloze' exercises. More extended writing may involve a response to a text, such as selecting a part of a text the student liked the best or found most interesting and writing about their reasons for this selection. Children may be invited to write an additional event or an alternative ending to the story, following modelling of this kind of writing by the teacher. Older children may be involved in scripting a story for a readers' theatre production – also following modelling by the teacher. The writing activities can also involve visual texts. Children may, for example, sort images into categories like 'offers' and 'demands', select/create alternative images for inclusion in texts studied, or scan images into a digital format and then manipulate them with computer software to construct alternative visual interpretations from those included in original texts.

Reviewing reading and writing

Again there are two phases to this final stage of the lesson. The first phase involves the children in *extension reading and writing*. There should always be extending activities available – and not just for those children considered to be more experienced or advanced readers. In some cases extension activities may be begun as a whole class activity with a good deal of teacher direction and then children allocated roles in completing the activity when time is available to them. An example for younger children would be the construction of a captioned collage of the scene from Pat Hutchins' story *The Wind Blew* (1978b), where all of the objects are mixed up in the sky. The children draw the background and then paste representations of the articles to form their collage. Some of these might come from advertisements in magazines etc. and could therefore include a cut-out label. In other cases the children may need to bring actual objects from home, such as a balloon, and for other objects, models may need to be used, for example cotton balls pasted to represent the judge's wig. Captioning of the latter objects would require the children to retrieve the print from the book. Such a task is quite demanding for many young children and could be undertaken initially as a whole class activity, which the teacher orchestrates, demonstrating how it is to be done. Children could then be encouraged to bring appropriate materials from home and keep these in a box so that they are available for later independent work on their own or small group collages. Other similar extensions of work done as a class might involve the construction and insertion of speech balloons into stories, the recording of children's retellings etc. As a further example, when children gain more experience with written language, the modelling by the teacher of the writing of short book reviews (such as those that appear on publisher's websites) and scaffolded practice of this activity organized as a part of 'working with the text' can be extended to independent work in 'reviewing reading and writing'.

Extension activities might also include simply supplying a 'book box' or Internet browser 'bookmarks' of texts related thematically to the one being dealt with in the lesson. For example, if the lesson was based on Pat Hutchins' story *The Very Worst Monster* (1986), a book box could usefully contain copies of David McKee's *Not Now, Bernard* (1987), Hiawyn Oram's *Angry Arthur* (1984), Rosemary Wells' *Noisy Nora* (1978) and Franz Brandenberg's *I Don't Feel Well* (1982). The children should always know that there is an interesting variety of activities in which they can engage when they have finished the particular task at hand. The second phase of this final stage and the conclusion of the lesson is the presentation of and reflection on work done during the lesson. This should take about five minutes.

Implementing the LDC focusing on writing

Although writing development activities will most frequently derive from related reading experiences, the writing of some genres, like personal recounts, is related more to students' own experiences. Young children may also be introduced to writing genres like 'personal responses' and 'reviews' – for example of picture books as indicated in the New South Wales *English K–6 Modules* (New South Wales Board of Studies 1998a: 177) and in the United Kingdom *National Literacy Strategy, Framework for Teaching* (DfEE 1998: 31). Here the writing obviously draws on knowledge of the picture book, but what the children need are models of, and guidance in, the writing of these genres. In these cases the implementation steps of the LDC are modified to focus on writing. The strategies of modelled, guided and independent practice are retained, but as with the integrative reading/writing activities, the modelling, guidance and independent practice are usually sequenced within the steps of the one lesson. The implementation steps, approximate duration, and the kinds of activities involved in each step focusing on writing development are outlined below:

- *Orientation to the text (10–20 minutes)*
  The orientation to writing involves establishing and/or reviewing the students' knowledge of the topic to be written about. The results of discussion and elicitation of responses from the children are scribed onto the display board as a systematic summary of the knowledge of the topic to be used in the writing. The social purpose of, and intended audience for, the writing is then discussed and a model of the genre to be used is provided. This model is explored in terms of its schematic structure, layout, font type, images etc.

- *Writing the text (20–30 minutes)*
  Using the summary of knowledge of the topic, the planning of the stages of schematic structure is undertaken by annotating the summary with coloured lines etc., grouping information to be included in particular stages. In modelling it is important that the teacher actually writes a version of the required text on a black/white board, overhead projector transparency or a computer with data projector, using the 'think aloud' technique to make his or her composition processes available to the students. Once a first draft is completed this is briefly reviewed and edited, and this process includes notes about the type and location of images to be inserted.

  In guided and independent writing it is useful for students to 'conference' with one or more other students about the drafts of their work. In modelling, teachers should try to invite another adult to comment on the draft and also seek feedback from the students. At this stage conferences should focus on how effectively the students have communicated their purposes to their peers as readers. The conferences should be a source of constructive advice about which aspects of the text are most effective and particular suggestions about how other aspects of the text might be clarified or improved. Students then redraft their work in preparation for a consultation with the teacher.

- *Reviewing writing (15–20 minutes)*
  The teacher consultation should encourage the student to discuss not only the content of the text but also the structuring of the language in terms of the stages of schematic structure of the genre, the grammatical choices designed to achieve particular effects, and selection of images with particular characteristics to contribute to the overall construction of meaning. The teacher should model effective, constructive editing and explain the explicit grammatical and rhetorical bases for the editorial suggestions. Students revise their texts in the light of teacher advice, then prepare final drafts and join with partners to proofread texts in preparation for publication.

- *Publishing writing (15–20 minutes)*
  This step may occur as a subsequent session. If the text has been prepared electronically, images should be drawn/scanned and inserted, background, borders, colour and font finalized and a hard copy printed. If the text has been prepared manually, corresponding hard copy steps should be completed. Finally, the text should be displayed in the classroom and, if relevant, also despatched to its intended audience.

'GRANDPA': LITERARY TEXTS AND MULTILITERACIES IN A YEAR 2 CLASSROOM

Introducing the unit of study

This unit of work on the theme of 'Grandpa' is for children who are about 7 to 9 years old and usually in their third year of schooling. Similar detailed programs using literary texts with children in the first and second years of schooling have been published in earlier work (Unsworth and O'Toole 1993). This unit will provide opportunities for children's exploration of, and reflection on, many issues involved in the relationship of children to their grandfathers in the context of learning how such relationships are constructed in contemporary picture books. As well as focusing on story, this unit will also contribute to children's knowledge of narrative structure and their understanding about how the resources of vocabulary, grammar and image are deployed to construct interpretive possibilities in story. In so doing the activities involved in this unit of study will enhance children's developing resources as code-breakers, text comprehenders and composers and critical text analysts (Freebody and Luke 1990). The following literary texts for children are the basis of the classroom activities.

Dan's Grandpa by Sally Morgan and Bronwyn Bancroft (1996)
Grandfather by Jeannie Baker (1994)
Grandpa by Lilith Norman and Noela Young (1998)
Granpa by John Burningham (1984)
Hannah and the Tomorrow Room by L. Gleeson (1999)

Dan's Grandpa (Morgan and Bancroft 1996) tells of a young Australian Aboriginal boy's experience with his grandfather and how he deals with his grandpa's death. Jeannie Baker's *Grandfather* (1994) recounts a young girl's experiences 'helping' her grandfather in his second-hand store. The book by Lilith Norman and Noela Young called *Grandpa* (1998) concerns a young boy's experience with his sometimes cantankerous grandpa and also with the way the young boy deals with his grandpa's death. John Burningham's *Granpa* (1984) constructs the relationship between Granpa and his granddaughter by depicting a selection of unrelated activities shared by the old man and the little girl over a period of perhaps a year. The activities are represented by highly elliptical dialogue and visuals that involve line drawings on the left-hand pages suggesting memories and imaginings, and coloured images on the right-hand pages indicating present events.

In *Hannah and the Tomorrow Room* (Gleeson 1999) Hannah's grandfather's illness necessitates his coming to live with Hannah, her baby sister, her older twin sisters and their parents, just on the eve of Hannah's planned move into a new room, which has been added to the house. Of course, this results in Hannah's having to continue to

Week	Session		Focus of learning experiences
1	1	Serial Reading	Writing recounts based on photos of grandfathers: Teacher modelling
	2	*Hannah and the Tomorrow Room*	Writing recounts based on photos of grandfathers: Guided writing
	3		*Grandfather* (Baker) – working with language
	4		*Grandfather* (Baker) – working with images
	5		*Dan's Grandpa* (Morgan and Bancroft) – working with language and images
2	1		*Granpa* (Burningham) – working with language and images
	2		*Grandpa* (Norman and Young) – working with language and images
	3		Comparison and review writing – four picture books and novel
	4		Children's choice reading and planning of presentation session 5
	5		Presentation day of work completed over the two week unit of study

Figure 6.3   Lesson schedule for a unit of work on 'Grandpa'

share with her older sisters. The story deals with Hannah's response to this situation and its eventual resolution. This book of 13 chapters and 88 pages is used to begin the unit of work and thenceforth as serial reading done by the teacher. It is written in the third person and in the present tense and the children are kept alert to these features – Hannah is a character in the story but she is not the one telling the story, and the language relates the events as if they are occurring now.

The lesson schedule for the unit of work on 'Grandpa' is indicated in Figure 6.3. For some classes this unit of work may need to be distributed over more lessons and/or a longer period of time, depending on their prior experience with the literacy practices involved. In the subsequent sections the sessions for the first week of the unit will be described in some detail, but the sessions for the second week will be only briefly outlined.

Session 1: Writing recounts – modelled practice

In preparation for this session children and parents have been advised that the children will have an opportunity to talk and write about their grandfather(s) and have been invited to bring in photographs of their grandfather(s) if this is possible.

Orientation to the text

- The teacher introduces the novel *Hannah and the Tomorrow Room* for serial reading and reads the first chapter, noting with the children the present tense narration.
- The following extract from the introduction to the book is displayed and read again to the children

  > It's funny how the same person has lots of names. It's like I say Grandpa but some kids say Pop and some Grandad and Annie says Grandy and Toula says Papou and Tui says Ong Noi.

- Children are given an opportunity to show the picture(s) of their grandfather(s) and to indicate the name(s) they use.
- It will be necessary for the teacher to explain some of the reasons why some people may not know their grandfather(s). An alternative task like writing about an uncle or family friend will need to be negotiated with any children in the class in this situation.
- The children's photographs are used to classify images in terms of actional/reactional; offer/demand; close-up/medium and long shot. Practice group categorizations such as: all long shots come to the front; all offers come to the front etc.
- The teacher shows a photo of her or his own grandfather and models talking about him (name, age, description, where he lives/lived, occupation, things he liked, special memories of being with him).

Writing the text

- The teacher models writing a recount of some experiences with her or his grandfather, labelling the schematic structure as she or he proceeds. The 'orientation' would include the grandfather's name, age, and description and optionally where he lives/lived etc. The next stage in the recount is the 'record of events'. Here the teacher would model writing a series of activities in which she or he engaged with her or his grandfather, for example walking to the newsagent on Saturday mornings, painting his boat every Christmas holidays. The construction of this section would also deal with the kinds of photographs and/or drawings that could be included – the appropriateness of actional or transactional offers to text dealing with events for example. The final stage is the re-orientation. This could be something like 'My grandad lives in a nursing home now, but I visit him once every month on Sunday afternoons and I still enjoy thinking about the things we did together.' Again the use of appropriate photographs and/or drawings should be included in the modelled writing.
- The teacher's model recount is then read and key elements of its construction are discussed. The schematic structure is rehearsed again and the teacher also notes the use of the present tense in the orientation (if the grandfather is alive), the past tense in the record of events, and the return to the present tense in the reorientation.

- As the first step in the guided writing to be undertaken by the children, they will be involved in talking about their grandfathers. In this session the talk will be focused on introducing their grandfathers in preparation for what they will write in the orientation stage of their recount. Some scaffolding prompts like 'name', 'whose father', 'what he does', 'where he lives' etc. will assist some children. These introductions can be shared in small groups and then some shared with the whole class. For homework the children can think about the things they have done with their grandfathers to be shared the next day.

Session 2: Writing recounts – guided practice

Serial reading and recapitulation of previous lesson

- The teacher reads the second chapter from *Hannah and the Tomorrow Room*.
- The teacher shows her or his recount from the previous lesson, reads this again with the children and consolidates their understanding of the structuring of the text.
- Some children who have not yet shared their oral introductions to their grandfathers do this and the teacher selects one or two to scribe onto to the display board. These are then read and edited to show how the children will undertake their writing of the orientation stage of their recounts.

Writing and reviewing writing

- The children draft the orientation stage of their recounts.
- The procedure adopted in preparing for the writing of the orientation is then repeated for the record of events. The children talk in small groups about the things they have done with their grandfathers. Again some scaffolding around 'what', 'when' and 'where' will be useful. Some of these can be shared with the whole class and some selections from one or two of the children can be scribed to demonstrate how they will write this part of their recount. Once the children have drafted the record of events the same procedure is used to scaffold their writing of the reorientation.
- Once most students have completed a first draft of their recounts, the teacher arranges groups of about three students so that they can 'conference' with one or more other students about the drafts of their work. At this stage conferences should focus on how effectively the students have communicated their ideas to their peers as readers. The conferences should be a source of constructive advice about which aspects of the text are most effective and particular suggestions about how other aspects of the text might be clarified or improved. These conference practices need to have been modelled by the teacher with individual children in previous lessons before this peer group conferencing is introduced. Students then redraft their work in preparation for a consultation with the teacher.

Teacher conferencing and publication of students' work

- Note that teacher conferencing with individual students may begin in this session but it will need to be completed during other lessons within this unit of work and also during opportunities at other times in the school day.
- The teacher consultation should encourage the student to discuss not only the content of the text but also the structuring of the language in terms of the stages of schematic structure of the genre, the grammatical choices, and selection of images. The teacher should model effective, constructive editing and explain the explicit grammatical and rhetorical bases for the editorial suggestions. Students revise their texts in the light of teacher advice, then prepare final drafts and join with partners to proofread texts in preparation for publication.
- Whether the draft is to be 'published' and in what form should be discussed between the teacher and the student. If it is to be published, this step may occur outside of class time or during class time in a subsequent session. If the text has been prepared electronically, images should be drawn/scanned and inserted, background, borders, colour and font finalized and a hard copy printed. If the text has been prepared manually, corresponding hard copy steps should be completed. Finally, published texts should be displayed in the classroom and, if relevant also despatched to its intended audience.

Session 3: *Grandfather* – working with language

Orientation to the text

- The teacher reads Chapters 3 and 4 of *Hannah and the Tomorrow Room*.
- Students read their published recounts about Grandpa.
- Introduction of new picture book, *Grandfather* by Jeannie Baker (1994). Students may note the surname above the shop window on the cover is the same as that of the author and speculate about the reasons for that. Also note that Jeannie Baker is the author/illustrator. The texture of the image on the front cover may remind some students who know other books by Jeannie Baker – *Where the Forest Meets the Sea* (1987), *Window* (1991) – that the images are the result of collage work.

Reading the text

- Teacher's introductory reading followed by children's initial comments on the story. In view perhaps of the previous lesson's dealing with names people call their grandfathers, students frequently comment on the formality of the use of 'Mother' and 'Grandfather'. They also ask what 'hatpins' and 'ephemera' are, and why the grandfather 'had cotton wool stuffed in his ears'. Australian children ask about the television set 'marked five pounds'. Frequently children comment on how 'real' some of the images are.

- In the first phase of collaborative reading the teacher pauses to encourage 'completion' reading by the children of sections containing less familiar vocabulary ('how to put my hands down into the upholstery', 'she asked if we sold antique hairpins', 'a man with a curly moustache') drawing visual attention to the words as they are read. This can also be done with sections the children find amusing such as 'A woman came in wearing a fox around her neck . . . I didn't like her and felt sorry for the fox'.
- In the second phase of collaborative reading the groups of children are allocated sections to read and given time to rehearse together, seeking assistance from the teacher as required. Either the teacher or the most proficient reader(s) in the class read the five pages of the 'orientation'. The remaining 11 events and the concluding reorientation have one page each ranging from two to seven lines of print. Two children are allocated to prepare each of these pages for oral reading.

Working with the text

- In exploring text meanings children frequently notice ways in which their grandfathers are similar to and different from the grandfather in the story. Some children are very interested in the grandfather being untidy in his shop and that the mother says he should tidy it up. The children see this as one way that the grandfather is like many of them. One common observation relates the text to the images of television sets in the orientation. The text indicates that 'Grandfather puts on all his televisions just to show they work'. However one of the television sets depicted with a picture on the screen clearly has the lead and plug for the electricity socket lying unconnected on the floor.
- The schematic structure of the text as a recount (Figure 6.4) was informally introduced in the allocations for oral reading. This can now be consolidated in noting that the orientation is mostly written in the present tense, while the record of events and the reorientation is mostly written in the past. It should be pointed out to the children that the present tense indicates events that are happening now or that continue to happen regularly like 'He lets me help in his shop'. On the other hand the past tense indicates events that have occurred like 'Grandfather showed me how to put my hands down into the upholstery'.
- It should also be noted that the little girl who is in the text is also the teller of this recount so it is told in the first person – by one of the people who actually participated in the events. The children frequently observe that she is not named and there is much speculation, drawing on the discussion of the image on the cover, that she is Jeannie Baker.
- In consolidating text processing the children are engaged in a close rereading of the text, providing further opportunity to confirm their decoding of the print, addressing the development of explicit grammatical knowledge and also learning how grammatical choices construct point of view in narrative. From the discussion of the narrator role, the teacher notes the occurrence of the pronoun 'I' indicating the

Stage	Text
Orientation	My grandfather is so old that he can't remember his age. He lets me help him in his shop. Mother said he ought to tidy it up, but Grandfather laughed and said that if it was tidy he wouldn't know where to find anything. Grandfather has an enormous number of clocks, of all shapes and sizes. There is a constant sound of clocks chiming. As soon as one finishes, another one begins, sometimes they overlap, making beautiful music. Grandfather puts on all his televisions just to show they work, but he doesn't turn on the sound. All you can hear is a buzzing noise. Sometimes I imagine what the people are saying. One set is a bit wrong, the picture keeps rolling round. Grandfather said he'd see to it later.
Record of events	I like Grandfather's old leather chair. It makes creaking noises when I move. Grandfather showed me how to put my hands down into the upholstery and feel for surprises. It made my hand sore, but I found an old penny, two buttons and a hairclip. A woman came in wearing a fox round her neck. She asked if we sold antique hatpins. Grandfather said he didn't. I didn't like her and felt sorry for the fox. I looked through a box labelled 'Ephemera'. It contained lots of postcards. Some were very old and had beautiful spidery writing. We sorted through some old clothes and I wondered about the people who used to wear them. I am a queen in my palace. I have to remember to lift my skirts as I walk, like the ladies in the olden days. Grandfather kissed my hand and said, 'Your majesty'. A man with a curly moustache looked at all the televisions. He spent ages scratching his head and turning the sounds up and down. He bought one marked five pounds. Grandfather said it was a real bargain and promised to deliver it tonight. Grandfather sat doing his football pools and soon his heavy breathing told me he was asleep. While he wasn't looking, I peeled more paint off the window frame. I like to see the shapes and colours of the paint underneath. Some children pressed their noses to the window and stared at me. I felt important sitting in the shop. I made Grandfather a cup of tea. The cat poked her head out of the chair stuffing in which she'd been hiding, and looked so thirsty that we poured her a saucer of milk. She jumped down purring. I sat on Grandfather's knee and he told me stories. I noticed that he had cotton wool stuffed in his ears. It makes him deaf so I had to shout.
Reorientation	Grandfather was pleased I had helped him so much. He gave me a photograph of a small boy, who, he said was my Great Great Grandfather.

Figure 6.4 Schematic structure of *Grandfather*
Source: Baker 1994. From *Grandfather* by Jeannie Baker. Text and illustrations copyright © Jeannie Baker 1987. Reprinted by permission of Scholastic Australia.

Action verbs	Thinking verbs	Saying verbs	Being verbs
I move	I imagine	*I tell**	*I am*
I found	I like	*I say*	*He is*
I had helped			

Figure 6.5 Verb categorizations
Note: * Italicized entries not from the Book.

narrator throughout the book. The teacher then models the identification of the word that follows 'I' in the orientation, the first (lounge chair) event in the record of events, and in the reorientation. These are initially written on the display board in the classroom ('I imagine', 'I like', 'I move', 'I found', 'I had helped'). Explain to the children that these words are called 'verbs' and there are two types in this list. One type tells what the narrator was doing (action verbs) and the other type tells what the narrator was thinking. Involve the children in sorting the verbs into these categories and add the categories of 'being' and 'saying' verbs with examples not drawn from the book. This model categorization of verbs should be displayed for student reference as indicated in Figure 6.5.

- The most proficient readers are located in one group and set the task of locating all of the occurrences of 'Grandfather' (or 'he' referring to 'Grandfather') and the associated verbs. The other children are divided into five groups of (about) four students. Each group has to complete a chart similar to that shown in Figure 6.5 by locating all of the instances of 'I' and the associated verbs in the remaining 10 event descriptions in the record of events. Once this first phase is finished these groups recombine into four groups of (about) five students, including the proficient readers group working on Grandfather, so that each new group has one member of each of the original groups. The students in the new groups now check their work, rereading the relevant sections of the book to ensure no instances have been overlooked. While this peer checking is proceeding the teacher can also check the students' categorizations. Each group then prepares a comparative table indicating the verbs in each category associated with the narrator and with Grandfather as shown in Figure 6.6. As the teacher monitors the finalization of this step in the groupwork tasks, the children are directed to think about the relative proportions of verb types associated with the narrator and the Grandfather.

Reviewing reading and writing

- The extension phase involves students in reviewing those segments of the text in which dialogue is reported, imaginatively creating the dialogue that might have occurred and inserting this into the text in the form of speech balloons. The children

	Action verbs	Thinking verbs	Saying verbs	Being verbs
Narrator	move found looked lift walk peeled made sat had helped	imagine like didn't like felt wondered have to remember like to see felt noticed	had to shout	am
Grandfather	lets help ought to tidy laughed puts doesn't turn see to showed didn't (sell) kissed sat doing wasn't looking gave	can't remember wouldn't know	said said said said promised told said	is has was was

Figure 6.6   Verbs associated with the narrator and with Grandfather

are provided with the page where the woman asks for an antique hatpin as a model (see Figure 6.7)

The children can choose from worksheets containing suitable pages from the book. For example:

> Mother said he ought to tidy it up, but Grandfather laughed and said that if it was tidy he wouldn't know where to find anything.

If some children exhaust these, more challenging examples can be provided where the full extent of the dialogue is implied but not actually reported in the text. For example:

> A man with a curly moustache looked at all the televisions. He spent ages scratching his head and turning the sounds up and down. He bought one marked five pounds. Grandfather said it was a real bargain and promised to deliver it tonight.

- The final phase of this lesson is the presentation and reflection on the work done. In this case the groupwork tables showing the distribution of verb types between the

Figure 6.7   Model of dialogue creation in *Grandfather*
Source: Baker 1994. From *Grandfather* by Jeannie Baker. Text and illustrations copyright © Jeannie Baker 1987. Reprinted by permission of Scholastic Australia.

narrator and Grandfather will be shown and the class as a whole will discuss the implications of this with the teacher. Some children may begin to see how the use of mental verbs indicating what the character is thinking is one way in which we are encouraged to see things from that character's point of view. Following this the teacher will read the book once more with children who have completed their speech balloons invited to interpolate these at a signal from the teacher as she or he reads.

Session 4: 'Grandfather' – working with images

Orientation to the text

- The teacher continues reading *Hannah and the Tomorrow Room*, and reviews with the children the story so far. They discuss any similarities between Hannah's grandfather and Jeannie Baker's grandfather.

Reading the text

- The class presents a group reading of the picture book *Grandfather*, using the same allocated sections from the previous lesson, but this time with nominated students interpolating the created dialogue as practised at the end of the last lesson. Move from this to preparing an informal readers' theatre presentation (Johnson and Louis 1985; Robertson and Poston-Anderson 1986; Nicoll and Unsworth 1990). The teacher prepares a script from the text of the orientation and the first event in the record of events. This script is essentially an annotation of the text of the book, showing the allocation of characters, the interpolation of dialogue and marks signalling changes in volume, pace, pitch etc. This is placed on a chart or overhead projector and the teacher models the readers' theatre presentation of this segment, explaining the use of the script. Six speaking parts are required for the whole book, so the class is divided into four or five groups of six students, each to prepare a readers' theatre presentation. This can be done relatively efficiently since the children are becoming confident readers of the book and much of the dialogue has already been constructed in the speech balloons activity.

Working with the text

- Exploring text meanings in this session deals with further opportunities for children to adopt a critical analytic stance in relation to the interpretive possibilities of the book and also to focus more on the images. The absence of the grandmother will already have occurred to some children. In *Hannah and the Tomorrow Room* we know that Hannah's grandmother had died. In Jeannie Baker's text, the children might speculate about why the grandmother is not mentioned. Children's awareness of the tendency toward stereotypical portrayal of grandfathers can also be heightened. One way to do this is to look at variation in age, appearance and behaviours among their grandfathers, compare this with Grandfather in Jeannie Baker's text and consider other ways in which grandfathers might be depicted.
- In the previous lesson some work was done in classifying the children's pictures of their grandfathers as offers/demands, close-up, medium and long shot, and action/reaction. This can be consolidated using images of men who might be grandfathers from magazines and newspapers. The children are given sets of such images in

groups of about four students and are asked to sort and then re-sort the images according to these dimensions. Once they are confident with this, a categorization worksheet for each image in the set is completed showing its classification on each of these dimensions.

- The next task is for the groups to do this for all of the images of the narrator and Grandfather in the Jeannie Baker text, to discuss any patterns in the types of images and how these image types affect your reading of the book.

Reviewing reading and writing

- An extension activity is for the children to explore the modality of the images in *Grandfather*. To do this the children are asked to look at each image in the book and to rate it on a scale of 1–5 ('very real', 'nearly real', 'a bit like real', 'not very real', 'not real at all'). They are then asked to indicate the features of the images that led them to the particular rating. From the children's specific responses it will be possible to derive categories for future work like background/context, full or limited range of colour, detail, sharp or blurred etc.
- The children's earlier work on the classification of images according to offer/demand, action/reaction etc. can then be presented and discussed. Significant points to note here are that the narrator and Grandfather are never depicted in 'demand' images. Other characters like the cat, the woman wanting the antique hatpins and the portrait from the ephemera are depicted as demands. The first image of Grandfather is quite a long shot – almost remote. Throughout the book then he is shown in medium to long shots and it is not until the penultimate page that he and the narrator are shown in close-up. The children could discuss the effect of this kind of progression.

Session 5: *Dan's Grandpa* – working with language and images

Orientation to the text

- The last two pages of Chapter 6 of *Hannah and the Tomorrow Room* are distributed to the class. The dialogue of Dad is underlined and that of Mum is double underlined, and one section of Hannah's silent rehearsal of her excuse is put in a 'thought cloud'. The teacher reads this final section of Chapter 6 again, indicating to the children that they will join in the next reading, taking the parts of Mum and Dad and Hannah rehearsing her excuse.
- The teacher continues with serial reading of Chapters 7 and 8 of the novel.
- The new picture book, *Dan's Grandpa* by Sally Morgan and Bronwyn Bancroft (1996) is introduced (Figure 6.8). Some children may recognize the distinctive 'dot painting' that characterizes much of the contemporary art work of Australian

Figure 6.8 *Dan's Grandpa* (Morgan and Bancroft 1996)

Aboriginal painters and they will notice that the characters are black. Some will also recognize the sulphur-crested cockatoo, which is common in many outback and urban areas of Australia. Although Grandpa is carrying spears, the contemporary setting of the story is suggested by the peaked cap that Dan is wearing. From the inspection of the cover, some predictions about the likely content of the text can be shared.

Reading the text

- Following the teacher's introductory reading of the story, children's initial responses are explored. From earlier work on Jeannie Baker's book, one thing to notice is that the grandmother is never mentioned. The distinctively stylized images with the turtles and fish, as well as the hills and paths being depicted in the colourful Aboriginal art motifs, can be related to the discussion of the modality in the Jeannie Baker illustrations. In *Dan's Grandpa* the images are not natural-

Stage	Episodes	Pages
ORIENTATION	Story preview: Dan reflecting on Grandpa's death	2
	Fishing with Grandpa	1
	Lessons about the bush and the Naml language	1
	Learning about dance and the corroboree	1
	Stories at night	1
COMPLICATION	Grandpa is ill and has to go to hospital	1
	School then visiting the hospital	2
	Mum picks Dan up from school and tells of Grandpa's death	1
	Cocky disappears	2
RESOLUTION	Cocky returns – symbolizing Grandpa's presence	3

Figure 6.9   Schematic structure in *Dan's Grandpa* (Morgan and Bancroft 1996)

istic. There is no detail in the drawing of any of the characters – their features are highly abstracted. It is almost as if what was important was their Aboriginality and the nature of the relationship rather than the individual characteristics of the participants.
- Some of the children may notice the difference from the Jeannie Baker text in that here Dan is a character but he is not telling the story, making explicit the difference between first and third person narration. This can be related to the serial reading where Hannah is a character but she is not telling the story.
- The teacher indicates that she or he will read the story again and children may notice other interesting things about it. The teacher can also point out the story structure (Figure 6.9) and that after the next reading the children will prepare their own group reading with different children reading different episodes.
- The most proficient readers are asked to prepare the orientation and resolution sections and then the children are allocated in pairs (or threes) to each of the remaining eight episodes to prepare for oral reading. The class is then regrouped into three groups of about 10. One group will present their reading now, one at the end of the lesson and one at the beginning of the next day's lesson.

Working with the text

- In exploring text meanings the children can return to the images. Further comparisons with Jeannie Baker's *Grandfather* will draw attention to the fact that all of the images in *Dan's Grandpa* are offers, and they are all long or long-medium shots. Most of the images are actional but some are reactional when, for example, Dan is sitting with his head on his knees. The children can then be asked to explore some of the patterns that occur in the images throughout the book. For example:

- When does Cocky actually disappear from the images? (the image of Grandpa in hospital).
- How do the sun's rays change throughout the book? (bright yellow dots at the beginning, white dots when Grandpa is in hospital, then disappear altogether until Cocky returns).
- Why does Cocky first reappear in a coloured circle? Is Grandpa really in the pool in first image? etc.

• In consolidating text processing the children return again to the schematic structure of the story (Figure 6.9). The teacher and the children look again at the episodes in the orientation, paying attention to the words that start each sentence. In most cases the sentences start with either Dan or Grandpa:

Dan loved to remember all the special things he and Grandpa had done together.
Grandpa loved fishing.
His favourite spot was down in the mangroves where the big turtles came in.

These participants that come first in the clause are referred to as the (topical) Theme. The final episode however starts with a circumstance of time – 'At night'. This is referred to as a marked topical Theme.

At night when it was cool Grandpa and Dan liked to sit on the verandah and talk about the old days.

Point out to the children that this could have been written elsewhere in the sentence:

Grandpa and Dan liked to sit on the verandah, when it was cool at night, and talk about the old days.

By shifting the circumstance of time then we can make the Theme of the sentence unmarked again. Discuss with the children how putting 'At night' at the beginning of the sentence and creating a marked Theme draws attention to the time.

• The children are then divided into five groups of about five or six students and their task is first to write down all the sentences which start with a circumstance of time – with marked Themes. Then they should note where these sentences occur in relation to the chart of the schematic structure of the text. Each group is allocated one episode from the complication and resolution stages and is asked to rewrite any sentences with a circumstance of time at the front, relocating this in a different

> *Even now, six months later*, Dan could feel a tear sliding down his cheek as he thought of Cocky and Grandpa.
>
> Dan could feel a tear sliding down his cheek _____
> _____.
>
> Dan could feel a tear sliding down his cheek _____ as he thought of Cocky and Grandpa.
>
> Dan could feel a tear sliding down his cheek as he thought of Cocky and Grandpa _____
> _____.

Figure 6.10 Cloze task based on Theme manipulation.

position so that the sentence still makes sense. This task can be scaffolded for children as a cloze task (Figure 6.10) with varying levels of guidance.

- Once this task is finished the children are regrouped so that each new group has one member of the original groups and therefore each episode with its rewritten sentences is represented in the new groups. Within these groups the children read the story interpolating their rewritten sentences and comment of the effect of the rewriting. With guidance from the teacher, the groups will notice that the marked topical Themes are confined to the beginning of each new episode in the complication and resolution sections of the story (Figure 6.11). These have the effect of marking off the episodes and drawing attention to the passage of time over which the story occurs. It may assist students to understand this by looking again at Jeannie Baker's *Grandfather* and noting that there are no marked topical Themes and the passage of time is over one day.

Reviewing reading and writing

- The extension task is to recontextualize the story as a first person narrative. The teacher models this for the preview section of the orientation stage (Figure 6.12).
- The children are then divided into eight groups of about three students and each group is allocated one of the remaining episodes to turn into first person narration (there is no change to the episode where Grandpa has to go to hospital). The groups of three work collaboratively on this rewrite of their episode then the class is re-grouped into three groups of eight students so that each rewritten episode is represented in the new groups. Each of the eight students reads his or her rewritten episode including the teacher's rewritten preview and the unchanged hospital episode. The effect of the first and the third person narrative versions are then discussed.
- After presentation and discussion of their groupwork on the manipulation of marked topical Themes, the teacher encourages the children to bring together the work they have done on this, the type of narrator and the schematic structure of the recount form of *Grandfather* (Baker 1994) and the story structure of *Dan's Grandpa* (Morgan

Stage	Episodes	*Themes*
ORIENTATION	Story preview: Dan reflecting on Grandpa's death	*Dan* stared into the still water
	Fishing with Grandpa	*Once* when Dan and Grandpa
	Lessons about the bush and the Naml language	*Grandpa* had taught Dan ...
	Learning about dance and the corroboree	*It* was Grandpa ...
	Stories at night	*At night* when it was cool ...
COMPLICATION	Grandpa is ill and has to go to hospital	*But, one day* Grandpa ...
	School then visiting the hospital	*At school*, Dan couldn't *Every afternoon* after school ...
	Mum picks Dan up from school and tells of Grandpa's death	*One day* Dan's Mum picked
	Cocky disappears	*The next day* Dan got up
RESOLUTION	Cocky returns – symbolizing Grandpa's presence	*Even now*, six months later

Figure 6.11 Relating schematic structure and Theme in *Dan's Granpa* (Morgan and Bancroft 1996)

Dan stared into the still water of the rock hole and thought about *his* grandpa. It had been six months since *his* grandpa had died. *Dan* really missed him. *He* had never had a dad, so *his* grandpa was very important to *him*. When *Dan* was sad *he* liked to escape to the bush, where *he* could sit quietly with *his* animal friends and remember Grandpa.	*I* stared into the still water of the rock hole and thought about *my* grandpa. It had been six months since *my* grandpa had died. *I* really missed him. *I* had never had a dad, so *my* grandpa was very important to *me*. When *I* was sad *I* liked to escape to the bush, where *I* could sit quietly with *my* animal friends and remember Grandpa.

Figure 6.12 Teacher modelling of changing from third to first person narrative

and Bancroft 1996). Through this kind of work the children are exploring both story and story form.

- Finally, the second group who prepared the oral reading in the orientation section reads this aloud to the class, providing further opportunities for the children's individual reflection on what has been learned.

Session 6: *Granpa* – working with language and images

Orientation to the text

- The teacher continues with the serial reading of Chapters 9 and 10 of *Hannah and the Tomorrow Room*.
- The third group who prepared the oral reading of *Grandpa* in the previous lesson presents their reading to the class.
- The teacher shows the front cover of John Burningham's *Granpa* (1984). Perhaps the children know other books by Burningham, which can be briefly recounted and noted. Some children may well have encountered this book before. Note the spelling of Granpa and relate this to the various names given to grandfathers. Notice that Granpa and the little girl are seated in a toy trolley. Predict with the children from this what kinds of things are likely to be dealt with in the story.
- Prepare and present on separate pages the text of each double page spread in dialogue format and ask the children to indicate the contexts in which they might occur.

Reading the text

- The teacher completes an introductory reading of the book as the children observe the text and image format. The children are often quite sombre at the end, asking what happened to Granpa. (This is why it is often useful to have dealt with a book like *Dan's Grandpa*.) It is important to discuss with the children that what happens to Granpa is left deliberately ambiguous and it is the reader's task to imagine the possibilities. Some children will want to know what wooden hoops are and Australian children might ask what a meadow is. It is also useful to explore children's familiarity with the biblical reference to Noah. Some may comment on the difference between the images on the left-hand side and those on the right-hand side of the double page spread.
- If the children do not notice, point out to them that the speech of the child is in italics and the speech of Granpa is in normal font. The children are then allocated parts to take in a whole class reading of the book. There are eight pages where both characters speak and pairs of children should be allocated one page each. Then there are two pages where the child speaks only and four where Granpa speaks only. If there are more than two children in the group, children can combine to read the child and Granpa-only pages.

Working with the text

- Remind the children of their understanding of first and third person narratives and point out that this book does not have a narrator at all. It also does not readily fit the schematic structure of a recount (orientation^record of events^reorientation) or a story (orientation^complication^(evaluation)^resolution). There is a beginning, middle and end structure with the opening 'And how's my little girl?', the shared events in the middle and the closure of Granpa's empty chair.

- Much of the impact of the book derives from the nature of the dialogue. One important part of this is the nature of the questions the little girl asks. The children could explore this by responding to questions like the following:

How many of the little girl's questions does Granpa answer?
Which questions do you think she already knew the answer to?
Why do you think she asked those questions?
Which questions do you think she really wanted an answer to?
Why do you think she really did want an answer to these questions?
Which questions do you think would have been the most difficult for Granpa to answer?
Why do you think Granpa would have found these difficult?

Children could also speculate about what prompted 'That was not a nice thing to say to Granpa'. They could also speculate on who actually said that, as well as who said 'Granpa can't come out to play today'.

- Exploration of the images could relate to the classifications the children have made in previous lessons, comparing the images in this book to the other books in terms of their modality, whether they are offers or demands, the social distance of the view etc. But it would also be productive to ask the children how much time passes from the beginning of the book until the end and how is this passing of time communicated through the images (passing of the seasons). They could also look at each double page spread and ask how the image on the right relates to the image on the left and what visual resources are used to construct this relationship (some of the line drawings on the left represent memories of things past, some represent imaginings related to the present and some are less determinate).

Reviewing reading and writing

- The presentation and discussion of the children's responses in exploring the questions in the dialogue and the ideas communicated by the images provides the basis for discussing the gaps or spaces left by the author, which the reader is able to fill in in a variety of ways. This leads to two extension tasks. The first is for the children to derive a third person narrative from Granpa thereby filling in certain gaps. They would need to name the little girl and could draw on Granpa for the content of the story. They could use previous work on *Dan's Grandpa* to assist in structuring the story. Some modelling of the first part of such a story by the teacher would be useful for some children, drawing attention to the schematic structure and grammatical resources such as the use of marked Themes to introduce episodes.

Kristin's Granpa always greeted her with 'And how's my little girl?' Kristen and her Granpa spent lots of time together and did lots of different things. In the spring Kristin helped Granpa in his greenhouse to prepare the seedlings to plant for the summer. They also played with Kristin's dolls and had tea parties in the garden. At night Granpa read Kristin stories. On sunny days they went to the beach or played in the park. In winter [etc.]

- A further extension task is to return to Jeannie Baker's *Grandfather* and reconstruct some of the events in the form of the kind of dialogue in Burningham's *Granpa*, adding the kinds of illustrations that might be appropriate to this form. Again the teacher could model this for a few pages of *Grandfather* to produce alternative text like the following:

    How old are you really Grandfather?
    As old as my tongue and a little older than my teeth.

    Was your shop ever tidy Grandfather?
    Your mother's bedroom used to look like the wreck of the Hesperus.

    You could have a concert with these clocks Grandfather.

Sessions 7–10: *Grandpa* (Norman and Young) plus review, extension and consolidation

The second session in the second week continues the serial reading of *Hannah and the Tomorrow Room* (Gleeson 1999) and introduces the children to *Grandpa* by Lilith Norman and Noela Young (1998). Following the orientation and reading of the text, initial responses deal with comparisons with the other books dealt with, including *Hannah and the Tomorrow Room*. This should lead beyond the story to the form of the texts, for example the intertextuality of the empty chair at the end of this story and at the end of Burningham's *Granpa*. The names given to grandfathers (drawn attention to at the beginning of Gleeson 1999) can lead to the significance of names in this story, where at the end of the story Grandpa calls Blake by his name instead of 'Sonny Jim'. In working with the text four groups rotate around the following activities:

- classification of the types of images as in work with previous texts in terms of modality, demands/offers, social distance, actional/reactional etc. The images in this book make significant use of demand, more realistic modality, and closer social distance (Figure 6.13) as well as many images where reaction processes are important to the story;
- using a digital camera to photograph the scenes in the book enacted by the children, so that the children can understand the point of view that is constructed in the presented images;
- comparison of the events recalled about the grandfather in this story and *Dan's Grandpa* in terms of both the types of events and the means of their depiction. For

My grandfather died last Saturday.

Figure 6.13 'Demand' image from *Grandpa*
Source: Norman and Young 1998. From *Grandpa* by Lilith Norman, illustrations by Noela Young. Text copyright © Lilith Norman 1998. Illustrations copyright © Noela Young 1998. Reprinted by permission of Scholastic Australia.

example Dan initially recalls his grandfather whose image appears in a pond, while Blake looks at a photograph. Dan's symbol of his dead grandfather's presence is Grandpa's white cockatoo, while Blake has the nail sculptures;

• listening critically to the teacher's reading of the story on tape and then preparing a group reading on tape.

The same group and regroup procedure is used to enable the sharing of work and engagement with different perspectives on understanding. The review section of the lesson involves the children presenting their comparison of the texts and their account of the types of images in *Grandpa*, including their ideas about the point of view constructed. An extension activity is to construct dialogue that can be inserted into the images in *Grandpa* using Post-it notes forming speech balloons. At the conclusion the class can listen to one or more of the four taped readings of the story by the student groups.

In session three the final (thirteenth) chapter of *Hannah and the Tomorrow Room* is read. This and the four picture books read are then reviewed and compared. In working with the text the children are guided in constructing first a comparison grid dealing with schematic structure, narrator role, types of images etc. The next step involves further guidance in using the grid in the collaborative writing of a review of *Hannah and the Tomorrow Room* for a children's literature Internet site. The reviewing and extending reading and writing then involves the children in writing a review in the same way as one of the picture story books.

Session four involves the reading of other texts about grandfathers brought in by the children and/or provided by the teacher. These could include different types of texts like the humorous story by Bob Graham called *Grandad's Magic* (1990) or humorous poems like 'Polishing Grandad' and 'Driving Grandad' by Jean Willis (Bennett 1993). This session also involves planning of the next and final day's work when the children will display work completed over the two weeks, including published recounts about their grandfathers, reviews of the books they have read, audiotaped readings, readers' theatre and computer-based text presentations.

Alternative selections of literary texts for classroom work

Of course many 'topic' units like Grandpa can be set up using literary texts. For example:

Bullying
Serial reading of *The Eighteenth Emergency* by Betsy Byars (1974)
Willy the Wimp by Anthony Browne (1984)
Willy the Champ by Anthony Browne (1985)

Fear of the sea
The Deep by Tim Winton (1998)
Stella – Star of the Sea by Marie Louise Gay (1999)
There's a Sea in my Bedroom by Margaret Wild and Jane Tanner (1989)

There are many other bases on which to plan units of work using literary texts. One of these is an author and/or illustrator study, focusing on several books by the same writer/ illustrator (Unsworth and O'Toole 1993), reading different versions of traditional and folk tales, children's books adapted to video and children's literature that has been published in conventional book format and on CD ROM.

USING INFORMATIONAL TEXTS IN THE EARLY YEARS OF SCHOOLING

The use of informational texts in conventional and computer-based formats in developing multiliteracies in the early years of schooling is just as important as the use of literary texts. The segment of a classroom program outlined here is derived from work undertaken by children of about 6 or 7 years of age in their second year of schooling near Campbelltown in New South Wales. Due to constraints of space the account of this work will be rather more skeletal than that provided in the previous section.

We will deal with the key elements of the second and third weeks of a four-week program about insects.

During the first week of the program the children had begun informal observation of insects at home and at school. By the end of the week pairs of students had selected particular insects that they were going to learn more about so that the class as a whole dealt with a variety of insects. They had begun a pinboard display of pictures of insects from magazines, photocopies from books and some photographs. The teacher had also purchased some phasmids (stick insects) from the Australian Insect Farm in Innisfail in North Queensland and with the children set up a vivarium to house them for observation during the unit of work. The children and their parents were advised of the Australian Museum's online 'search and discover leaflets' as a ready source of information about phasmids (http://www.austmus.gov.au/is/sand/phasmid.htm).

From the second week the teacher was bridging from the informal knowledge base of week one to more systematic understanding of the characteristic features of insects as a particular category of arthropods. In terms of visual literacy she was dealing with conceptual analytic images showing part/whole relations as well as very simple forms of classificational images. The work on analytic images focused on the common practice of colour coding of body parts for identification. Recognition literacy in relation to verbal text involved the children moving toward familiarization and hesitant command in reading and writing the new vocabulary. Grammatically they were learning how 'relating' verbs like 'is' are used to categorize or classify and how 'possessive relating' verbs like 'have' are used to describe. Reproduction literacy involved beginning to learn the conventional form of an information report in science, beginning with a general classification and then a description. In the latter part of the unit of work the children began to add information about insect behaviours. Digital literacies included learning how to navigate and use different sections of a CD ROM on insects, exploring a website on 'entomology for beginners', which featured interactive material on insects' body parts, accessing a website produced by an American year two class on insects and (in week four) emailing their responses and information about their own study of insects to their counterparts in the US. An overview of the lesson sequence for week two of the program is shown in Figure 6.14.

The book for the modelled reading lesson in session one included a table of contents page and an index with the body of the book consisting of six pages (Drew and Pride 1997). Each of these six pages dealt with a different insect indicated as a heading at the top of the page. The main text on each page took the form: 'All ——— are insects.' On each page there was a top-down view of a naturalistic drawing of the insect and directly underneath that a colour coded drawing highlighting the main body parts. Beside this drawing to the left was the colour code key naming the body parts. This format not only assisted young inexperienced readers to learn the conventions of the contents page and how to use the index, but also the repetitive structures assisted them in learning to recognize the new vocabulary. These aspects were the

Session	Organization Whole Class (W) Groupwork (G)		Teaching/learning activity	Textual resources
1		W	Modelled reading	Drew and Pride 1997
2		W	Guided reading	Drew and Pride 1997
		W	Modelled reading	CD ROM – CSIRO 1994
3	4 groups. 2 groups swap halfway through lesson	G	Guided reading	Drew and Pride 1997
		G	Independent descriptive writing and drawing	Phasmids vivarium
		G	Guided reading	CD ROM – CSIRO 1994
		G	Drawing of 'special study' insect	Dubosque 1998
4	Repeat lesson 3 procedure so all groups do all activities	G	Guided reading	Drew and Pride 1997
		G	Independent descriptive writing and drawing	Phasmids vivarium
		G	Guided reading	CD ROM – CSIRO 1994
		G	Drawing of 'special study' insect	Dubosque 1998
5	W		Modelled writing	Teacher writes proto report on insects

Figure 6.14   Overview of the lesson sequence for week two of the 'insects' program

focus of the first modelled reading. The guided reading in session two consolidated the recognition literacy learning of lesson one and then focused on the colour coded diagrams and how they help us to recognize and understand the insect's main body parts.

Some features of the CD ROM introduced in session two (CSIRO 1994) were discussed in Chapter 3 in the section on classifying images and in the section on analytic images (see pages 84 and 87 respectively). This CD also has a computer graphics feature that allowed students to select predrawn body parts of insects and assemble these to draw different kinds of insects. It has a 'paint' facility that allowed the students to colour code their drawings. The modelled reading in session two was to demonstrate to the children how to navigate the different features of the CD and how to use the draw facility in preparation for one of the groupwork tasks in sessions three and four.

In session three the children were divided into four groups. Halfway through the lesson two groups swapped tasks, so that all of the students at the end of the lesson had completed two of the four activities. The first group undertook further guided reading of the main text (Drew and Pride 1997). This kind of recurrent context is important for young readers to consolidate their learning of recognition literacy. In this task pairs of students within the subgroup were asked to compare two different insects in the book and discuss their findings. The object was to note that all insects have the same three main body parts and legs but some have wings and some don't. The first aspect of this understanding was made explicit on page 8 of the book but the second aspect needed to be made explicit. The second group wrote any descriptions and observations they could about the phasmids in the vivarium and also attempted to draw the phasmid. The third group had access to the CD ROM to locate and learn more about the insect she or he chose for special study and then to use the draw and paint facility to produce a digital image of their insect. Logistically it was helpful to have the pairs who were studying the same insect in the same subgroup for this task. This meant that two students could use the CD for the same purpose simultaneously (many classrooms in Australia have two, sometimes three, computers and therefore can only accommodate a maximum of about four to six students at a time). The fourth group followed the detailed instructions on how to draw a wide variety of insects freehand in Dobosque (1998). The variety of insects included in this book meant that most children found specific visual instructions for the insect they chose for special study. In session four the procedure for session three was repeated so that at the end of session four all students had completed all four activities.

In session five the teacher demonstrated the writing of a 'proto' report on insects. This session also explicitly taught the students the first two stages of the report genre – Classifying statement and Description. The report was drawn from information that the children by then knew quite confidently. The modelled report would typically begin as follows:

| Classifying statement | Insects are creatures with three main body parts and |
| Description | legs. The main body parts of insects are the head, thorax and abdomen. All insects have six legs. Some insects have wings and some do not . . . |

Grammatical features that were emphasized included the use of the relating verbs to classify and describe, and the use of the plural to indicate the generic terms. It was further noted that 'insects' was likely to be in the Theme in most of the sentences, since this was what the report was about and what was therefore the common point of departure. The overview of the lessons in the next week of the program is indicated in Figure 6.15.

The text for guided reading in session one was a double page spread, which included a diagram of the main types of arthropods, a large image of a honeybee with the main body parts labelled, and an image of ladybirds in winter (Cooper 1988: 6–7). The text introduced the term arthropods, located insects within this group and extended previous work on the structure of the report genre to include Behaviour.

Session	Organization Whole Class (W) Groupwork (G)		Teaching/learning activity	Textual resources
1		W	Guided reading	Cooper 1988
2	4 groups 2 groups swap halfway through lesson	G G G G	Prep of images for report on special study insect Discussion of downloaded webpage from US yr2 class Reading of unseen texts on insects (research) Researching internet site for more info on study insect	Digital photograph, scanner, photocopy, children's drawings http://www.greeceny.com/wr/jones/btrfly.html MacLulich 1996 Oppenheim Broda 1998 Loves 1992 http://www1.bos.nl/homes/bijlmakers/ent omology/begin.htm
3	Repeat lesson 3 procedure so all groups do all activities	G G G G	Prep of images for report on special study insect Discussion of downloaded webpage from US yr2 class Reading of unseen texts on insects (research) Researching internet site for more info on study insect	Digital photograph, scanner, photocopy, children's drawings http://www.greeceny.com/wr/jones/btrfly.html MacLulich 1996 Oppenheim Broda 1998 Loves 1992 http://www1.bos.nl/homes/bijlmakers/ent omology/begin.htm
4	W		Guided writing	Report on phasmids
5	W		Independent writing	Report on special study insect

Figure 6.15 Overview of the lesson sequence for week three of the 'insects' program

Classifying statements	Insects belong to a big group of animals called **arthropods**. Our picture shows how they fit into this group. An arthropod is an animal with **joints** in its body and legs. The joints help it move easily.
Description	Our picture shows the main parts of an insect – the head, the **thorax** and the **abdomen**.
Behaviour	Insects cannot keep warm in winter. They stay still like these ladybirds. In summer they warm up and move around.

The first activity in the groupwork in session two involved the children in preparing images for use in writing their own reports on their special study insect, which they would finalize in session five. The children copied images for colour coding, drew simple taxonomic diagrams locating their insect and scanned these for eventual inclusion in an electronic version of their report. In the second activity the teacher discussed with the subgroup downloaded material from the website prepared by Ms Patricia Jones' year two class from West Ridge School in the US. The site included pages from the children's diary observations of their insects, butterfly drawings done by the children with a computer graphics program, trivia and jokes about insects, link pages as well as photographs of the children and email contacts. In this session, as well as reading and discussing the material, the teacher planned with the students how they would communicate some of their work to this group of children in the US using email. In the third activity the children read some very simple, but interesting additional insect books at their independent reading level (Loves 1992; MacLulich 1996; Oppenheim and Broda 1998). This consolidated their recognition literacy learning and also provided an opportunity to seek more information for inclusion in their reports in session five. The fourth activity centred on an 'entomology for beginners' website. The 'insect body parts' used the colour coding idea the children explored in the Drew and Pride text (1997). Clicking on a body part of a generic insect brought a hyperlink to another drawing with that body part coloured and some brief text with information about it. Some of the vocabulary was unfamiliar but the texts were brief and with some support the children could access useful additional information. In session three the groupwork procedure of lesson two was repeated so that all students completed all four activities.

In the guided writing in session four the teacher and the children jointly constructed a report on phasmids. The children drew on what they learned through the preceding weeks' work and their observations of the phasmids in the classroom vivarium. The teacher scribed the children's responses onto a display board and then guided the editing of them to re-scribe a class report. The teacher and the class then prepared the illustrative material to accompany the report. In session five then, the children repeated this process individually to draft their own report on their special study insect. Once drafted they 'conferenced' about their writing with their peers who wrote about the same insect and made any revisions they saw as appropriate in preparation for an individual conference with the teacher about the report in the next week. In week four these reports were 'published' and some sent to the year two class in the US.

CONCLUSION

The examples of classroom work outlined here are not intended as exemplars or models for uniform application. They represent some possibilities in attempting to address the complex demands of early literacy pedagogy in contemporary schooling. The examples here indicate ways in which the teaching of traditional fundamental recognition literacy practices can be integrated with the teaching of the literacy practices required to critically negotiate changing contexts of text and image in conventional and computer-based media. This entails the development of meta-semiotic understanding – understanding how the various visual, verbal and electronic meaning-making systems construct interpretive possibilities and how these are interconnected with the parameters of the social contexts in which texts function. The development of such understanding can and should be a fundamental aspect of early literacy pedagogy and the lesson materials here indicate practical learning experiences that incorporate this. It is hoped that the ideas presented in this chapter will encourage investigative approaches to the management of classroom teaching and learning that will provide all young children with the beginnings of a critical apprenticeship to the multiliteracies of the culture.

CHAPTER 7

Developing multiliteracies in content area teaching

INTRODUCTION

Developing the range of literacies needed by students from diverse backgrounds to effectively negotiate learning in school curriculum areas is the complex task of class-room teachers. Although there is no diminishing this complexity, the previous chapters have shown how systemic functional accounts of language and image as social semi-otic resources can contribute to delineating the knowledge about language and image and the literacy practices students need to acquire in critically negotiating curriculum area learning. We have noted that in both science and humanities, as students' initial everyday understanding of topics shifts to specialized knowledge and critical engage-ment, the language of the texts they encounter becomes increasingly nominalized and characterized by lexical and grammatical patterns of *written* medium that distinguish the texts of particular subject areas. We have also noted that the initial emphasis on genres of recounting and reporting gives way to more emphasis on explaining and critiquing. In addition, there is a shift in the deployment of images, so that in science for example, the use of naturalistic narrative images tends to give way to conceptual images and initial, more concrete representation gives way to the more abstract. (Such changes in the visual and verbal forms of curriculum area texts occur in both con-ventional book and computer-based formats. In computer-based texts these changes are augmented by increasingly complex dynamic hypertextual and intermodal composi-tional structures.) Students are expected to accommodate these semiotic shifts as they advance their learning of particular topics, but often the meta-semiotic knowledge entailed in such shifts is not made explicit in classroom work. The purpose of this chapter is to describe a framework for designing and managing coherent programs of learning experiences that will facilitate the practicalities of implementing such explicit teaching about how texts and images mean, and to provide some specific examples of this kind of classroom work.

THE CAMAL FRAMEWORK

The Curriculum Area Multiliteracies And Learning (CAMAL) framework draws on and extends previous work applying systemic functional accounts of language and image to the articulation of pedagogic models of literacy and learning in school curriculum areas (Derewianka 1990b; Macken-Horarik 1996, 1998; New London Group 2000). The basis of this work rests on systemic functional linguistic views of the complete interconnectedness between the grammatical structures people select in using language, and key variables of the situation in which their use of language is involved. The situational variables are field, tenor and mode (see Chapter 2). These situational variables are a feature of all social contexts, and contexts can be distinguished by their particular configurations of the values of field, tenor and mode. This view of context was adapted by Macken-Horarik (1996, 1998) to show how learning could be related to progression through a series of contexts, each with its own values of field, tenor and mode. The field is concerned with the type of knowledge – from incidental, everyday knowledge to critical, systematic understanding. The tenor is concerned with the nature of the relationships between those involved in the learning – solidary, communal roles to more formal, institutional, educational roles. The mode is concerned with the genres and the grammatical forms of spoken and written medium – from the language forms that accompany and describe reality to those that construct and challenge reality. The theoretical models constructed by Macken-Horarik dealt with learning development in terms of field and mode. She relied on case studies to exemplify changes in tenor as the learning progressed from one context to the next. The focus of her work was verbal text in conventional formats and she did not consider visual literacy or electronic texts.

The Curriculum Area Multiliteracies And Learning (CAMAL) framework adopts the view of Macken-Horarik (1996, 1998) that the advancement of students' learning in units of work within curriculum areas can be understood as a progression through a series of contexts, each with distinctive features of field, tenor and mode. The shifts in field are concerned with advances from informal, everyday understanding to systematic, discipline-based knowledge, to critical, transformative knowledge. The shifts in mode are concerned with changes in grammar towards the more nominalized forms constructing technicality and abstraction, shifts in genre from those of observing and recording to those of explaining and critiquing, and shifts in the use of images from concrete, narrative representations to abstract, conceptual images. These mode shifts entail changes in literacy practices – from recognition to reproduction to reflection literacies. The CAMAL framework also builds in tenor – theorized as the pedagogical orientation – the nature of the teacher–student relationship as the learning advances.

In elaborating the CAMAL framework we will first discuss in turn, the nature of the shifts in each of the contextual variables of field, tenor and mode. Next we will discuss the articulation of the distinctive types of knowledge, pedagogic orientations and literacy practices within each of the series of contexts constituting development in the curriculum area learning. Integral to this articulation is the elaboration of the teaching/ learning strategies that relate the types of knowledge and associated literacy practices within each context and facilitate progression from one context to the next. These teaching strategies form the Literacy Development Cycle (LDC) incorporating 'modelled', 'guided' and 'independent' comprehension/composition practice. In describing the implementation steps for modelled, guided and independent practice, we will address the differentiation of learning tasks to facilitate the participation of learners with varying literacy proficiencies in the same learning activity. Once these parameters of the CAMAL framework have been described, its application will be demonstrated in an account of a four week program of classroom work dealing with the greenhouse effect and its relationship to global warming.

DIMENSIONS OF LEARNING CONTEXTS

Learning contexts in schools have both instructional and regulatory dimensions, which are largely interrelated (Bernstein 1996; Christie 1997, 2000). Here it will be necessary to restrict the focus to the instructional, but it needs to be noted that this is a skewed perspective. Implicit in the framework for pedagogic practices that will emerge are the concomitant practices of classroom interaction that contribute to the role of the school as an agent of social control. The instructional dimensions of learning contexts and their key parameters to be discussed here are shown in Figure 7.1. Each dimension is discussed in the following sections.

The knowledge/content dimension – shifts in field

Informal knowledge is the understanding individuals develop largely incidentally through personal and/or communal experience. It has been referred to as everyday knowledge or commonsense knowledge. Knowledge of this kind is often passed on through casual interaction or at points of perceived need. It is frequently also acquired through observation and trial and error. However, the informal knowledge acquired by people is clearly not uniform across the social spectra of the culture. Depending on socio-economic and sociocultural positioning, the informal knowledge different groups of students bring to schooling may be more or less aligned with the kinds of knowledge that are highly valued within systems of formal education. Some kinds of informal knowledge may be marginal to school curricula, but often school learning means developing a different view of phenomena from that afforded by informal knowledge. For example, students need to understand the perspective that classifies a tree as a plant in favour of their informal view that '[a tree] was a plant when it was little' (Osborne and Freyberg 1989). Constructively unsettling informal knowledge and opening up differences between informal and systematic knowledge is crucial to the initial phases of curriculum area pedagogy.

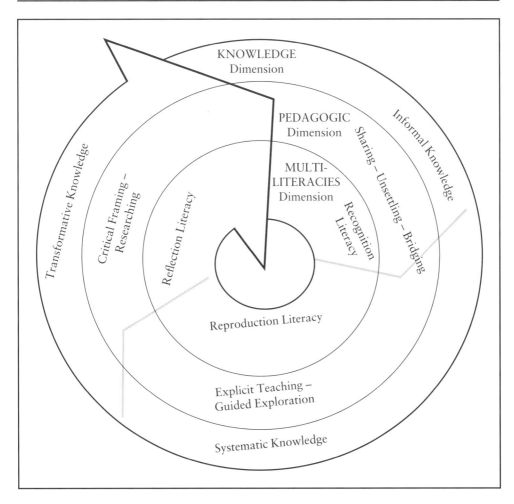

Figure 7.1   Dimensions of learning contexts

Systematic knowledge is the specialized learning of societal institutions reflected in the content of formal school curricula. It includes the fundamental concepts and hegemonic perspectives within recognized disciplines like maths, science, geography, history, economics etc. Systematic knowledge builds up an alternative construction of reality alongside that of commonsense experience. Systematic knowledge in areas like science and geography is concerned with ordering reality in terms of classificational (types of) and decompositional (parts of) taxonomies according to technical criteria, which are often not observationally obvious. For example, glass, rubber, plastic and air do not seem to constitute an obvious utilitarian categorization from a commonsense point of view. But from a scientific perspective, they do form an important category of 'non-conductors' of electricity or 'insulators'. These taxonomic relations are then used in explaining how and why phenomena are as they are, as well as the nature of potential change. History and humanities on the other hand, do not so much construct technical reconfigurations of commonsense reality as reconstrue records of the experience of participants in events as abstract entities like 'full employment' and 'immediate post-war migration'. These abstractions are then used to reason about generalized social phenomena – 'full employment leads to economic inflation'. School learning is very much concerned with inducting students into these forms of systematic knowledge. This may suggest a conservative view, preserving the prevailing hegemonic orders of knowledge, but school learning can also introduce students to competing discourses within and across discipline areas, facilitating the development of transformative knowledge.

Transformative knowledge initially involves questioning the taken-for-grantedness of systematic knowledge, understanding that what appears to be the 'natural' view of phenomena is actually a view produced by particular combinations of historical, social and political influences, and that alternative combinations of these influences could produce different views. This denaturalizing of systematic knowledge may occur as students are confronted with competing accounts of phenomena. For example, education packs or kits produced by forestry or mining companies, construct accounts of environmental issues quite different from those in the literature of environmental groups like Greenpeace. School textbooks are replete with conflicting information about apparently straightforward issues such as whether 'air friction' slows down cars and aeroplanes, whether gravity in space is zero, and the number of colours in a rainbow (Beaty 1996). Critique can also result from students encountering different perspectives on the same phenomena. For example, Macken-Horarik (1998) notes how students in a Year 10 biology class studying *in vitro* fertilization, as well as understanding the technology, began to confront issues such as consumer cost and the ethics of freezing embryos for research purposes etc. In addition, critique can occur at the intersection of informal and systematic knowledge, resulting in critique of aspects of both kinds of knowledge, as students weigh the institutionally-endorsed systematic knowledge against evidence of informal learning. But transformative knowledge extends beyond critique to a remaking of understanding emerging from the negotiation of conflicting and complementary perspectives. The result may be enduring tension rather than resolution, but it is transformative knowledge that leads to new understandings and the potential for social action.

The pedagogic dimension – shifts in tenor

In the first phase of teaching any curriculum area unit of study students' existing knowledge and extra school experience as well as their interests are recruited as an integral basis for new learning. This involves a sharing of students' current understandings in a secure environment and planning to take their affective and sociocultural needs and identities as learners into account. As part of this process the teacher provides experiences that begin to unsettle and/or extend students' understanding, bridging towards systematic knowledge. Such experiences could include demonstrations that involve counter-expectation such as showing how a sheet of paper over the top of a glass appears to support water inside when the glass is inverted. They could involve 'agree/disagree' surveys including items like 'all the hair on your head is dead', or explorations like sticking a small piece of cloth in the middle of a larger piece of white cloth, hanging this out in the air for a few days, and then removing the small piece of cloth to reveal how clean the air is.

Having provoked or engaged a need to know, it is then important to preview with students how the ensuing lessons will provide opportunities to explore the issues and to indicate the utility of doing so. The utility may be in terms of the practical usefulness to the individual, the relevance to understanding aspects of the wider social and material world of significance to the learner, and the role of this work in making future learning easier. In addition, students need to know how the work will address the immediate learning outcomes required by the school system. In this sharing–unsettling–bridging phase the authoritative knowing of the teacher is initially backgrounded as teacher and students adopt the roles of sharing, co-explorers of the issue(s). Then the teacher begins to lead the exploration as she or he moves to coordinate the unsettling–bridging activities and the students become observers, recorders and contributors with the teacher as guide.

The next phase of the pedagogic dimension involves both guided exploration and explicit teaching. The teacher as expert scaffolds learning experiences, including direct teaching, making students aware of his or her interpretation of the task and its relation to other aspects of learning. Scaffolded learning experiences provide structured support to students, enabling them to accomplish tasks more complex than they would be able to accomplish independently. Direct teaching does not imply a simple transmission model of learning with drills and rote practice. But it does mean that at times the teacher will engage in overt instruction providing explicit input to students. The role of the teacher here is much more of the expert, authoritative (but not authoritarian) manager of student learning. As an acknowledged academic leader, the teacher is inducting students into the knowledge and ways of knowing of the discipline. The students are apprentices, assimilating and reproducing the contents of specialized knowledge and taking on the roles and relationships of an incumbent member of the discipline and advancing towards institutionally recognized expertise. The pedagogic orientation in this phase then, is one of balancing direct, explicit teaching with opportunities for students to engage in both independent and collaborative, guided exploration of the curriculum area topic.

Once students have developed substantial systematic knowledge of a topic, it is possible to shift the pedagogic emphasis more to critical framing and the kind of research that teaches students how to problematize and critique their own learning. This is not a strictly lock-step sequence. It is certainly possible to introduce learners to critical orientations as they develop systematic knowledge and it is possible to introduce these orientations to children in the early years of school (Unsworth 1993a). However, as students progress through schooling, and as they develop familiarity with systematic knowledge of particular topics, they are better able to draw on this experience to consider contemporary issues related to such topics. Critical framing and research then, assumes a greater role in units of classroom work as students progress through schooling. In this phase of the pedagogic orientation, the relationship between the students and the teacher with respect to authoritative knowledge of the topic again shifts, so that the teacher and the students are now more like co-critics. However, the teacher has the role of facilitating student access to different interpretive perspectives on aspects of systematic knowledge in question. Teachers also have the role of facilitating students' opportunities to extend critique to creative application, so that students are re-creating knowledge as they engage with it for their own purposes (New London Group 2000). This means balancing a critical approach to incorporate one that celebrates emancipatory, humanity-enhancing advances in knowledge and understanding (Martin 2000).

The multiliteracies dimension – shifts in mode

Recognition literacy obviously includes the literacy practices with which students are already familiar. It also includes the recognition and familiarization phases in their learning of new technical/specialized vocabulary, distinctive grammatical structures typical of the subject area, new genres and/or genre variations, new forms of images, new layouts and new aspects of the digital rhetorics of electronic texts. From the point of view of developing curriculum area literacies, the recognition literacy practices most students will be familiar with are those related to direct personal experience. These involve genres like observation, anecdote, personal response, procedures or instructions and commentary (accompanying activity). The grammatical forms will be similar to those of spoken medium and images are likely to be narrative rather than conceptual and concrete rather than abstract. Again this experience will not be uniform. The recognition literacy practices of students will be influenced by their experiences outside of schooling and also by prior learning in school. Where contemporary media coverage relates to curriculum topics, students may well develop recognition and familiarity with the nominalizations of specialized and technical terms (like 'land degradation' and 'salination' – frequent in the Australian press) and the use of conceptual images (like those showing the effect of land clearing on the water table in Australia). Similarly, through advertisements like those for 'green' energy supply companies, which include genres like explanation and exposition dealing with the greenhouse effect and global warming, students may begin to recognize and develop some familiarity with the structuring of such genres. Such experience and also prior school learning indicates that students may have some recognition of, and familiarity with, the forms of language and image that extend beyond immediate experience and are central to the new learning to be undertaken. The importance of such recognition of literacy practices needs to be acknowledged and fostered as a bridge to the reproduction literacies entailed in developing systematic knowledge of the topic.

Reproduction literacy involves understanding and producing the conventional visual and verbal text forms that construct and communicate the established knowledge of the discipline area. The student moves from familiarization to tentative command of new technical vocabulary, the distinctive grammatical forms of written medium, specialized conceptual and abstract images and a wider range of genres for different social purposes. The genres typical of reproduction literacies distance us from direct experience via written and visual meaning making. These include genres like reports, explanations, historical accounts and interpretive responses. Genres of this type reconfigure reality as discipline knowledge. In fact, learning in school curriculum areas means learning to control the discourse forms that distinguish the particular curriculum areas (see Chapter 4). While the distinctive textual forms of the various curriculum areas may represent specialized use of language for most members of the community, it is the dominating classes that engage in literacy practices that most approximate those required by school curriculum area learning (Hasan 1996). Consequently, since reproduction literacies are integral to demonstrations of student success in school learning through either formal examination or informal school-based assessment procedures, the explicit teaching of reproduction literacies can make a crucial contribution to issues of equity in access to the benefits of formal education. Such explicit teaching relies on a clear description of the visual and verbal textual forms that reproduction literacies require students to be able to comprehend and compose. Hence the role of meta-language (visual and verbal grammar) is crucial to the explicit teaching of reproduction literacies, but it is also a fundamental resource for developing the critical practices of reflection literacy.

In reflection literacy students learn to interpret and construct texts that deal with controversial and competing points of view on issues. They compare texts with different perspectives and they analyse visual and verbal texts to make explicit how the choices of language and image privilege certain viewpoints and how other choices of visual and verbal resources could construct another view. This means adopting a critical stance with respect to genres typical of recognition and reproduction literacies and also constructing genres whose social purpose involves critique and transformation, such as expositions, discussions and critical reviews etc. Reflection literacy is critical engagement as a basis for reworking knowledge and, as such, means schooling for producing new knowledge (Hasan 1996). Explicit knowledge about the systems of meaning-making resources of language and image (meta-semiotic knowledge) of itself is not sufficient for the development of reflection literacy. However the socially responsible, systemic functional accounts of genre, grammar and image described in this volume have been acknowledged by many as fundamental resources in facilitating reflection literacy development (Janks and Ivanic 1992; New London Group 2000).

THE LITERACY DEVELOPMENT CYCLE

Designing learning experiences

The Literacy Development Cycle (LDC) is a set of strategies for designing learning experiences that will bring about the articulation of the knowledge, pedagogic and multiliteracies dimensions within learning contexts and facilitate progression through successive learning contexts. In its most generalized form the LDC (see Figure 6.1) incorporates modelled, guided and independent practice in the comprehension/composition of multimodal texts in conventional and electronic formats.

The cycle can be entered at any point in planning learning experiences within a unit of work. If students are very familiar with a particular genre, modelled and guided practice may not be necessary. On the other hand, in introducing new genres, it may be advisable to extend modelled practice, curtail guided practice and postpone independent practice until a subsequent unit of work. It may also be the case that the LDC is applied differentially to a range of comprehension/composition activities within a unit of work. Some activities might involve modelled, guided and independent practice while some require extended modelling and others are undertaken as independent practice. The ways in which the parameters of the LDC are adapted will depend on the prior learning of the group as a whole and the range of experiences among students within the group. The broken lines indicate this kind of flexibility as well as the lack of rigid boundaries around the categories of practice.

The LDC can be applied in this flexible manner within any of the contexts defined by particular combinations of phases within the knowledge, pedagogic and multiliteracies dimensions of learning contexts. This means that teachers can model the recognition literacy practices associated with sharing of informal knowledge but they can also provide guided and independent practice. In the same way both reproduction and reflection literacy practices can be undertaken as modelled, guided or independent learning experiences.

The development of students' reading of curriculum area materials is integrally related to the development of their capacity to compose the texts required of them in curriculum area learning. The organization of teaching needs to take this into account. The LDC maintains the strategies of modelled, guided and independent practice for both reading and writing development, but the implementation steps differ for reading and writing. However, within reading and writing, the same implementation steps are used for modelled, guided and independent practice, as shown in Figure 7.2.

In fact the 'orientation to text' in the application of the LDC to writing, includes the *reading* of texts which are models of the genre to be dealt with in the writing session. Some of the genres students need to write in school curriculum areas are rarely found in curriculum reading materials. For example, persuasive genres like analytical expositions were found to be very infrequent in junior secondary school history textbooks, despite being one of the key genres students were expected to master by the end

Literacy Development Cycle		
Strategies	Implementation steps	
	Reading	*Writing*
Modelled practice ⎫ Guided practice ⎬ Independent practice ⎭	• Orientation to the text • Reading the text • Working with the text • Reviewing reading	• Orientation to text • Writing the text • Reviewing writing • Publishing writing

Figure 7.2   Strategies and implementation steps in the Literacy Development Cycle

of their tenth year of schooling (Coffin 1996). In cases like these, the model texts for teaching writing cannot be those previously dealt with in focusing on reading. Consequently, the writing session needs to maintain its embedded reading of model texts written by the teacher or by past students or obtained from sources beyond those usually included in curriculum area reading. However, if students are developing their writing of genres that are readily available in curriculum reading materials, the 'orientation to text' may well be a review of a text dealt with in a prior reading session.

Organizing whole class, small group and individual learning

The following principles of dynamic, functional organization of classroom groups for learning underpin the implementation of the LDC:

Composition of groups
• There are no permanently set groups.
• Different classroom groupings of students are formed from time to time on varying functional criteria, which may sometimes include proficiency in managing particular learning tasks.
• Groups are periodically created, modified or disbanded to reconcile changing student needs and task demands.
• There are times when there is only one group – consisting of the entire class.
• Group size will vary from two or three to nine or ten or more, depending on the group's purpose.

Management
• Students should encounter some choices relating to how, when and what work is to be done so that they can exercise some responsibility in organizing their own learning.

- Student commitment is enhanced if they know how the groupwork is related to the overall class program.
- There should be clear, context-sensitive strategies for monitoring and recording students' participation and progress in learning activities.
- There should be a principled distribution of teacher-interactive, teacher-supervised and teacher-independent tasks among group work activities.

Scaffolding learning tasks
- Learning experiences should be based on functional texts in genuine communicative contexts rather than fragmented exercises.
- Task structure, level of demand and forms of scaffolding should be differentiated to accommodate the range of experience and proficiency among students in the class, insuring that all students are supported in improving their learning.
- Clear models and demonstrations of work required should be provided.
- Directions for completing tasks should be clear and able to be referred to if forgotten.
- Group tasks should lead to some form of corporate production, display or exchange involving the whole class and sometimes interaction with other groups within and/or outside the school.

The 'group-then-regroup' strategy

The objective of the 'group-then-regroup' strategy (Unsworth 1993b) is to provide support for less proficient learners so that they can participate with more proficient peers in developing strategies for learning from a range of curriculum area resources that they would have difficulty dealing with independently. This involves a two stage learning activity where the first stage is preparatory to the second. In the first stage the students are grouped homogeneously according to relative proficiency. The less proficient students are given supportive versions of the learning tasks containing additional guidance and/or are supported by explicit instruction from the teacher in the first phase of the task. At the same time the more proficient learners complete the task without such scaffolding. The students are then regrouped and asked to undertake a follow-up or review task that relies on the understandings developed in phase one. Because the less proficient students have been supported in the first phase, they are better able to participate collaboratively with their more proficient peers in the second follow-up or review phase.

GUIDELINES FOR IMPLEMENTING THE LDC – CURRICULUM AREA READING

The LDC makes use of two teaching/learning strategies known as 'structured overviews/ concept maps' and 'graphic outlines'. Various versions of these strategies have long been included in approaches to developing content area literacies (Davies and Greene

1984; Lunzer and Gardner 1984; Morris and Stewart-Dore 1984; Anstey and Bull 1996). The structured overview or concept map is a succinct visual representation of students' understanding of a topic in terms of relationships among central and more peripheral ideas. It consists of a set of key words arranged in clusters or hierarchical groups with lines or dots showing the interrelationships. An example, showing students' emerging understanding of the greenhouse effect and global warming, is provided in Figure 7.6. The graphic outline was designed to assist students to survey chapters or topic sections of textbook and other content area reading materials (Morris and Stewart-Dore 1984). It is a graphic summary representation of the organizational markers in texts like headings, subheadings and illustrations of various kinds, located in rectangles whose relative size indicates the amount of space devoted to this section in the text. The graphic outlines used here are similar, except that, in order to take account of compositional meanings, they preserve the layout of the original (electronic or conventional) page, rather than abstracting this to a more schematic representation. An example of a graphic outline for a double page spread dealing with the greenhouse effect and global warming is provided in Figure 7.7.

Modelled reading practice

Orientation to text
- Review with students their understanding of the text topic derived from previous lessons.
- Scribe notes of student contributions onto a display board and edit with students to form a structured overview/concept map.
- Establish purpose(s) for reading the text related to prior knowledge (note that these could be related to recognition, reproduction or reflection literacies).
- Ensure all students are able to see the text (using an epidiascope or coloured overhead projection transparency of copies of the pages).
- Identify the text and its context – book section, magazine article, website etc. Note the author, date and location of publication.
- Survey the text segment from which the selection is to be read. Note title, text sections, main headings, subheadings, illustrations, captions, hypertext links etc. Sketch a graphic outline and predict the genres included and the likely content.

Reading the text
- Confirm that all students can see the text.
- Indicate that you will read the text aloud and that you will interpolate a commentary explaining when you refer to illustrations or other particular text features as you are reading.
- Invite the students to observe and note for subsequent discussion, aspects of your oral reading. These might include emphases in your voice while reading, miscues in your recoding of the text, changes in pace related to technical information etc.

Working with the text
- Invite the students to contribute their observations of your reading.
- Model your response as to whether reading the text achieved the purpose(s) set. Invite the students to indicate whether this was the case for them as listeners.
- Indicate how the initial survey of the text related to the experience of reading it.
- Identify the genres, their social purposes, the stages in their schematic structure and how these advanced the text's purpose.
- Comment on grammatical features of the text whose significance became apparent during reading.
- Describe the types of images and the effect of their form on your understanding of the text as a whole.
- Comment on an aspect of the text that suggests a need for closer attention based on your reading.

Reviewing reading
- Review the structured overview/concept map and purposes for reading, as well as aspects of the text warranting closer attention.
- Ask all students to reread the text silently with you addressing issues raised in the above review.
- Discuss the outcomes of the second reading of the text and the effectiveness of the strategies that were modelled.

Guided reading practice

Orientation to text
- Review with students their understanding of the text topic derived from previous lessons.
- Scribe notes of student contributions onto a display board. Students work in pairs to form from notes a structured overview/concept map on an overhead projector slide. Display and compare concept maps.
- Establish purpose(s) for reading the text related to prior knowledge.
- Identify the text and its context – book section, magazine article, website etc. Note the author, date and location of publication.
- Provide students with a graphic outline guide to survey the text. Students complete the labelled boxes for title, text sections, main headings, subheadings, illustrations, captions, hypertext links etc.
- Discuss the completed graphic outlines and ask students to predict the genres included and the likely content.

Reading the text
- All students to read the text silently, with pairs of students nominated to subsequently take responsibility for shared reading aloud of a text section allocated to them.

- Pairs prepare text section for reading aloud. Each pair of students reads their allocated sections aloud.
- Monitor students' oral reading, noting quality of any student miscues and strategies for dealing with unfamiliar vocabulary.
- Ask students to indicate the meanings conveyed by the images in the text.

Working with the text
Allocate students guided reading task with different levels of scaffolding support according to students' proficiency in reading such texts. The following examples indicate some of these kinds of tasks relevant to the development of *reproduction* literacy:

- Provide efficient readers with an acetate overlay for the text and ask them to divide the text into functional stages, label the stages and name the genre. For less experienced readers stencil the name of the genre and the labelled stages of schematic structure onto the sheet and ask students to use water-based marker pens to mark off the stages of schematic structure according to the labels provided. A third version of this task provides students with the acetate overlay showing the text segmented into stages of schematic structure. The labels are provided separately as adhesive Post-it notes and students are asked to stick them onto the appropriate stage. After completion of the initial task, student groups are reconstituted comprising one member from each of the previous three task groups. Responses are discussed briefly in the new groups. The teacher then displays the genre and stages of schematic structure, consolidating with students the functional role of these text segments.
- Teach students about the significant grammatical features of the text. For example, model 'talking out' nominalized structures, typical of written mode, into the grammar of oral language. A written text segment like 'The drainage of wetlands and conversion to residential land is a favoured practice of tourism developers' might be talked out as 'Businessmen who want to increase the number of tourists in an area like to drain wetlands and convert them to land where they can build houses and hotels.' Efficient readers can be asked to identify the nominalized text segments and generate spoken grammar equivalents. Less experienced readers might be provided with the identified nominalized segments and the verbs around which to generate the spoken grammar versions. Least efficient readers could also be given the nominalized segments and a 'clozed' version of the spoken text: '_____ who want to increase the number of _____ in an area like to drain _____ and convert _____ to land where _____ can build _____ and _____.' Again upon completion students are regrouped to compare responses and then the whole group is reconvened so that the teacher can ensure students can describe grammatically the key changes they made to the written text.
- Generate similar tasks to teach students about images and their role in the construction of the text's meaning. For example, in focusing on interactive meanings, use examples from magazines to introduce students to 'offer', 'demand', close-up, medium and long shot, high shot and low shot etc. Have students sort additional

images to consolidate understanding, and have them identify these aspects of images in the target text and comment on their effect. You could scan the target text, scan alternative images and then use a computer graphics program to replace the images in the original text and ask groups of students to compare the original and edited text in terms of the meaning making of the images. Similarly, students could locate alternative images to change aspects of the text's meaning.

In the same way tasks can be designed to focus on students retrieving literal information, inferring from the text and interpreting the writer's stance in relation to the topic – in the case of the latter dealing, for example, with the use of modal verbs (may, must, have to etc.), modal adverbs (of course, perhaps, certainly, even etc.) and comment adverbs (unfortunately, hopefully, surprisingly etc.) as well as the 'colouring' of meaning through vocabulary selection.

Reviewing reading
Students work in pairs or groups of three to read the text again in order to complete review tasks such as the following:

- Complete an entry for a computer-based bibliography manager. Such databases include, as well as standard bibliographic information, sections for key words, abstract and notes. Students could use their knowledge of genre and stages of schematic structure to organize the abstract. The notes section could require specific factors to be commented upon. These could include factors relating to reflection literacies, for example the number and type of images and their role in the text; indications of the author's stance in the interpersonal meaning of the text; points of view that were not represented and questions that remain unanswered etc.
- Students could 'mark up' a copy of the text with editorial changes. The editors' brief could be specified – delete peripheral information, suggest more examples, ensure all new technical terms are defined, remove authorial comment (or change it to another specified perspective) etc.

Similar tasks can be targeted to address a range of specified aspects of the text:

- Generate a series of questions for the author(s) and/or editor(s) of the text. Students could be asked to consider questions about genre, grammar, images, the author's opinions etc.
- Use different coloured highlighters to show significant patterns in the language of the text, for example causal conjunctions, marked topical themes, comment adjuncts etc.
- Complete a teacher-prepared cloze summary of the text.
- Annotate the images to show their relationship to the verbal text and the kinds of visual meanings they contribute.

Provide time for students who completed different tasks to exchange and discuss their responses. Convene the whole group to discuss similarities and differences in thinking about the text that emerge from their responses to these tasks.

Independent reading practice

Orientation to text
- Ensure the availability of a range of texts relevant to the unit of work at varying levels of difficulty either in the classroom or by arrangement with the librarian.
- Encourage access to a variety of text formats including textbooks, general knowledge books, magazine articles, pamphlets, CD ROMs and websites.
- Take time to introduce the students to some interesting texts in a variety of formats.
- Draw attention to relevant reviews of texts of various kinds, especially those in newspapers and on websites. Involve students in displaying reviews of texts relevant to the topic on the classroom display boards.
- Encourage students to bring texts they have found, which are relevant to the topic.
- Establish with the students a system for maintaining a record of their independent reading.
- Identify with students their purposes for reading and use these to assist in text selection.

Reading the text
- Specify some regular class time for independent reading.
- Indicate when/how information from independent reading will be able to be used in the classroom program of work on the topic.
- Schedule guided reading practice with one group (on a rotational basis) during this time.

Working with the text
- Make it possible for students to photocopy/download/print material from the texts they are reading.
- Provide opportunities for students in pairs or groups of three to share responses to the different texts they have been reading.

Reviewing reading
Institute opportunities for systematic responding to and sharing of responses such as the following:

- List the available texts on the class display board and a number of categories of response such as 'Why we should all read this text in class'; 'Why we should delete this text from our list'; 'Why this text was useful/interesting to me' etc. Provide Post-it notes for students to contribute their responses. Alternatively this could be set up on a computer-based class data base for the purpose.
- Organize a competition for the best text on the topic. Texts must be nominated by at least four students and students may nominate one text only. Once nominations

are closed (in most classes this means a maximum of about six texts can be nominated), chief nominators read the texts to the whole class and votes are taken. Some suitable recognition may be given to the winning nominators.

GUIDELINES FOR IMPLEMENTING THE LDC – CURRICULUM AREA WRITING

Modelled writing practice

Orientation to the text
- Review with students their understanding of the text topic derived from previous lessons.
- Scribe notes of student contributions onto a display board and edit with students to form a structured overview/concept map.
- Discuss the social purpose(s) and intended audience of the writing to be undertaken and the genre(s) to be used.
- Show the students a number of published examples of the genre dealing with the topic of study or one related to it (for example if the topic of study was the nitrogen or nutrient cycle, show explanations of this or explanations of the water cycle). Discuss who wrote these texts and why.
- Select one such text example and display this so that the whole group can read the text.
- Read the text to the group.
- Discuss the layout of the text, the type(s) of image(s), font etc.
- Identify the stages of schematic structure in the verbal text explaining the functional role of each.

Writing the text
- Rehearse the social purpose of the text to be written and its stages of schematic structure. [For relatively short texts, model the actual draft writing of the text in the classroom. For longer texts prepare a draft version prior to the lesson.]
- Refer to the structured overview/concept map constructed in the orientation phase. Use coloured chalk/pens to circle and colour code elements to be included in particular stages of schematic structure. Then number the coloured circles to indicate the sequencing within stages.
- Draft the first stage of schematic structure on a black/white board, overhead projector transparency or a computer with data projector, using the 'think aloud' technique to make your composition processes available to the students. Briefly review and edit this stage. Proceed with drafting the rest of the text, including notes about the type and location of images to be inserted.
- Revise and edit the draft text, again using thinking aloud to make the reasons for the changes and the grammatical description of them explicit to the students.

Reviewing writing
- Invite the students to read the text again, asking questions and/or making suggestions about further editing. (If possible include another teacher as a reader of your text.)
- Make any final revisions of the text in preparation for publication.

Publishing writing
This step may occur outside of class time or during class time as a subsequent session. If the text has been prepared electronically, images should be drawn/scanned and inserted, background, borders, colour and font finalized and a hard copy printed. If the text has been prepared manually, corresponding hard copy steps should be completed. Finally, the text should be displayed in the classroom and, if relevant, also despatched to its intended audience.

Guided writing practice

Orientation to text
- Review with students their understanding of the text topic derived from previous lessons.
- Scribe notes of student contributions onto a display board and edit with students to form a structured overview/concept map.
- Discuss the social purpose(s) and intended audience of the writing to be undertaken and the genre(s) to be used.
- Show the students a number of published examples of the genre dealing with the topic of study or one related to it. Discuss who wrote these texts and why.
- Select one such text example for deconstruction and display this so that the whole group can read the text.
- Read the text to the group.
- Discuss the layout of the text, the type(s) of image(s), font etc.
- Identify the stages of schematic structure in the verbal text, explaining the functional role of each.
- Select some of the significant grammatical features of the genre as target student learning outcomes for this session. (In an explanation such a selection may be that relational processes tend to occur in the Orientation and Closure stages and to compact/summarize the cause/effect chains of events of the Implication Sequences, while material processes tend to dominate the Implication Sequences. The pattern of Rheme to Theme progression in the Implication Sequences and the role of causal conjunctions may also be addressed.) Analyse the text for each of these grammatical aspects in turn, modelling the identification of the elements and consolidating student understanding by eliciting from them identification of subsequent examples in the text. Explain the functions of these grammatical patterns. For the Theme progression show that what is new in the Rheme of one clause becomes the given information to orient the next clause and so on though the Implication Sequence.

- Select some significant aspects of the image(s) as target student learning outcomes for this session. For example, in explanations of the greenhouse effect and global warming the focus may be the ways in which arrows of various kinds are used to depict processes like radiation, absorption, reflection etc. Analyse the image, explaining the conventions used in representing the different processes and then consolidate student learning by asking them to identify the vectors for the various processes and indicating how they conventionally constructed that meaning.

Writing the text
- Rehearse the social purpose of the text to be written and its stages of schematic structure.
- Refer to the structured overview/concept map constructed in the orientation phase. Elicit from the students the elements to be included in particular stages of schematic structure. Use coloured chalk/pens to circle and colour code these elements. Then elicit from the students the ordering of the elements with the same colour coding and number these accordingly.
- Draft the first stage of schematic structure on a black/white board, overhead projector transparency or a computer with data projector, eliciting the suggested wording clause by clause from the students.
- Negotiate the editing of these clause by clause contributions with the student group, guiding the students toward the use of the grammatical structures of written mode, as students' suggestions are initially phrased using the grammatical structures more typical of spoken language.
- Briefly review and edit this stage. Proceed with drafting the rest of the text in this manner, including discussion about the type and location of images to be inserted.
- Revise and edit the draft text, reminding students of the grammatical features discussed in the model text and asking them to review this text for the use of these grammatical forms.

Reviewing writing
- Invite the students to read the text again, asking questions and/or making suggestions about further editing.
- Make any final revisions of the text (including spelling) in preparation for publication.

Publishing writing
The steps involved here are similar to those described for publishing in modelled writing practice.

Independent writing practice

Orientation to the text
- Ensure that students have developed substantial knowledge of the field about which they are to write through consolidation of classroom work, independent study and research.

- Students specify the social purpose(s) and intended audience of the writing to be undertaken and the genre(s) to be used. As far as possible there should be a genuine social purpose beyond simply fulfilling the teacher's requirements (letters to the editor; material to send to e-mail partnership classes; resources to use in working with younger children in peer tutoring schemes; an addition to the class homepage on the school website etc.)
- Students' preparatory notes and text outline should include the use to be made of images in developing the text.
- Organize a roster of brief planning consultations with the teacher so that students can outline their intentions for developing the text. This could be combined with peer collaborative conferences while the individual teacher/student roster is operating.

Writing the text
- Students construct a first draft of their text and then conference with one or more other students about the drafts of their work. At this stage conferences should focus on how effectively the students have communicated their purposes to their peers as readers. The conferences should be a source of constructive advice about which aspects of the text are most effective and particular suggestions about how other aspects of the text might be clarified or improved.
- Students then redraft their work in preparation for a consultation with the teacher.

Reviewing writing
- The teacher consultation should encourage the student to discuss not only the content of the text but also the structuring of the language in terms of the stages of schematic structure of the genre, the grammatical choices designed to achieve particular effects, and selection of images with particular characteristics to contribute to the overall construction of meaning. The teacher should model effective, constructive editing and explain the explicit grammatical and rhetorical bases for the editorial suggestions.
- Students revise their texts in the light of teacher advice, then prepare final drafts and join with partners to proofread texts in preparation for publication.

Once students are able to control the conventional construction of the prototypical genre, the teacher should encourage them, in subsequent independent writing, to explore the creative exploitation of the genre and its possibilities. This may involve for example, embedding scientific explanations and reports in a narrative of scientific discovery (Coffin 1996; Humphrey 1996).

Publishing writing
Again, the steps involved here are similar to those described for publishing in modelled writing practice.

DESIGNING LESSON SEQUENCES USING THE CAMAL FRAMEWORK AND THE LDC

The application of the CAMAL framework and the LDC in planning lesson sequences for units of study within curriculum areas is indicated here in a program of work on the greenhouse effect and climate change. This unit of study is designed for students of about 11 to 13 years of age in the senior elementary, middle or junior secondary school. It extends over four weeks and is taught in one lesson of about 30–45 minutes each day. Space will not permit a comprehensive account of each lesson here. A skeletal synopsis of the program is provided in Figure 7.3. The first two weeks of the

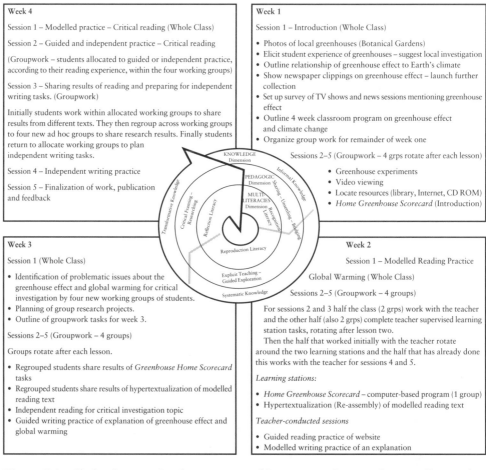

Week 4

Session 1 – Modelled practice – Critical reading (Whole Class)

Session 2 – Guided and independent practice – Critical reading

(Groupwork – students allocated to guided or independent practice, according to their reading experience, within the four working groups)

Session 3 – Sharing results of reading and preparing for independent writing tasks. (Groupwork)

Initially students work within allocated working groups to share results from different texts. They then regroup across working groups to four new ad hoc groups to share research results. Finally students return to allocate working groups to plan independent writing tasks.

Session 4 – Independent writing practice

Session 5 – Finalization of work, publication and feedback

Week 1

Session 1 – Introduction (Whole Class)

- Photos of local greenhouses (Botanical Gardens)
- Elicit student experience of greenhouses – suggest local investigation
- Outline relationship of greenhouse effect to Earth's climate
- Show newspaper clippings on greenhouse effect – launch further collection
- Set up survey of TV shows and news sessions mentioning greenhouse effect
- Outline 4 week classroom program on greenhouse effect and climate change
- Organize group work for remainder of week one

Sessions 2–5 (Groupwork – 4 grps rotate after each lesson)

- Greenhouse experiments
- Video viewing
- Locate resources (library, Internet, CD ROM)
- *Home Greenhouse Scorecard* (Introduction)

Week 3

Session 1 (Whole Class)

- Identification of problematic issues about the greenhouse effect and global warming for critical investigation by four new working groups of students.
- Planning of group research projects.
- Outline of groupwork tasks for week 3.

Sessions 2–5 (Groupwork – 4 groups)

Groups rotate after each lesson.

- Regrouped students share results of *Greenhouse Home Scorecard* tasks
- Regrouped students share results of hypertextualization of modelled reading text
- Independent reading for critical investigation topic
- Guided writing practice of explanation of greenhouse effect and global warming

Week 2

Session 1 – Modelled Reading Practice

Global Warming (Whole Class)

Sessions 2–5 (Groupwork – 4 groups)

For sessions 2 and 3 half the class (2 grps) work with the teacher and the other half (also 2 grps) complete teacher supervised learning station tasks, rotating after lesson two.

Then the half that worked initially with the teacher rotate around the two learning stations and the half that has already done this works with the teacher for sessions 4 and 5.

Learning stations:

- *Home Greenhouse Scorecard* – computer-based program (1 group)
- Hypertextualization (Re-assembly) of modelled reading text

Teacher-conducted sessions

- Guided reading practice of website
- Modelled writing practice of an explanation

Figure 7.3   Skeletal synopsis of a program of lessons on the greenhouse effect and global warming

program are subsequently described in some detail, including a more fully elaborated account of two lessons exemplifying the LDC and dealing with modelled and guided reading practice using conventional and computer-based texts. Weeks three and four of the program are then briefly outlined.

Week 1

The initial learning experiences in week one are intended to survey, recruit and build students' informal knowledge relevant to the greenhouse effect and global warming. By engaging students' interest in local facilities and activities and exploring their understanding of the relationships to global climate, both students and teachers become aware of the nature and extent of students' knowledge of the topic. This is important in planning learning activities for particular students and groups within the class and also for the selection of learning resources. The collecting of newspaper and magazine clippings and surveying of television shows and news items on the topic also assist in engaging students' interest and in moving from the sharing of informal knowledge to unsettling current understandings and beginning to bridge into systematic knowledge. At the time of writing there were many news articles in the Sydney press concerning the greenhouse effect. Some dealt with the federal government taking over the existing state government responsibility for approving projects that would result in high greenhouse gas emissions, and others with Australia's role in international conferences about the greenhouse effect. There were also many advertisements dealing explicitly with this topic. One prominent advertisement encouraged people to subscribe to 'greenpower' electricity suppliers, which generate electricity from renewable sources such as the sun, wind and water. These common community texts would be largely accessible to the students through their existing recognition literacy practices. This can be seen in the non-technical, somewhat simplistic, explanatory introduction to the greenpower advertisement previously alluded to:

> Human activity, such as burning coal for electricity, is increasing greenhouse gas emissions by billions of tonnes in addition to what is produced naturally. These heat-trapping gases create a blanket-like effect around the planet, increasing our Earth's temperature and changing our climate.
>
> (*Sydney Morning Herald*, 29 April 2000: 43)

Advertisements like this also tend to bridge into the technical discourse of reproduction literacies. For example, a later section of the greenpower advertisement refers to 'clean renewable sources such as solar, wind, hydro and biomass'. The advertisement includes a website address and this site provides additional, slightly more technical, information, naming carbon dioxide as a prominent greenhouse gas and including a 'frequently asked questions' button, where it is possible to find a definition of 'biomass' as an energy source. For many students this kind of exploration will utilize their recognition (cyber)literacies and begin bridging from informal knowledge to systematic knowledge and reproduction literacies. But texts like this advertisement should also subsequently become subject to students' reflection literacy practices as they develop more knowledge and understanding of the field and the semiotic resources used to construct a variety of accounts of phenomena within the field.

The groupwork in week one is designed to further bridge from informal to systematic knowledge. The students work in four groups of about six students and, after each lesson, the groups rotate to the next learning activity. The activities have been selected so that they require teacher supervision rather than intensive teacher interaction. This provides an opportunity for the teacher to monitor the groups differentially, according to student needs, and to gather more detailed observational data about individual student's understandings, interests and literacy and learning practices. This information will further guide the design of the learning tasks and allocation of students to working groups in week two.

The greenhouse effect experiments are readily accessible curriculum materials for students of this age (House n.d.; Wong 1991; Sustainable Solutions 1995). They involve activities like putting a thermometer in a sealed glass jar in the sunlight and another thermometer outside a jar in the same vicinity and then recording the temperature of each thermometer every minute for about 20 minutes. An inside alternative is to use similar desk lamps shining over thermometers in cardboard boxes, but with one box covered by a sheet of glass. The students should work in pairs, and at the end of the lesson, meet as a group of six to compare their results. The recognition literacy practices involve reading and implementing a procedural text, and, at the conclusion of the activity, writing up a procedural recount recording the outcomes of the activity.

While there are many video documentaries about the greenhouse effect in libraries, for example Gell (1987) and Vaughan (1988), more recent video productions of programs on the greenhouse effect produced specifically for students of this age are also available (Australian Broadcasting Commission Education Television 2000). In this activity a group of six students views the video produced by the Australian Broadcasting Commission, which is about 15 minutes long. Students are given a viewing brief which asks them to confirm or contest specific information about the greenhouse effect noted in the introductory lesson and draws attention to specific features of the video. For example, students are asked to note before viewing, what Antarctica has to do with understanding the greenhouse effect and to review their response after viewing (the video deals with research into the composition of air extracted from the ice at Antarctica – possibly 1000 years old). Once the students have viewed the tape, there is time for reviewing and cueing the tape to explore particular issues again.

Another group of about six students works in pairs to locate and record sources of information on the topic for subsequent use. If possible, this could be undertaken with the support of the librarian. Students could search (on-line?) library catalogues, locate texts and record details on a (computer-based?) data base or bibliography manager like *Endnote*. Students should also search CD ROM-based encyclopedias like *Encarta*, *Britannica*, *World Book* etc. as well as undertaking Internet searches using World Wide Web search engines.

The final group activity in the week one rotation is a computer-based program called the *Australian Home Greenhouse Scorecard* (Sustainable Solutions 1995). This is an interactive program that enables students to evaluate the contribution of their household to the greenhouse effect. The program enables students to answer questions about those household activities that contribute to the greenhouse effect. It then calculates the contribution of the activity to the greenhouse effect, and provides hints on how the contribution can be reduced. It also allows students to compare the contribution of their household to greenhouse gas emissions with those of other households, including some examples stored in the program. During this first week the groups of students are introduced to the program and learn how to navigate it. During the second week this will also be a groupwork task, and by then students will have had an opportunity to gather relevant information about activities in their households in order to respond to questions asked in the program. Other introductory computer-based learning activ-ities on the greenhouse effect, for example House (n.d.) could be used in much the same way.

Week 2

The organization of the learning experiences for week two is indicated in Figure 7.4. The first lesson is a modelled reading lesson undertaken with the whole class. At the conclusion of this whole class session, the groupwork plan for the remainder of week two is negotiated with the class, including allocation of students to groups and order-ing of task completion. The *Home Greenhouse Scorecard* and follow-up work with modelled reading text are essentially 'learning station' activities requiring teacher

Learning activities for week 2	Sessions				
	1	2	3	4	5
Modelled reading practice	CLASS	Groups			
Home Greenhouse Scorecard		A	B	C	D
Follow-up work with modelled reading text		B	A	D	C
Guided reading practice of website		CD		AB	
Modelled writing practice of explanation			CD		AB

Figure 7.4   Organization of the learning experiences for week two

supervision. The guided reading practice of website and modelled writing are both activities in which the teacher is interacting more intensively with the students. The teacher then, is working intensively with half the class at a time and supervising the other half at the two learning station activities.

The text for the modelled reading practice session is shown in Figure 7.5. It is a double page spread from a text about the weather (Ellyard 1996: 58–9).

In the orientation to the text session, the teacher works with the students to jointly construct a concept map similar to that shown in Figure 7.6. This summarizes the group's knowledge of the topic at this point.

A number of newspaper articles brought into the classroom mentioned the role of trees:

The primary Australian goal was reducing emissions . . . but planting forests which would store carbon and cut down the amount of gases released into the atmosphere was an important option.

(*Sydney Morning Herald*, 15 April 2000)

Democrats environment spokesman . . . warned it did not pick up the key problem of land clearing, which reduced the absorption of carbon dioxide.

(*The Weekend Australian*, 6–7 May 2000)

Figure 7.5   Text for modelled reading practice (Ellyard 1996: 58–9)
Source: Illustrations (main image and top left) from pages 58–59 *Discoveries: Weather* © Weldon Owen Pty Ltd.

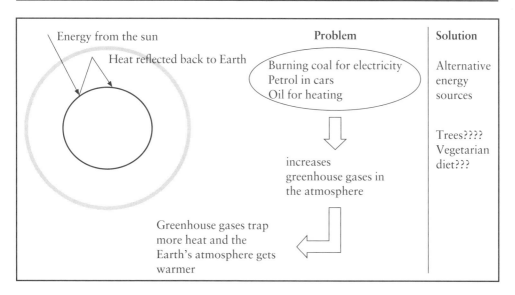

Figure 7.6   Structured overview/concept map of class learning about the greenhouse effect and global warming

The students' need to clarify the role of trees in reducing the increased greenhouse effect is intensified by another headline: 'Vegetarians produce less greenhouse gas' (*The University of Sydney News*, 18 May 2000). These concerns inform the main purposes for reading the text selected for modelled reading.

   Following a discussion contextualizing the extract in relation to the text as a whole, its author, his or her credentials, the date and location of publication, a graphic outline (Figure 7.7) is produced surveying the double page spread in terms of headings, sub-headings, illustrations etc. in relation to the purposes for reading.

Reading the text

The text is read essentially in the order indicated in the graphic outline in Figure 7.7 of Figure 7.5. After reading the section on disappearing forests, note the impact of the size and nature of the main image. Its domination of the page seems to reflect the domination of the industrialization over the countryside. It is a high angle image, which appears to put the reader in a position of relative power, but the parallel frontal angle also seems to include the reader, so that she or he is travelling along the road to industrial pollution. (One might normally expect to see part of the highway travelling in the other direction!) The exhaust fumes of the cars are clearly visible, although the number plates aren't, so the 'naturalism' of the image may have been adjusted to make its particular message clearer. The curve of the main image seems to lead to the greenhouse explanation at the top of the page and then down to the

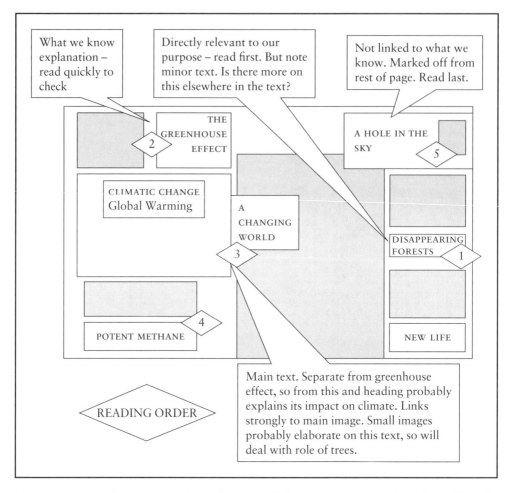

Figure 7.7   Graphic outline of text for modelled reading practice (based on Ellyard 1996: 58–9)

main text. The subheading 'A changing world' also seems to guide the reader in the direction of the main text. However, the greenhouse effect explanation does seem to be marked off as prerequisite at the top of the page, so this is next in the order of reading.

Being on the left, the diagram showing the greenhouse effect is read first. Note the arrows showing light from the sun being reflected by the atmosphere is new information to what is recorded on the class concept map, as are the arrows indicating something escaping from the atmosphere into space. After reading the explanation, note that these arrows are not mentioned in the text. Also note that the explanation mentions other gases as well as carbon dioxide increasing in the atmosphere. The classwork to date has not mentioned any of these other gases.

After proceeding to read the main text, note that this further addresses our specific purpose for reading. Then read 'A changing world', noting the identification of methane as one of the other increasing gases, as well as the possible explanation of the newspaper headline about vegetarians producing less greenhouse gas. However, upon proceeding to the image and text about potent methane in rice paddy fields and wetlands, note that the issue regarding vegetarians may remain problematic.

Finally after reading the section on 'A hole in the sky', note that the connection of this with the greenhouse effect and global warming is not made explicit. This may be why this section has its own distinct border and colour background.

Working with the text

Having done some earlier work on the greenhouse effect and having set clear purposes for reading, it might be conceded that there is a tendency to 'skip' reading the explanation of the greenhouse effect at the top of the page and go directly from the initial reading of 'Disappearing forests' and 'New life' to the main text on 'Climatic change and global warming'.

Discussion with the class can confirm that the purposes for reading have been substantially achieved. The relationship between maintaining and extending forests and the reduction in greenhouse gases has been clarified, but the contribution of vegetarianism to this issue remains problematic. Perhaps it depends on the proportion of methane in greenhouse gases? Perhaps there are other ways that vegetarians use less energy produced by fossil fuels? More exploration is required on these matters.

In identifying the genres and their schematic structuring, it might be decided to focus on 'The greenhouse effect' and 'Global Warming'. The schematic structure of the first of these explanations is quite simple. The orientation consists of the heading and the first sentence, which function as a Phenomenon Identification. The remaining sentences are the Implication Sequences and there is no Closure stage. This can serve as a preparatory experience to the introduction of the introduction of the more elaborated schematic structure of 'Global Warming', which is shown in Figure 7.8.

In pointing out the components of the elaborated 'orientation', it is important to indicate to students the role of the phenomenon contextualization in locating the theoretical status of the greenhouse effect's relationship to global warming. The role of the explanation summary is also significant for strategic reading since it alerts the reader to the main focus of the 'implication sequences'. The conclusion brings about the 'closure' of the explanation, but the indefinite 'some' and the mental process 'believe', maintain the tentativeness of the conclusion.

Commentary on the grammar of the text might indicate that the mood and modality does not include mood adjuncts like 'perhaps', 'possibly', 'maybe' or modal verbs like 'may', 'might', 'could', despite the contested nature of the theoretical link between the greenhouse effect and global warming. One might also comment on the significance of Theme selection in some clauses. For example, the marked Topical Theme 'Each year'

Global Warming Phenomenon	ORIENTATION
The Earth is getting warmer. Identification	

Most of the hottest years during the twentieth century have
occurred in the last decade.
Scientists are still arguing   Phenomenon
whether this is due to the greenhouse effect or some other cause.   Contextualization

One of the key factors in the greenhouse effect is carbon dioxide.

Explanation summary

This greenhouse gas traps heat in the Earth's atmosphere.
Each year, more than 5,000 billion tons (5,100 billion tonnes) of
carbon dioxide are absorbed by green plants
to make food in a process called photosynthesis.
This process produces oxygen,
which living organisms need   IMPLICATION
to breathe.   SEQUENCES
However, the level of carbon dioxide in the atmosphere is
increasing dramatically because of pollution, deforestation,
farming methods and the burning of more fossil fuels (coal, gas
and oil).

Some scientists believe   CLOSURE
that the Earth's atmosphere will continue to rise   Conclusion
as more carbon dioxide is released into the atmosphere.

Figure 7.8   Schematic structure of the global warming explanation (from Ellyard 1996: 58)

has a particular impact, which would be different if this Circumstance of location in time were positioned elsewhere in the sentence (it could be positioned after 'green plants'). Some commentary on the transitivity choices has already been alluded to. The small number of mental and verbal processes are very significant in contextualizing the status of this account. What might also be pointed out is the typical pattern of relational processes occurring in the orientation and the material processes being concentrated in the implication sequences. The orientation, of course, is concerned with identifying and describing the phenomena. It introduces the ways things are, hence the predominant deployment of relational processes. The implication sequences have to account for how things come to be the way they are and so they deal with the events that brought them about. Hence the deployment of material processes, the Actors involved and the Goals they act upon. This typical pattern of deployment of process types in explanations is illustrated in Figure 7.9.

A further issue about the material processes to point out to the students is the use of passives like 'are absorbed', noting the importance of the Actor role of 'green

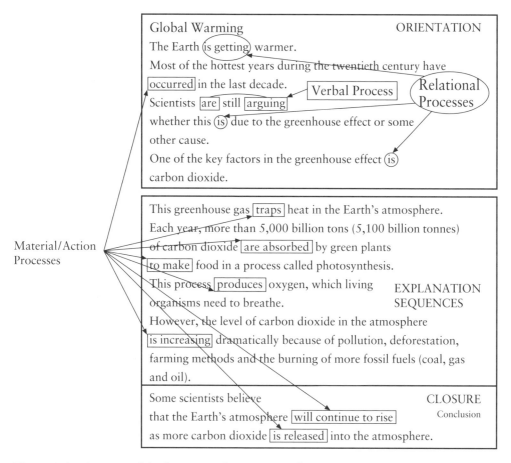

Figure 7.9 Pattern of deployment of process (verb) types in the global warming explanation (from Ellyard 1996: 58)

plants', and also the significance of the ellipsed Actor in the passive 'as more carbon dioxide is released'.

Some responses to the impact of the images were included in the section above on reading the text. One might also point out the emphasis given in the images, due to their relative size, to the role of motor vehicles in contributing to greenhouse gas build-up. The compositional feature of the large central image as nucleus and the smaller images as satellites might be noted as lending itself to a hypertextual recon-figuration in electronic mode, which is to be explored in later sessions.

Closer attention might be given in subsequent reading to the relationship between 'the greenhouse effect' explanation and the 'global warming' explanation. One way to consider this is to ask whether hypertextual links could be inserted to link the explanations, and if so, how many and which text segments would be selected for highlighting as links?

Matters for further exploration include the relationship of the hole in the ozone layer to the greenhouse effect and global warming and the question of the contribution increased vegetarianism might make to reducing greenhouse gases.

Reviewing reading

In reviewing the structured overview/concept map in the light of reading this text, it might be observed that the section in solutions relating to planting of trees could now be improved. The question of the role of methane gas, and vegetarianism as a partial solution, remain problematic. As well as grappling with the 'what' of this text, the modelled reading demonstrated a concern with the 'how' – the effect of the choices of language and image. The class should reread the text silently with the teacher to further address these issues of what and how. Subsequent discussion may raise further issues, such as what is meant by 'methane is 20 times stronger than carbon dioxide' and how does the use of the passive with the ellipsed Actor influence our understanding in 'forests are being cleared throughout the world'? Students are encouraged to see how their work in this unit of study could follow up such questions.

Group work sessions 2–5 in week 2

Groups were prepared for the work on the *Home Greenhouse Scorecard* (Sustainable Solutions 1995) in the introductory groupwork session in week one. The 'follow-up work with the modelled reading text' deals with exploring potential 'hypertextual' relations among 'The greenhouse effect' and 'Global Warming' explanations and between the latter and the images and texts concerning 'Potent Methane', 'Disappearing Forests' and 'New Life', as intimated during the modelled reading lesson. Students are provided with a partial model showing some hypertextual links and invited to generate others, initially within the existing material from the double page spread in Ellyard (1996), but then using additional materials. If sufficient computers are available for the group of six students to work in pairs on this task, it should be done electronically, cutting and pasting from scanned text, using software like *Microsoft Powerpoint* or a basic web page editor like *Claris Homepage* or *Microsoft Frontpage*. If sufficient computers are not available, the task can be done using conventional cut and paste. Again a partial model is provided to the students. Once the work is complete the pairs swap their 'hypertextualized' materials, comparing and sharing the rationales for the links they have constructed.

Guided reading practice

The guided reading practice activity is based on the greenhouse website maintained by *USA Today* (http://www.usatoday.com/weather/tg/wghwrmng/wghwrmng.htm), which is shown in Figure 7.10.

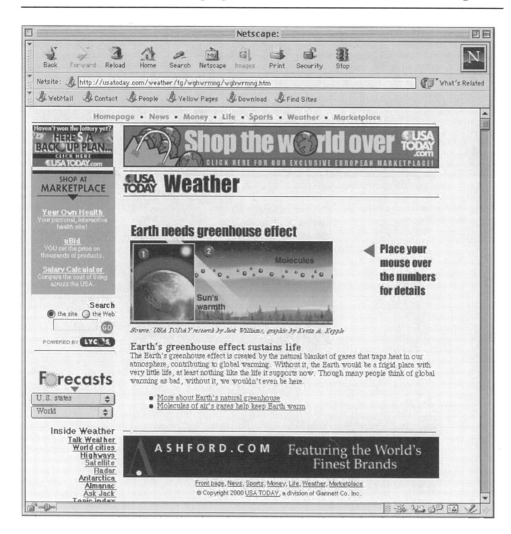

Figure 7.10   Website for guided reading practice
Source: Copyright, *USA TODAY*. Reprinted with permission.

Orientation to text

The orientation to the text largely follows the steps described in the general outline of guided reading practice. Due to constraints on space we will not detail the application of all of these steps for this lesson. However, updating the evolving structured overview/concept map of the topic jointly constructed with the class is an important stage in negotiating the purpose(s) for reading this new text. The issue to focus on here is the discrepancy noted in the modelled reading lesson between the diagram of the greenhouse effect in the text and the one produced in the class concept map.

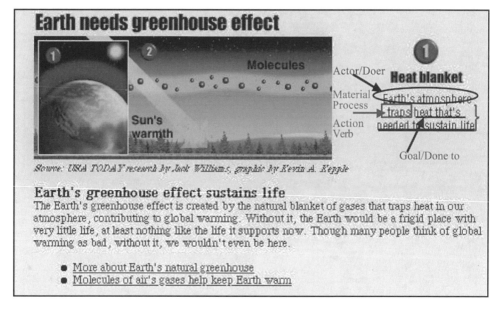

Figure 7.11   Image 1 in the website for guided reading practice

The modelled reading text left some of the arrows in its diagram unexplained, so a purpose for the reading of this website text is to clarify the actual processes whereby energy is received by the Earth and how it is trapped or escapes.

Reading the text

Again this follows the general steps previously outlined. In this case two groups of students, about 12 altogether, will work on this text simultaneously. All students read the main page and are directed to read the page accessed by the hyperlink 'Molecules of air's gases help keep Earth warm'. The more proficient readers are then asked to prepare, in pairs, allocated segments of this hyperlinked page for oral reading, including one pair to 'read' the visual text. The less proficient readers are similarly allocated sections of the main page.

Working with the text

In the first stage of working with the text the teacher works with both groups combined. Image 1 is read and the material process (action verb), Actor and Goal in the caption are identified, as indicated in Figure 7.11. Note that image 1 does not indicate action and hence it is a conceptual analytical (or Whole/Part) image.

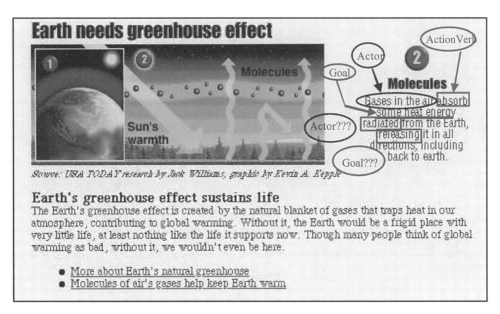

Figure 7.12   Image 2 in the website for guided reading practice

Image 2 is read and students are asked to identify the material processes (action verbs) in the caption text (Figure 7.12). The teacher elicits from the students the Actor and Goal involved in the process 'absorb' and also notes with the students the Actors and Goals implicit with the processes 'radiated' and 'releasing'. It can then be pointed out that these actions are indicated in image 2 by the vectors, so, in contrast to image 1, this is a narrative image (in fact on-line image 2 is dynamic, showing the wavy arrows moving upwards and one then moving back to Earth). It is then useful to discuss how image 2 'explains' image 1 – there is a shift from 'given' information in 1 to new information in 2.

The students are asked to look at the main text to answer the question 'How does the blanket of gases trap heat?' The answer, of course, is not in the main text but in the images and captions. Students could be asked to comment on the role of the modal adverb 'even' in the last sentence by asking them what the effect would be if it were deleted. This draws students' attention to aspects of interpersonal meaning in these texts. Finally, in this first stage of working with the text, note with students the effect of the Theme selections. In the first clause the passive is used to get the 'given' information (The Earth's greenhouse effect) into Theme position and the cause, which is the new information, is appropriately located in the Rheme at the end of the clause. The repeated use of the marked Theme, 'Without it', maintains continuity with the previous clauses, in each case being linked to 'global warming' by the reference item 'it' (for further information on reference see the final section in Chapter 2). Note with the students different ways in which these clauses could be written – the active form

Macro-cloze Version 1	Macro-cloze Version 2
_____ traps _____	A natural _____ traps _____
_____ radiates _____	The Earth _____ radiates _____
_____ absorb _____	Gases _____ absorb _____
_____ release _____	These g _____ release _____
_____ is called _____	This _____ is called _____
_____ contributes to _____	The gr _____ contributes to _____
_____ sustains _____	The gr _____ sustains _____

Macro-cloze Version 3	Macro-cloze Grammar Version
A natural _____ traps heat _____	ACTOR/DOER ACTION VERB GOAL/DONE TO
The Earth _____ radiates h _____	_____ traps _____
Gases _____ absorb Some of this radiated _	_____ radiates _____
These g _____ release the r _____	_____ absorb _____
This _____ is called the gr _____	_____ release _____
The gr _____ contributes to global _____	RELATING VERB
The gr _____ sustains 1 _____	_____ is called _____
	_____ contributes to _____
	_____ sustains _____

Figure 7.13   Macro-cloze activity

in clause one, and repositioning the phrase 'Without it' so that it is not in Theme position, and hence note how these changes would detract from the effectiveness of the text.

In the second stage of working with the text, the less proficient readers are given reading tasks based on this main page and the more proficient readers are given tasks based on the hyperlinked page.

The less proficient group is divided into pairs and, according to their reading competence, students are allocated one of the three versions of a macro-cloze based on the website's main text, as shown in Figure 7.13. Each pair completes the cloze task and the students then swap partners to compare responses. After this, the whole group reconvenes to read the completed macro-cloze and to review its grammatical structure as indicated in the final version in Figure 7.13. At the same time the more proficient readers are asked to complete the following tasks based on the hyperlinked page, which is shown in Figure 7.14.

How "greenhouse effect" works

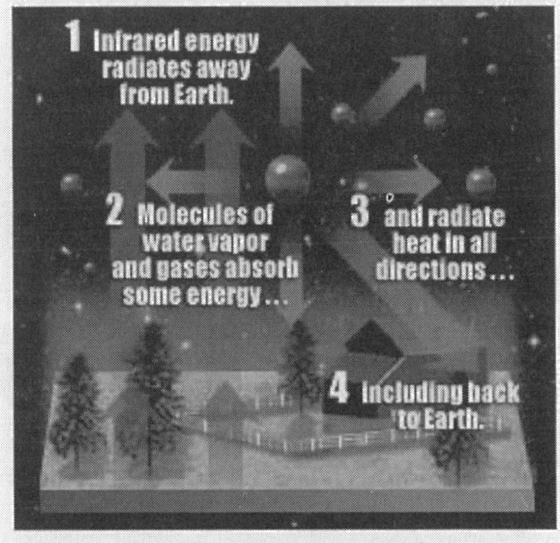

1 Infrared energy radiates away from Earth.

2 Molecules of water vapor and gases absorb some energy...

3 and radiate heat in all directions...

4 Including back to Earth.

USA Today research by Jack Williams

Air's gases help keep Earth warm

The sun supplies the energy that keeps the Earth warm enough for life. Once this energy reaches Earth, it follows complex paths. Some solar energy is reflected back into space and the rest absorbed by the atmosphere and the Earth's land and oceans. The absorbed energy warms the earth, which in turn radiates heat back towards space as infrared energy. Water vapor, carbon dioxide and other gases in the atmosphere absorb some of the outgoing infrared energy, which heats them. These molecules then radiate the energy in all directions, including back to Earth. In effect, some of the energy remains trapped in our atmosphere, warming the planet. This process is often called the "greenhouse effect," but it doesn't work quite like a greenhouse. A greenhouse stays warm because the glass roof allows solar energy in. But it doesn't allow heated air to rise and mix with cooler air aloft as warmed outdoor air would.

- More information, data on greenhouse gasses
- Relation between greenhouse effect and climate change
- Understanding climate change

Figure 7.14 Hyperlinked page from *USA Today* greenhouse effect website
Source: Copyright, *USA TODAY*. Reprinted with permission.

Compare the images of the greenhouse effect from the top left of the modelled reading text (Figure 7.5) and from the hyperlinked page on the website (Figure 7.14). Indicate which arrows on the book image correspond to which arrows on the website image. Which arrows remain unexplained in the images? Are these explained in the website text?

Look at the way in which new information in the Rheme of the one clause becomes the given information in the Theme of the next clause in the following extract from the text:

THEME   RHEME

The sun supplies | the energy [[that keeps the Earth warm enough for life]]. |

Once this energy   reaches the Earth,

it   follows complex paths.

Find another example of this Rheme → Theme progression.

Complete the following macro-cloze task (Figure 7.15) based on the text.

Actor	Material Process (Action Verb)	Goal	Circumstance
The —— and —— and ———	absorb	some ———	
———————————————	warms	———————	
———————————————	radiates	———————	into ———
————— and —————	absorb	———————	
———————————————	heats	———————	
———————————————	radiate	———————	in ———
———————————————	traps	———————	in ———

Figure 7.15   Macro-cloze task based on hyperlinked text page

Look at the following 'passive' sentence and notice that the 'doer' is not in Theme position at the beginning of the clause:

A lot of playground rubbish (done to) *was collected* (action) *by students in this class* (doer).

Find 'passive' sentences in the Main Screen and Hypertext 2 which are written like this.

Main text: _____

Hypertext 2: _____

Rewrite these sentences putting the 'doer' into Theme position at the beginning of the sentence.

Main text: _____

Hypertext 2: _____

Explain why the texts on the web pages use the passive sentence constructions.

_____

_____

Make a list of other features that appear in the Main Text and Hypertext 2.

Figure 7.16 Text comparison guide

Reviewing reading

At this stage of the session the more and less proficient readers are regrouped so that each student works with a new partner from the other original group. The review task for the pairs is to compare the main page of the website with the hyperlinked page and to identify those features of both the language and the images that are common, those peculiar to the main page and those peculiar to the hyperlinked page. Comparison guides on particular features of the texts can be used to focus student work. The guide shown in Figure 7.16 deals with the use of the passive and Theme selection in the structuring of written explanation, while Figure 7.17 indicates the kind of comparisons among these particular texts for which similar guides could be constructed.

When they have had an opportunity to complete the tasks, the students swap partners once to compare their findings. They then reconvene as a whole group to discuss the outcomes of the review task and the ways in which the reading experience addressed the original purposes set and perhaps raised new issues for investigation.

The last of the group work activities for week 2 is the modelled writing of an explanation. This follows the general guidelines as outlined on pages 236–7.

Week 3

The third week maintains the previous pattern of lesson organization, but the emphasis is now shifting to developing transformative knowledge, so the teaching strategies are beginning to involve more critical framing and researching and the development of

Features distinctive to Website main page	Features distinctive to Hyperlinked page
Image Source of the Earth's heat energy from the sun Labels in the image and accompanying captions outside the image Shift from concrete realism of image 1 to abstract scientific coding of image 2 Interactivity – use of mouse to manipulate screen	**Image** Infrared radiation away from the Earth Numbered labels/captions within the image Abstract Conceptual feature of 'flat earth segment' suspended in space
Text Mention of people Use of thinking verbs Judgement of greenhouse effect (bad) – Why is this the case? Where does the website discuss the reasons for this?	**Text** More technical treatment of the topic e.g.: • Sun supplies 'energy' not 'heat' – later referred to as 'solar energy' • Some naming of gases in the atmosphere – 'carbon dioxide' • Energy radiated away from the Earth referred to as 'infrared energy' Note also the different hypertext links provided at the bottom of hypertext 2

Figure 7.17   Comparisons between main page and hyperlinked page

reflection literacies. The first session involves the teacher working with the class as a whole to identify problematic issues about the greenhouse effect and global warming for further critical investigation. Such issues might include:

- the relationship between the hole in the ozone layer, the greenhouse effect and global warming;
- evidence for and against the theories relating the greenhouse effect and global warming;
- different views of the proposed effects of global warming;
- the relative impact of the practices of individual householders in reducing greenhouse gas emissions.

New working groups of students are formed to investigate issues such as these. They also plan genuine social purposes for the research and writing tasks they will undertake. These could include writing improved information on the greenhouse effect and global warming for other students of their age; writing a 'parent pack' informing parents about the topic; generating a class webpage on the greenhouse effect (such as that produced by the Johannes-Kepler secondary school in Reutlingen in southwest Germany – http://www.schwaben.de/home/kepi/green1.htm).

Over the remaining four lessons in the week the students work in four groups and rotate over the four learning activities shown in Figure 7.3. Students are encouraged to research their own sources in undertaking independent reading for their critical investigation but the teacher also provides access to provocative texts like 'Scepticism Net: Global Warming' (http://www.skepticism.net/global_warming/index.html) and 'Global Warming: Early Warning Signs' (http://www.climatehotmap.org).

Week 4

Although the teacher still plays an important role in critical framing, especially in the first two sessions (see Figure 7.3), the orientation in week four is much more toward independent and collaborative work by students. By this stage they are advancing from their systematic knowledge of the field to critically constructive enquiry and socially productive transformative knowledge.

CONCLUSION

The Curriculum Area Multiliteracies and Learning (CAMAL) framework and its Literacy Development Cycle (LDC) need to be seen as evolving approaches to describing theory–practice relations in developing content area literacies and learning. These approaches are quite inclusive of other such work based on social-semiotic perspectives on school subject area learning, and can comfortably subsume specific teaching techniques such as 'writing frames' (Wray and Lewis 1997), broader genre-based writing pedagogies (Feez and Joyce 1998), and scaffolded support for literacy development and learning in content areas (Polias 1998). In attempting to link a clear theoretical rationale to both general frameworks for professional practice and detailed descriptions of classroom implementation, what is provided here is a basis for encouraging ongoing renewal of content area multiliteracies and learning through consolidation of effective teaching as well as constructive critique and transformation.

CHAPTER 8

Teaching multiliteracies in the English classroom

THE CURRICULUM AREA MULTILITERACIES AND LEARNING (CAMAL) FRAMEWORK IN THE ENGLISH CLASSROOM

This chapter is concerned with practical classroom applications of knowledge about genre and functional accounts of visual and verbal grammar in teaching English in the upper primary and junior secondary schools. In Chapter 7 we discussed the knowledge, pedagogic and multiliteracies dimensions of learning contexts (Figure 7.1). We noted that these dimensions are interrelated and that learning in curriculum areas could be seen as a progression through different learning contexts defined by changing characteristics of the knowledge, pedagogic and multiliteracies dimensions. In the English classroom informal knowledge frequently concerns familiarity with story content of various kinds as well as the content of various texts of popular culture. Systematic knowledge relates to taxonomic knowledge of types of story and their textual forms, as well as perhaps authorship and cultural and historical location and valuing. Transformative knowledge entails contestation of hegemonic views of the bases of such taxonomic accounts of story and their valuing, as well as understanding that what counts as story varies according to alternative sociocultural perspectives. The pedagogic dimension maintains the parameters discussed in Chapter 7. Initially there is the sharing of informal knowledge and bridging by the teacher toward systematic knowledge, which is then dealt with via principled balancing of direct teaching and guided exploration. Then the pedagogy moves to critical framing, research and opportunities for transformation. The literacy practices concomitantly move from the recognition literacies associated with text forms encountered informally, to reproduction literacies reflecting the comprehension and composition of text forms identified as culturally significant in English syllabuses, and then to the reflection literacies associated with critique and the remaking of text forms.

In this chapter we want to indicate some practical examples of the progression of these articulated knowledge, pedagogic and multiliteracies dimensions through the changing contexts of sequences of lessons in the English classroom. The classroom programs described here are designed for students in the middle years of schooling – from about 10 or 11 years of age through to about 13 or 14 years of age. It will not be possible to address the range of literary texts, media texts and texts of popular culture with which the teacher of English is concerned. The emphasis on literary narratives here is not intended to privilege literature in the curriculum, but rather to highlight less common selections of such texts for older students and also to draw on widely available texts, which readers can readily access to follow up the ideas suggested. First, a one-week program using picture books is outlined. Next a more detailed account of a two-week program integrating the use of picture books, illustrated stories and novels is described. Then some classroom work on television sitcoms and romance novels and films is briefly reported and, finally, there is a note on technoliteracies and English teaching.

The classroom programs described here make use of the systemic functional analyses of language (Chapter 2) and image (Chapter 3) to explicate the ways in which the texts construct meanings. The relevant aspects of these analyses are explicitly taught to the students in the context of negotiating the meanings of the texts they are investigating. This means that the students develop a meta-language for describing the visual and verbal meaning-making resources that have been used. The Literacy Development Cycle (LDC), which was described in Chapters 6 and 7 (Figure 6.1), is also adapted in this chapter to provide modelled, guided and independent practice in text comprehension and composition as appropriate. The principles of dynamic, functional organization of classroom groups for learning underpinning the implementation of the LDC (and detailed in Chapter 7) including the 'group-then-regroup' strategy are also fundamental to the programs described here.

USING PICTURE BOOKS IN THE ENGLISH CLASSROOM

Picture story books initiating interpretive textual practices with older students

The use of picture books in secondary school English teaching has been an established practice for many years. The initial surprise of some 17-year-old students encountering this at the beginning of their A level English course in the United Kingdom is recorded by Aidan Chambers in his 'Tale of the High School Levellers' (Chambers 1985). Contrary to the students' expectations of beginning their studies with Shakespeare and the Victorian novelists, their teacher put before them a collection of 20 or more picture books 'including such standards as Pat Hutchins' *Rosie's Walk* (1968) at one extreme and Raymond Briggs' *Fungus the Bogeyman* at the other (1977)'. Following some exploration of these books however, the students began to assert that they were far too complicated for young children, pointing out 'subtle interweavings of words and pictures, varieties of meanings suggested but never stated, visual and verbal clues to intricate patterns, structures and ideas' (Chambers 1985: 126).

Through their exploration of the picture books these 17-year-olds learned about the 'constructedness' of text and how this influenced its interpretive possibilities. They came to understand

> that criticism is not about error, not about finding right or wrong, but that there never can be a definitive reading, but only additional readings, all of them in some way revealing, on the one hand of the reader him/herself, and on the other hand of the patterns contained within the mythos we call a text.
>
> (Chambers 1985: 127)

Picture books have been included in senior secondary school syllabuses in Australia (Prain 1998: 82), and a number of scholarly publications discuss both theoretical and practical bases for the inclusion of picture books in the secondary school English curriculum (Michaels and Walsh 1990; Stephens and Watson 1994; Keifer 1995; Watson and Styles 1996; Prain 1998). Such publications argue that picture books are suitable texts for study because they are valued cultural artefacts in their own right with a history extending over 200 years. Stephens and Watson (1994) argue that the form of many contemporary postmodern picture books means that they are especially useful resources for introducing students to key concepts of 'critical' literary and cultural theories. According to them such picture books offer a very manageable resource for teaching students about particular ideologies such as feminist, multicultural and post-colonial perspectives and also teaching knowledge about contemporary narrative forms and the reading practices they entail. In developing visual literacy and other advanced integrative visual and verbal literacy practices increasingly necessitated by the influence of information technology, picture books are seen by Prain (1998) as offering a stable starting point for classroom work, compared with the currently still emerging conventions of digital texts.

There are two interrelated aspects of previous work encouraging the use of picture books with older students that need further development. The first is the need for explicit teaching of meta-semiotic understanding based on functional theoretical descriptions of visual and verbal grammar. The New London Group, comprising 10 members and including academics from the UK, US and Australia, advocated in the *Harvard Educational Review* that what is needed to develop multiliteracies for the future is . . .

> an educationally accessible functional grammar; that is, a metalanguage that describes meaning in various realms. These include the textual and the visual, as well as the multi-modal relations between the different meaning-making processes that are now so critical in media texts and texts of electronic multimedia.
>
> (New London Group 2000: 77)

The kind of functional visual and verbal analyses of picture books which was demonstrated in Chapter 5 contributes to such a basis for the teaching of meta-semiotic understanding using picture books with older students. The second aspect of previous work in this area needing further development is pedagogy. In much of the literature the suggested 'classroom practices' offer little more than a series of discussion questions on particular texts to be put to students. What is needed is a pedagogy that balances explicit teaching, modelled and guided practice, with opportunities for collaborative and independent exploratory work by students. The following outline of a classroom program illustrates this kind of approach.

Picture books and classroom practice – a sample outline program

This classroom work is based on Maurice Sendak's *Where the Wild Things Are* (1962), *Rebel!* by Allan Baillie and illustrated by Di Wu (1993), Anthony Browne's *Zoo* (1994) and *Voices in the Park* (1998) and *The Great Bear* by Libby Gleeson and illustrated by Armin Greder (1999). The program focuses on the role of the framing of images and parallelism in language in the literary construction of experiences of transformation in these books.

Over a period of nearly four decades readers young and old have been fascinated by Maurice Sendak's story of the transformation of young Max's banishment to his bedroom without any supper into his enchanting journey to 'where the wild things are' – and back again. In Chapter 5 (see pages 172–4) we noted the role of visual framing in constructing this transformation. When we first see Max making mischief it is in framed images on the right-hand side of the page and these images do not fill all of the right-hand page. The pictures become bigger and the frames smaller as Max is sent to his room, until they fill the entire right-hand page. As Max begins his journey to the wild things the images creep across onto the left-hand side of the page. Upon the arrival of Max in his boat the images extend fully across the double page spread, framed by the edges of the page and about a quarter of the page of white paper at the bottom of the double page spread where the print is contained. For the duration of the wild rumpus the images completely take over every bit of space on the double page spreads. Then we find that the framing changes reverse, the images gradually receding to the right-hand side of the page, but significantly the final image of Max in his bedroom fully takes up the right-hand page, in contrast to the first image of Max in his bedroom.

We could also explore the role of verbal parallelisms as a complementary verbal framing technique in constructing the transformation. Prior to his 'journey' Max 'was sent to bed without eating anything', and upon his return to his bedroom 'he found his supper waiting for him and it was still hot'. In departing Max 'sailed off through night and day and in and out of weeks and almost over a year to where the wild things are'. Then he 'sailed back over a year and in and out of weeks and through a day and into the night of his very own room'. The enduring popularity of 'wild things', and perhaps fairly widespread recognition of these visual and verbal textual features of the story, make this book a very useful starting point for engaging older readers in an exploration of the role of visual and verbal framing in the construction of transformations of various kinds in contemporary picture books.

The picture book, *Rebel!* (Baillie 1993) tells the story of a General defeated by school children. The General arrives with his army to take over a sleepy Burmese village. While proclaiming his rules to the forcibly assembled townspeople, he is hit by a small battered thong, flung from the school building. Furious, the General sets out to find and punish the culprit who dared to attack him. Students and teachers are marched before him so that he can identify the child with the missing thong, however he had not counted on the ingenuity of the children. In the school house was a great pile of thongs. The General's departure from the village was very different from his arrival.

In *Rebel!* the text and image are on a white background framed by a pink border. Initially the framing of the arrival of the General extends from the left-hand page onto the right-hand page so that the image of the village occupies just over one-third of the double page spread. This is also the case on the next double page spread. Then the occupation of the village by the General and his army is depicted in the one frame extending over the entire double page spread. After the incident of the thong throwing and the failure of the General to identify the culprit, we have a mirroring of the framing of the images in the first part of the book. The three double page spreads prior to the final one in the book, show the village people framed over the left-hand side of the page and extending to the right-hand side so that now the General occupies less than one-third of the double page spread. The last double page spread is taken up entirely by the framed image of the village people.

Verbal parallelism also frames the transformation in the story. At the beginning of the story we read:

> The General came across the dusty plain of Burma in the early morning. He came with great clanking tanks, and lorries. And long columns of crunching hard-faced soldiers. They marched over the bridge, past the pagoda and the quiet shops, until they stopped outside the open playground of the school.

This is paralleled at the end of the story with:

> The General went past the noisy shops, past the ancient pagoda and over the bridge. He went with great clanking tanks, and wheeled guns, and columns of crunching – grinning soldiers. The General marched across the dusty plain of Burma in the late afternoon. But he could still hear the laughter.

Further examples of parallelism can be identified by comparing grammatical features such as circumstances (adverbial phrases), adjectives in nominal groups and process (verb) types as indicated in Figure 8.1.

Grammatical features	Before thong throwing	After thong throwing
Circumstance	early morning	late afternoon
Adjectives in noun groups	hard-faced soldiers	grinning soldiers
Adjectives in noun groups	quiet shops	noisy shops
Process (verb) types	stroke his baton	broke his baton
Process (verb) types	The stars on his hat flashed in the sun	shone his stars
Process (verb) types	The rows of medals clinked proudly on his chest	tinkled his medals

Figure 8.1   Parallelism in the selection of grammatical features in *Rebel!* (Baillie 1993)

The visual framing in Anthony Browne's *Zoo* has been discussed in Chapter 5 (page 173). Once the family have arrived at the zoo, the humans are consistently on the left-hand page and the animals on the right. The framing around the images of the family is not prominent nor straight – as if the images had been cut out from somewhere else. By contrast the images of the zoo animals are all heavily framed with thick black straight border lines. This pattern is maintained until we see a much more distinct, albeit not quite straight, grey-black bordering around the image of the boys wearing their monkey hats. Then we see a distinct yellow border around the image of the family and other members of the public looking at the orang-utan. Then the second to last image of the book shows the older son, the narrator, who had a very strange dream in his room that night. This image has the same thick, black, straight black border that surrounded all of the images of the animals in the zoo, so the transposition of framing is complete. Suffice it to say that the use of framing is far from incidental to the construction of the interpretive possibilities of this book. In Chapter 5 we also looked at the verbal grammatical patterns in *Zoo* such as the marked Topical Themes reflecting the transition from one episode to the next (page 151) the mother being the only character engaged mental processes (page 155) and the dominance of the father's commands and repeated jokes (page 157).

The effects of the visual and verbal framing in Anthony Browne's *Voices in the Park* are perhaps not as transparent as those in *Where the Wild Things Are*, *Rebel!* and *Zoo*. However, it is interesting to note the ways in which the framing changes, reflecting the transformation that occurs when Charles and Smudge meet up in the park.

- The images in the First Voice all have very regular, distinct frames. The only image where the participant extends beyond the frame is where she is shouting for her son, concerned at the 'frightful types' that may be in the park. The only image extending over the full page is where she has left the park to walk home.

- The framing of the images in the Second Voice are more varied. The initial image has no frame. The two framed images have borders that are much less regular and there are three images that extend over the full page – going to the park, the dogs in the park, and coming home from the park.
- In the Third Voice there is a significant progression in the framing of the images. The first two images including the young Charles are bordered with distinct black lines. The next image of Charles and Smudge together on the bench has black lines only on the bottom and left hand sides – where Charles is located. The top and right-hand side has no black line border on the frame – the side where Smudge is located. The next image of Charles and Smudge and the slippery slide, shows the slide protruding over the bottom black border line as Charles is about to slide down. Subsequently we see the lack of border around Smudge and Charles on the climbing frame and the very irregular frame, without any black border, around the image of Charles and Smudge climbing the tree.
- In the Fourth Voice it is the images of Charles and Smudge playing in the park that take up the whole page.

Again complementary verbal parallelism could be explored across the 'voices'. For example the First Voice section concludes with 'We walked home in silence', while the Second Voice concludes with 'She chatted happily to me all the way home'. In the Third Voice, Charles indicates that his departure was imposed by his mother because he was talking to Smudge – 'Then Mummy caught us talking and I had to go home'. On the other hand, Smudge, the Fourth Voice, simply recounts 'Then his mother called and he had to go'.

The Great Bear by Libby Gleeson and illustrated by Armin Greder (1999) won the 2000 Bologna Ragazzi Award for best picture book. It tells the story of a circus dancing bear, which finally breaks free from the cruel conditions, mindless repetitive performances and torments of village audiences. The story has minimal text and the last six of the 15 double page spreads have no print at all. In fact, from the seventh double page spread the coloured images on the right-hand side begin to encroach onto the left-hand side. By the tenth double page spread the print has disappeared completely and the images fill both sides of the double page layout. The print begins with a short sentence, 'Once there was a bear'. The next page contains two nominal groups only – 'A circus bear. A dancing circus bear.' The next page contains a sentence of two lines, and the following one a sentence of three lines and so on. But the second to last page containing print has four short Actor/Process clause structures:

Sticks poke.
Sticks prod.
Chairs yank.
Stones strike,
         strike,
            strike.

The interaction of the patterning of the language and of the illustrations is a very significant feature of the telling of this story.

The classroom program using these books extends over one week with daily sessions of about one hour's duration. The first session is based on *Where the Wild Things Are* (Sendak 1962). This involves modelled and guided reading activities in which the visual and verbal framing in this book are made explicit as a basis for the students' investigation of the other picture books. In session two, after reviewing the discussion from session one, the teacher models the writing of an interpretive response to *Where the Wild Things Are*, explicating the role of visual and verbal framing. The remainder of this session is used to introduce and read the other picture books and to negotiate the organization of the investigative work with them in the subsequent lessons. The class is divided into four working groups – each of which in turn can divide into two subgroups each of about three students. The less experienced readers are encouraged to work initially in the groups investigating *Rebel!* (Baillie 1993) and *Zoo* (Browne 1994), while the more proficient readers are encouraged to form groups working with *Voices in the Park* (Browne 1998) and *The Great Bear* (Gleeson and Greder 1999). But what is important is that all students will eventually work on all of the books. In subgroups of three, all students in the class investigate the role of visual and verbal framing in one of the four picture books listed. Reading guides can be provided to support students as necessary (see below). The students' task is to write an interpretive response dealing with the nature and role of visual and verbal framing in the book, drawing on the model based on *Where the Wild Things Are* provided by the teacher. After their initial collaborative efforts in session three in these groups, the students are then regrouped so that each new working group represents all four picture books, having at least one member who has worked on each different title. The students then share and discuss their work and revise and edit their interpretive responses as appropriate. The next day published versions of these responses are submitted and displayed. Then new discussion groups are formed to read and respond orally to the visual and verbal framing aspects of another selection of picture books, perhaps this time picture books dealing with transformations in relationships like Anthony Browne's *The Tunnel* (1989), *The Wolf* by Margaret Barbelet and illustrated by Jane Tanner (1991), Bob Graham's *Rose Meets Mr Wintergarten* (1992) and *John Brown, Rose and the Midnight Cat* by Jenny Wagner and illustrated by Ron Brooks (1977).

INTEGRATING THE USE OF PICTURE BOOKS, ILLUSTRATED NARRATIVES AND NOVELS

Comparative study of literary texts in the classroom

Students can often develop clearer understandings of the distinctive features of a literary text if they can make comparisons with other texts (Prain 1998). The classroom work with picture books for younger students described in Chapter 6, as well as the outline of work with older students described earlier in this chapter, make use of scaffolded and systematic comparison. In earlier work (Unsworth 1993b) I have detailed classroom programs using comparisons of junior novels dealing with similar subject matter like bullying (Aidan Chambers' *The Present Takers*, 1983, *Josh* by Ivan Southall, 1971, and Betsy Byars' *The Eighteenth Emergency*, 1974) or illustrating different narrative techniques (Gene Kemp's *The Clocktower Ghost*, 1981, Robin Klein's *Hating Alison Ashley*, 1984 and *Cannily Cannily* by Simon French, 1981). As Prain (1998) suggests, comparisons can be usefully made across literary genres, and the unit of classroom work described in the next section involves students in comparisons across the novel, picture book and illustrated story genres.

Fox – a unit of work exploring a motif in the literary construction of other worlds

The fox has been a prominent motif in literary texts from D.H. Lawrence's 'The Fox' (1971) to Roald Dahl's *Fantastic Mr Fox* (1974) and the realist fiction of Betsy Byars' *The Midnight Fox* (1970). Some more recent books for young readers have centred on the association of the fox with the supernatural and other worlds. One of these is the illustrated story, *Grandad's Gifts* by the popular Australian writer Paul Jennings and illustrator, Peter Gouldthorpe (1994). In this story pre-adolescent Shane and his family move into his grandfather's old house in the country. Shane's bedroom, formerly his father's room, contains a wardrobe which the late grandfather has warned should never be opened. Mysterious guidance leads Shane to discover a fox skin fur wrap inside. Further mysterious influences result in Shane's transporting lemons from the trees under which the remains of the fox and his grandfather were buried, to the fox in the wardrobe. Ultimately, one night the family discovers the forbidden wardrobe door open and observes a blue-eyed fox at the edge of the garden.

The novel for young adolescents, *Foxspell* (Rubinstein 1994) negotiates the delicate transitions between fantasy and reality and between human, spirit and animal worlds, as the main character, Tod experiences events beyond his control dragging him into adolescence. His fascination with foxes, which inhabit the quarry near his grandmother's house leads him into a world whose simplicity seems to offer relief from his everyday life of complexity and compromise, until one day he finds he has to choose between two very different worlds.

This two-week unit of study, based on about one hour of classroom work each day, draws on pre- and early adolescent readers' interest in stories involving transitions into supernatural worlds. This is evidenced in the contemporary success of J.K. Rowlings's 'Harry Potter' series (1997, 1998, 1999, 2000), but also the enduring popularity of the Narnia stories by C.S. Lewis (1950) and a good many novels for young readers that suggest that extrasensory perception and worlds in dimensions beyond the here and now could be reality. These include Mary White's *Mindwave* (1980), Allan Baillie's *Megan's Star* (1988), Victor Kelleher's *The Hunting of Shadroth* (1981) and *The*

Forbidden Paths of Thual (1979), as well as Ruth Park's *Playing Beatie Bow* (1988) and Nadia Wheatley's more complex *The House That Was Eureka* (Wheatley 1985).

This classroom program focuses on a close reading of *Grandad's Gifts* and *Foxspell*, but it also encourages wide reading to take in other 'fox' stories like the recent picture book entitled *Fox* (Wild and Brooks 2000) and novels like *The Midnight Fox* (Byars 1970). Both of the books for close study are engaging stories with interesting characters and raise important social questions centrally related to the issues individually confronting young readers in the transition to, or in early adolescence. They also provide opportunities for the exploration of narrative conventions in stories of this type like the establishment of an entrance to the supernatural world (like the wardrobe into the land of Narnia). Matters like these, as well as critical understanding of the construction of point of view and other narrative techniques can be addressed. However, the main focus in this two-week program will be the visual semiotic and linguistic means of foreshadowing the emergence into the supernatural world and at the same time sustaining the viability of a rational perspective on unfolding events.

Week 1: Session 1

- Elicit from students their recollections of stories about foxes they have read (perhaps *Rosie's Walk* by Pat Hutchins, 1968, Roald Dahl's *Fantastic Mr Fox*, 1974, etc.)
- Display the range of books this unit of work will draw on (*Foxspell* by Gillian Rubinstein, *The Midnight Fox* by Betsy Byars, *Grandad's Gifts* by Paul Jennings and Peter Gouldthorpe, *The Fox* by Leith Morton and Yukuo Murakami and *Fox* by Margaret Wilde and Ron Brooks).
- Introduce *Foxspell* and read the first three chapters.
- Introduce *Grandad's Gifts* (between four to six copies of both the illustrated version and the earlier unillustrated version by Paul Jennings published in *Unbearable* (1994) will be needed for classroom work).
- Mask the text pages in the illustrated version and form half the class into groups of two or three students to read the images only. The other half of the class (more proficient readers) read the print only version.
- Those reading the images jot down what they think the story is about. Regroup this half of the class to share ideas across the small groups.
- Regroup again so that each new group of about three to four students contains students who have read the images and students who have read the text only version.
- Students share their interpretations of the story based on the mode of reading they experienced and discuss how the addition of the textual/visual dimension affected their original ideas of what the story was about.
- Raise with the whole class group the question of foreshadowing – how does the author/illustrator gradually suggest the emergence of the supernatural before it actually does emerge? Indicate that this will be the focus of the next session.

Week 1: Session 2

- Review the impact of the relationship between the images and the text in the interpretation of *Grandad's Gifts* and the focus in this session on visual and verbal foreshadowing of the supernatural and the simultaneous sustaining of a rational perspective prior to the actual emergence of the supernatural.
- Form the students into four subgroups. The most proficient readers will be asked to identify the segments of the verbal text in which this foreshadowing occurs and to explain how these choices of language achieve this purpose. The second group (of less experienced readers) may be given a reading guide for this task. This guide would be based on Figure 8.2, which could be modified in the level of support provided. Most proficient students would simply receive the relevant text indicated by double page spread with no coding of foreshadowing resources or key. The next level of support would have the key added. The next level of support after that would have the key and some of the text (three double page spreads) coded according to the key. The third group of students (judged likely to deal most effectively with independent interpretation of images) are asked to indicate how the images achieve this foreshadowing. The fourth group is provided with a viewing guide based on Figure 8.3. Again the level of support could be graduated by modifying the amount and type of information provided in the guide. The first level of support includes only the right-hand column showing the relevant features of the images according to page location. The next level of support would include these and a cloze format of the text in the column of visual cues. Further support would have in addition full description for pages 1, 2 and 4 as indicated in Figure 8.3.
- Once these tasks are completed, regroup the first two groups to compare the results obtained in the original groups and similarly regroup the third and fourth groups working on the images.
- Then regroup these groups so that we now have four new groups each consisting of some students who have investigated foreshadowing in the language and some who have looked at foreshadowing in the images. Students discuss the effects of the verbal and visual foreshadowing separately and in combination.
- Read aloud to the class Chapter 4 of *Foxspell*, inviting the students to note and indicate examples of foreshadowing as the reading of the chapter progresses.

Week 1: Session 3

- Read aloud to the class Chapter 5 of *Foxspell* (it is useful to recruit some proficient readers in the class in advance to read ahead in preparation for working with the teacher in the reading aloud of the book).
- The class now begins to work in groups on *Foxspell* as well as *Grandad's Gifts*. In this session two groups will work on each book.
- The first two groups will investigate further the images in *Grandad's Gifts*. They are asked to consider the following issues:

Double page spread	Relevant text	Key to grammatical resources for foreshadowing
2	It was (almost) *as if* a gentle voice was stirring the shadows of years gone by. The stillness seemed to echo my name, 'Shane . . .	(Modal adverb)
3	That's when I saw the two lemon trees for the first time.	
4	I turned my back on the secret cupboard and tried to listen to the gentle voice lapping inside my head. 'Shane . . . Once again I peered through the keyhole. This time I thought I saw two points of light twinkle in the darkness.	Circumstance/Adverb Phrase:location *conjunction*
5	I tried to prise up the board but it wouldn't budge. Suddenly it gave way and sprang out. It was (almost) *as if* a hidden hand had helped it up.	Phased verb: reality
6	It (the key) didn't seem to fit. I jiggled and wiggled it. Then, just like the floorboard, it moved without warning. *As if* hidden fingers had twisted it.	Nominal group
7	*Its mouth opened a fraction.	
8	Why had Grandad locked the door and made everyone promise not to open it? What was it about that fox?	Mental verb: thinking
9	A voice seemed to call me. It wanted me to go to the large lemon tree. The voice inside my head told me to go out into the night and pick a lemon. *The cupboard door had swung open. The fox's eyes glinted in the moonlight. I thought it moved. It seemed to sigh gently. My hand seemed to have a life of its own.	

Figure 8.2   Foreshadowing in the verbal text of *Grandad's Gifts* (Jennings and Gouldthorpe 1994)

Note: * The grammatical structure suggests that this event just happened without an agent bringing it about (see Halliday 1994a: 163–72 on ergativity).

Double page spread	Relevant visual cues	Visual grammatical resources for foreshadowing
1	Miniature fox icon superimposed on the first letter of the first word opening the story (repeated on all double page spreads). The woodgrain pattern on the door of the wardrobe is in the form of a fox head.	Symbolic attribute
2	The image of Shane seen through a keyhole suggesting something is watching him.	Framing
4	Image is now on the left-hand rather than the usual right-hand side of the page. The uneasiness of sleeping in the room at night is what is given (left-hand side). We are still to find out the new information about what causes this uneasiness. The moonlight shining into the bedroom highlights the woodgrain image of the fox on the wardrobe. The vectors of the bars on the windows reinforce the gaze of Shane towards the wardrobe (and the highlighted fox image).	Given/New Framing – vectors Transactional Reaction
6	Woodgrain image of the fox again.	Symbolic attribute
7	Startled (non-transactional) reaction of Shane when the door is opened, indicating fear. Again on the left-hand side instead of the right as is the predominant position of images in this text. Again what is given (left) is the fright – the new information we don't yet know is the cause of the fright. Presented as a low angle, demand as if the viewer is in the position of whatever frightened Shane.	Given/New Non-transactional reaction Demand Low angle
9	This image is back to the left-hand side of the page, emphasizing that the strange, unsettling events are now what is given, but we are still to find out whether something supernatural is behind them. The image is a high angle shot with Shane presented as relatively powerless. It is also a demand with his gaze of trepidation directed to the viewer. The aura surrounding Shane's hand and the lemon he is about to pick suggest some other force involved.	Given/New Transactional Action Demand High angle

Figure 8.3   Foreshadowing in the visual text of *Grandad's Gifts* (Jennings and Gouldthorpe 1994)

Demands in which Shane's gaze is directed to the viewer			
Pages	Vertical angle	Process type	Assumed phenomenon
2	Eye-level	Reaction:Non-Transactional	Whatever is in the wardrobe
3	Low angle	Reaction:Non-Transactional	Fox's grave
5	Low angle	Reaction:Non-Transactional	The key under the floorboards
7	Low angle	Reaction:Non-Transactional	The fox in the wardrobe
9	High angle	Reaction: Transactional	Lemons
12	Low angle	Reaction:Non-Transactional	Dad cutting down lemon tree
13	Eye level	Reaction:Non-Transactional	Lemons

Figure 8.4   Images and positioning of the viewer in *Grandad's Gifts* (Jennings and Gouldthorpe 1994)

- Look again at the images that are 'demands' where the gaze of Shane is directed to the viewer. How does the vertical angle and the 'reactional' process in which Shane is engaged position you in relation to Shane? How does this change as the story progresses?
- Is there any significance in the selection of images that appear on the left-hand side of the double page spreads?
- Look at the parallelism between some of the images in the book. For example the small lemon tree on the title page and the same tree, shown as dead on the final page. Now look at the image containing the fox in the penultimate section of the story. Compare this with the image on the front cover. Does this add any significance to the vertical angle of the cover image?

- 'Scaffolding' guides can again be provided based on Figures 8.4 to 8.5. The first two of these would be modified in a manner similar to that shown previously in accordance with the level of support required. Figure 8.4 assists students to come to the understanding that up to page 9, after which the nature of the fox becomes clear, the features of the images position the viewer as if she or he were the spirit of the fox watching Shane. Figure 8.5 shows that the images on the left-hand side of the double page spreads in each case indicate the boundary between one key episode and the next. Further guidance can be provided juxtaposing copies of the cover image and the penultimate image in the book and annotating these to show that the fox in the penultimate image occupies a position not dissimilar to that indicating the position of the viewer with respect to the cover image.
- The other two groups work on the foreshadowing in *Foxspell*. In session two they identified two features. The first is the use of the verb 'trotted' to describe Tod's movement and also the direct foreshadowing:

Pages	Image description	Marking end of episode	Marking start of episode
4	Shane in bed at night	Orientation – the forbidden wardrobe and the fox buried under the lemon tree	
7	Shane discovers the fox in the wardrobe	Shifting the bed, finding the key and unlocking the wardrobe	
9	Shane reaching for lemons		Rejuvenating the fox with lemons
12	Shane calling from the window		Realizing the glass eyes require more lemons
15	The fox walking away	The complete rejuvenation of the fox	

Figure 8.5   Images and the episodic structure of *Grandad's Gifts* (Jennings and Gouldthorpe 1994)

'Tod is an old word for fox', Leonie said. 'I think it's Scottish' . . . 'You'll change into one if you're not careful,' she warned him. 'Specially if you go around covering yourself in mud and calling them.'

(Rubinstein 1994: 51)

In this session they look at how this foreshadowing changes in Chapter 6 and read Chapter 7 to track any further changes. One group works with the teacher support, while the second group works independently locating the verbs associated with Tod and noting the shift from simply the use of material/action verbs to those concerning the senses: 'loping', 'lapping' → 'sniffing', 'his new sharp hearing'.

Week 1: Session 4

In this session the groupwork tasks of the previous lesson are reversed so that those who worked on the images in *Grandad's Gifts* now work on *Foxspell* and vice versa. The groups then come together and the class shares what has been learned from the previous two lessons about both books. The next stage of the unit will involve investigating how the foreshadowing develops in *Foxspell*, looking at a model review in preparation for writing a review of *Grandad's Gifts*, and browsing some of the other stories about foxes.

Week 1: Session 5

- Read aloud to the whole class Chapters 8 and 9 of *Foxspell*.
- Two groups of students (more proficient readers in the class) reread Chapters 8 and 9 to note how the author is using different language choices to develop the foreshadowing of Tod's transition into a different world. Again differential scaffolding may be

provided to the students based on the close reading guide shown in Figure 8.6. Some students may simply address this task without the need for such guidance. Other students may be provided with part 1 or with parts 1 and 2 of the guide, depending on their experience/confidence in working with texts in this way.

- Group three (students requiring more teacher support) works with the teacher on the guided writing of a review of *Grandad's Gifts*. Lesson organization for guided writing is described in Chapter 7 (see pages 237–8). A sample review of *Harry Potter and the Philosopher's Stone* (Rowling 1997) is provided in Figure 4.8. The review of *Grandad's Gifts* from *The Dragon Lode*, Spring 1994, and published on Paul Jennings' Internet homepage (http://www.pauljennings.com.au/books/info/gdgrev.htm), can be used as both a model review and also as a base text that can be modified by students to produce their own reviews. (This review is included here as Figure 8.7.)
- Group four can browse the classroom collection of 'fox' stories, including the picture books *The Fox* (Morton and Murakami 1989) and *Fox* (Wild and Brooks 2000). For the latter picture book students can also visit the publishers' website (http:www.allen-unwin.com.au/kidzone/trfox.htm) and make their own responses to the comments on and interpretations of the book that appear there.
- About half way through the lesson, groups one and two 'regroup' to share their responses to the task and groups three and four swap activities.

Week 2: Session 6

- Read aloud to the class Chapters 10 and 11 of *Foxspell*.
- In this session the two groups of more proficient readers who worked on Chapters 8 and 9 of *Foxspell* in the previous lesson undertake the writing of a review of *Grandad's Gifts*. One group of these students can be reminded of the stages of schematic structure of a review (Context, Text Description and Judgement) and then asked to generate an initial draft. The other group can be asked to critically discuss the review from the Paul Jennings website (Figure 8.7). Then these groups can swap tasks and further refine the drafts of their own reviews.
- Groups three and four from the previous lesson now undertake with the teacher the study of foreshadowing in Chapters 8 and 9 of *Foxspell* completed by the first two groups in the previous lesson. The teacher will work through the close reading guide with each of groups three and four in turn. While the teacher works closely with one of these groups, the other group visits the Paul Jennings website where the students can find out about the author, read information about his other books and enjoy a free story published on the Web.

Week 2: Session 7

- Read aloud to the class Chapters 12 and 13 of *Foxspell*.
- In this session two groups of students further explore *Foxspell*, students in a third group finalize the publication of their reviews of *Grandad's Gifts* and the fourth

Close reading guide – part 1

Compare the sections below from Chapter 7 where Tod cannot find the fox tunnel and from Chapter 9 where he finds it easily:

Tod was using the fox trail he'd followed before, picking up the scent, noticing the landmarks and signs almost unconsciously. But when he came through the olive trees he realised he was disoriented. There were no huge ash trees up here. And though there were rocks and boulders in front of him, cast about as he might he could not find the fox tunnel.

(Chapter 7: 88)

Following the scent of the fox, he had no trouble finding the tunnel through the fallen rocks.

(Chapter 9: 115)

In both cases Tod was picking up/following the scent, what has happened between Chapter 7 and Chapter 9 that might explain his success on the second occasion?

When you have noted down your ideas about this, turn to part two of this guide.

Close reading guide – part 2

Read again the following sections of Chapter 9:

When Tod woke up it was bright daylight. A train was clattering down the hill towards the city. Perhaps it was the 12.01, or the 1.01. Tod yawned and stretched, not bothering to check his watch. There was no need to get up yet, he thought lazily. No need to move until the sun disappeared from the sky and night fell. But he didn't exactly think it in words, and he didn't think in precise times either. He saw a series of images inside his head – the sun, the night, himself set within each frame, part of the sun, part of the night, not a person who thought things out and planned them with clocks and dates and timetables.

(Chapter 9: 109)

Tod couldn't understand why he hadn't been able to find the way through the ash trees when he had been there with Adrian. He kept thinking about all the different paths and tracks he had explored, running through them in his mind with his new way of thinking as if he were watching himself running along them, ears pointed, tail swinging.

(Chapter 9: 110)

Look at the types of processes Tod is involved in as a participant indicated by the verb types associated with him. How do they represent a further progression from the one we noted in the previous two lessons ('loping', 'lapping' → 'sniffing', 'his new sharp hearing')? How does your reading of these paragraphs relate to your response to part one of this guide?

Figure 8.6   Reading guide – foreshadowing in *Foxspell* (Rubinstein 1994)

Grandad's Gifts Jennings, known for his short stories (turned into an Australian children's television series), transforms a most captivating tale into a picture book.	Context
Shane and his family move into Grandad's old house in the hills. But what is in the cupboard in Shane's bedroom that he has been warned not to open? What has remained in there, undisturbed for nineteen years? It seems to call to Shane and he soon becomes involved in the contents of the forbidden cupboard. As always, Jennings adds an unexpected twist to the ending. This story can be a springboard for sharing family stories or enjoyed for its suspense and surprise ending. Gouldthorpe's illustrations add to the spellbinding effect of the story. His technique of black acrylic paint, used like watercolour, and coloured pencil on watercolour paper; gives the reader the feeling of being part of the illustration with its depth and realism.	Text Description
This book was named an Honor book in the Picture Book category by the Australian Children's Book Council for 1993. Both the story and the illustrations will stay with the reader for a long, long time. (Fresch 1994)	Judgement

Figure 8.7   Review of *Grandad's Gifts* (Jennings and Gouldthorpe 1994)

group works with the teacher reading the picture book *Fox* by Margaret Wild and Ron Brooks.

- The first group working on *Foxspell* considers what has been resolved at the end of Chapter 13 and what remains to be resolved. Tod has rejected his participation in the world of the fox. How is the book likely to end? What will be the outcome of Tod's and Charm's relationship with Shaun and his gang, the breakers? What will happen between Dallas and Rick? Will Tod's father return and reconcile with his mother Leonie?
- The second group looks at the images that are included in this novel – the map of the district in which Tod's grandmother's house is situated and the comparative drawing of the dog and fox paws, as well as the images on the book cover. Why were these particular illustrations included? What other illustrations might have been included? Could this story be turned into an illustrated story as occurred with the illustrating of the earlier published version of *Grandad's Gifts*?
- These two groups swap tasks halfway through the session.
- The third group considers the picture book *Fox* with the teacher. In this story Dog, with one blind eye, rescues Magpie with a damaged wing, and they become friends. Then fox – charismatic, damaged, restless and unhappy – comes into the bush. Magpie knows that he is not to be trusted, and yet, when he tempts her away, she succumbs. He abandons her in the hot red desert. To die in the heat would be the easiest way, but Magpie thinks of Dog waking to find her gone, and sets out on the long journey home. Suspense is created in the story by the

After the rains, when saplings are springing up everywhere, a fox comes into the bush; Fox with his haunted eyes and rich red coat.
He flickers through the trees like a tongue of fire, and Magpie trembles.
. . .
Dog beams, but Magpie shrinks away. She can feel fox staring at her burnt wing.   foreshadowing
                                                                                                   physical harm
. . .
Now and again Fox joins in the conversation, but Magpie can feel him watching, always watching her.
And at night his smell seems to fill the cave – a smell of rage and envy and loneliness.   foreshadowing
                                                                                                   psychological
                                                                                                   harm
Magpie tries to warn Dog about Fox.
'He belongs nowhere,' she says. 'He loves no one.'

He turns and looks at Magpie, and he says,
'Now you and Dog will know what it is like to be truly alone.'

Figure 8.8   Foreshadowing in *Fox* (Wild and Brooks 2000)

author's choice of words that foreshadow the fox's harmful intentions (as well as by images such as the fox's 'haunted' eyes). This foreshadowing suggests not only physical harm but also the sinister motivation for the fox's actions, made disturbingly explicit at the end of the story, as indicated in Figure 8.8. The nature and extent of the students' discussion of this use of language provides some indication of the learning that has taken place in the related work on *Grandad's Gifts* and *Foxspell*.

- The fourth group finalizes publication of their reviews of *Grandad's Gifts*.
- Groups three and four also swap tasks halfway through the session.

Week 2: Session 8

In this session the two groups who explored the possible resolutions of the story and the use of images in *Foxspell* now finalize their publication of their reviews of *Grandad's Gifts* and discuss the language of foreshadowing in the picture book *Fox*. Correspondingly, groups three and four from the previous lesson now explore the resolutions and images in *Foxspell*.

Week 2: Session 9

- Read aloud the final two chapters (14 and 15) of *Foxspell*.
- Discuss the 'unexpectedness' of the tragic conclusion to *Foxspell*. Discuss also how the 'ending' section maintains the story as somewhat unresolved. Compare this to the somewhat unresolved nature of the ending of the picture book *Fox*.

- Elicit from the students suggestions for concluding activities for the next and final session in this unit of work. These might include:

  - Sharing of written reviews of *Grandad's Gifts*;
  - production of images to accompany *Foxspell* (for example Tod's rock painting; a new cover design);
  - display of other 'fox' stories located by students;
  - design of a 'fox' stories page for class website;
  - discussion of other stories by Paul Jennings and Gillian Rubinstein;
  - writing a 'fox' story;
  - issues for discussion might include:

  the gendering of the animals in *Fox*;
  the unusual orthography and layout;
  why so many of the stories about foxes (*Grandad's Gifts*, *Foxspell* and *The Midnight Fox*) have male main characters;
  the unfavourable portrayal of Mum (Leonie) in *Foxspell* and Dad in *Grandad's Gifts*.

MEDIA TEXTS, TELEVISION, VIDEO AND FILM – FUNCTIONAL ANALYSES OF TEXTS AND TEACHING

The English classroom engages with texts beyond literary narratives, and the application of systemic functional analyses of language (Chapter 2) and image (Chapter 3) to texts of popular culture has provided detailed accounts of visual and verbal text forms as a basis for teaching about the meaning making resources deployed in news stories (Iedema *et al.* 1994; Iedema 1995, 1997; White 1997, 2000) advertisements (Shirato and Yell 1996) television video and film (van Leeuwen 1991, 1996). The practical use of these functional semiotic analyses in English teaching is described in a range of publications. The Queensland Government's School English syllabus for Years 1 to 10 (Queensland Department of Education 1994) provides descriptions of the genre and grammar of short news stories and guidelines for developing students' critical reading and writing of such texts. Collerson (1997) reports on the teaching of the genre and grammar of news stories at Dulwich Hill Public School in Sydney. Here the submission to a local newspaper of a story about the vandalizing of the students' school garden project resulted in a visit to the school by a reporter and photographer and the subsequent publication by the paper of its own story under the headline 'Kids robbed of green dreams'. There are many other such programs covering a variety of textual forms. Work with a Year 7 class on advertisements was reported on the Australian National Professional Development Program's CD ROM, *Literacy for Learning Years 5–8* (1997). The New South Wales Disadvantaged Schools Program published a unit of work for junior secondary school English on *Exploring Narrative in Video* (Rothery 1994). There are also published examples of classroom programs exploring the genres of popular television situation comedies (Macken-Horarik 1996) and comparing the genres of popular romance novels and similar contemporary films (Macken-Horarik 1998). A very detailed systemic functional linguistic analysis of the Emmy award-winning wildlife documentary, *Kangaroos: Faces in the Mob*, and associated texts and news stories have been the basis for extensive work on the explicit teaching of critical literacy practices in both senior and junior secondary school English classrooms (Miller 1995; Miller and Howie 2000). Space will not permit detailed descriptions of examples of classroom work of this kind, but in order to indicate their consistency with the detailed programs that have been described here, we will outline some of the main features of the work on television sitcoms and romance novels and films reported by Macken-Horarik (1996, 1998).

In the Year 10 English classroom program dealing with television sitcoms (Macken-Horarik 1996), the researcher observed that the students were very familiar with meta-language from systemic functional descriptions of language. The students freely talked about 'genre', and the situational variables 'field', 'tenor' and 'mode' (Chapter 2), as well as grammatical terms like 'modality', 'process type' and 'connectives'. The unit of study considered a number of sitcoms but primarily focused on *Mother and Son* and *The Golden Girls*. The broad goal was to understand the structure of the sitcom genre and then to critically appraise the genre considering ways in which these examples serve to naturalize a particular view of old people. The initial phase of the pedagogy involved sharing informal knowledge about these shows, employing recognition literacy practices of recounting and describing. Then, as the work bridged to systematic knowledge, the teacher took a more directly instructive role in establishing more technical understanding of the structural form and narrative technique of the sitcom. This included the teacher's writing of model texts such as an essay evaluating *Mother and Son* as a successful Australian sitcom, which the class read and deconstructed with the teacher, prior to writing a similar essay evaluating *The Golden Girls*. As the students developed their understanding of the sitcom genre, the work moved toward the critical stance of transformative knowledge. This involved research on 'ageism' and age-discrimination in Australia, investigating materials from a range of sources such as the New South Wales Anti-Discrimination Board. Finally the students produced a feature article about the construction of ageism in television situation comedy, after studying the feature article genre in well-known popular magazines.

The work on the romance genre in novels and film (Macken-Horarik 1998) took place in a Year 9 classroom at a Sydney girls' school. First the students studied the features of the genre in book form. Next they wrote their own romance story and eventually wrote a critique of romance films like *Pretty Woman*. Through deconstructing romance stories and then writing them in accordance with the formulaic plot options derived from the schematic structure of the genre, the students developed meta-level awareness of not only generic structure but also the grammar that typified the different stages of the genre (such as extended nominal group structures with heavily descriptive pre- and post-modification of the head noun – 'the most entrancing and tender woman that his dazzling yellow-green eyes had ever encountered'). The students were then guided in deconstructing the films *Pretty in Pink* and *Pretty Woman* to explicate their schematic structure and narrative techniques. As in the program about sitcoms, the next move was towards a critical stance. Again the teacher provided a model essay discussing the assertion that notwithstanding its close adherence to the romance formula, *Pretty Woman* is a dangerous lesson for today's woman. The students then wrote a similar essay discussing the film *Pretty in Pink*.

These accounts of classroom work have in common the key features of the Curriculum Area Multiliteracies and Learning (CAMAL) framework. First they move from informal knowledge of the topic to systematic technical knowledge to transformative knowledge. Second, the initial pedagogy of sharing familiar understandings bridges to direct teaching and guided exploration of new understandings and then to research and critical framing. Finally, from recognition literacies of familiar genres and language forms, the students move to reproduction literacies, reading and generating the established text forms, and then to reflection literacies, critiquing and challenging established text forms. Facilitating this kind of progression is the differential use of modelled, guided and independent practice in the reading and writing of the relevant genres – formulated as the Literacy Development Cycle.

TECHNOLITERACIES AND ENGLISH TEACHING

In Chapter 1 we noted that rather than trying to squeeze new technologies into familiar literacy education procedures, we need to attend to the reality of new and emerging literacies. But we also noted that conventional, hard-copy forms of 'linear' texts will continue to co-exist with electronic hypertext for some time, and that old and new literacy technologies will frequently have complementary roles in a range of contexts. If the English classroom is concerned with both traditional and popular literature for children, there is every reason to believe that it will have growing support from complementary resources in conventional and computer-based formats. The daily newspaper, *The Sydney Morning Herald*, on 19 August 2000, reviewed 23 websites dealing with various aspects of J.K. Rowling's Harry Potter books (1997, 1998, 1999, 2000). We have noted that children can access the author Paul Jennings' website and read web-published versions of his stories. Australian author, John Marsden, also currently includes on his website (http://www.ozemail.com.au/~andrewf/john.html) a story in hypertext format entitled 'Cool School', which children can visit and explore. A number of publishers such as Allen and Unwin (http://www.allen-unwin.com.au/kidzone/Suckitki.htm) in Australia, provide for children on their websites with opportunities for obtaining information about authors, illustrations from books, extracts to read and activities based on books to participate in. There are a number of sites now, like Bibliobytes (http://www.bb.com/index.cfm), which enable visitors to read online or download from a huge online library free books sorted into science fiction, horror and fantasy with a very wide range, from the poetry of Edgar Allen Poe to contemporary pieces. Children can publish their reviews of books online (http://lausd.k12.ca.us/~cburleso/Lessons/), publish their own writing (http://www.kidpub.org/kidpub/), create e-zines (magazines online) (http://www.nexus.edu.au/TeachStud/students/FUTURES/KIDSET), or enter story-writing competitions (http://www.writearound.com.au/home/). These of course, are just some of the opportunities afforded by the Internet. There is also the role that email can play in English teaching (Warshauer 1999) and various kinds of chat rooms not to mention the offline multimedia texts and authoring software that is now available. Technoliteracies are distinctive because of the particular affordances of computer-based and networked technologies for information and communication (see Chapter 1, page 12). However, technoliteracies are also sites for the integrative deployment of visual, verbal and acoustic semiotic resources and, in the foreseeable future will coexist with multiliteracies required to negotiate contemporary hard copy texts.

In conclusion, the work of the English teacher clearly involves developing students' use of multiliteracies in the composition and comprehension of texts in computer based and conventional formats. But it also involves developing students' meta-semiotic understanding and the associated meta-language to facilitate critical understanding of how meaning-making systems are deployed to make different kinds of meanings in texts and how these may be oriented to naturalize the hegemony of particular interests. The concern here has been to indicate a practical basis for this kind of work.

References

Allen, P. (1991) *Black Dog*. Ringwood, Victoria: Penguin/Puffin.

Anderson, M. and Ashton, P. (1993) *Focus on Australian History*. Melbourne: Macmillan.

Anstey, M. and Bull, G. (1996) *The Literacy Labyrinth*. Sydney: Prentice Hall.

Applebee, A.N. (1981) *Writing in the Secondary School*. Urbana, IL: National Council for the Teaching of English.

Ardizzone, E. (1982) *Little Tim and the Brave Sea Captain*. London: Viking Kestrel.

Astorga, C. (1999) The text–image interaction and second language learning, *Australian Journal of Language and Literacy*, 22(3): 212–33.

Australian Broadcasting Commission Education Television (2000) *Education Programme Guide. Schools, Lifelong Learning*, January–June. Sydney: Australian Broadcasting Commission.

Baillie, A. (1988) *Megan's Star*. Melbourne: Nelson.

Baillie, A. (1991) *Drac and the Gremlin*. Ringwood, Victoria: Penguin/Puffin.

Baillie, A. (1993) *Rebel!* Sydney: Ashton Scholastic.

Baker, J. (1987) *Where the Forest Meets the Sea*. London: Walker Books.

Baker, J. (1991) *Window*. London: Julia MacRae.

Baker, J. (1994) *Grandfather*. Sydney: Ashton Scholastic.

Barbalet, M. and Tanner, J.I. (1991) *The Wolf*. Melbourne: Puffin.

Barlow, A. and Hill, M. (1987a) *Australian Aborigines: Families*. Melbourne: Macmillan.

Barlow, A. and Hill, M. (1987b) *Australian Aborigines: Meeting People*. Melbourne: Macmillan.

Barton, M. (1987) *Animal Rights*. London: Franklin Watts.

Bates, J. (1990) *Hands on Science: Seeds to Plants*. London: Franklin Watts.

Bawden, N. (1974) *Carrie's War*. London: Puffin.

Beaty, W. (1996) Recurring misinformation in science books, *Science Education Notes*, 45(2): 17–19.

Bender, L. (1988) *Today's World: Insects and Simple Creatures*. London: Franklin Watts.

Bennett, J. (1993) *Early Years Poems and Rhymes*. Sydney: Ashton Scholastic.

Bernstein, B. (1996) *Pedagogy, Symbolic Control and Identity: Theory, Research, Critique*. London: Taylor & Francis.

Biesty, S. and Platt, R. (1996) *Stephen Biesty's Incredible Explosions*. Ringwood, Victoria: Viking/Penguin.

Bird, B. and Short, J. (1998) *Insects*. Sydney: Scholastic.

Bloor, T. and Bloor, M. (1995) *The Functional Analysis of English: A Hallidayan Approach*. London: Arnold.

Bolter, J. (1998) Hypertext and the question of visual literacy, in D. Reinking, M. McKenna, L. Labbo and R. Kieffer (eds) *Handbook of Literacy and Technology: Transformations in a Post-typographic World*. Hillsdale, NJ: Erlbaum.

Braddock, R., Lloyd-Jones, R. and Shoer, L. (1963) *Research in Written Composition*. Champaign, IL: National Council of Teachers of English.

Bramwell, M. (1986) *Rivers and Lakes*. London: Franklin Watts.

Bramwell, M. (1987) *Earth Science Library: Planet Earth*. London: Franklin Watts.

Brandenberg, F. (1982) *I Don't Feel Well*. Harmondsworth: Puffin.

Briggs, R. (1977) *Fungus the Bogeyman*. London: Hamish Hamilton.

Bright, M. (1987) *Saving the Whale*. London: Franklin Watts.

Bright, M. (1988) *Killing for Luxury*. London: Franklin Watts.

Browne, A. (1983) *Gorilla*. London: Julia MacRae.

Browne, A. (1984) *Willy the Wimp*. London: Julia MacRae.

Browne, A. (1985) *Willy the Champ*. London: Julia MacRae.

Browne, A. (1986) *Piggybook*. London: Julia MacRae.

Browne, A. (1989) *The Tunnel*. London: Julia McRae.

Browne, A. (1994) *Zoo*. London: Random House.

Browne, A. (1995) *Hansel and Gretel*. London: Walker Books.

Browne, A. (1998) *Voices in the Park*. London: Doubleday.

Burbules, N. (1997) Rhetorics of the web; hyperreading and critical literacy, in I. Snyder (ed.) *From Page to Screen: Taking Literacy into the Electronic Era*. Sydney: Allen & Unwin.

Burnett, F.H. (1992) *The Secret Garden*. London: Sainsbury Walker.

Burningham, J. (1977) *Come Away from the Water, Shirley*. London: Cape.

Burningham, J. (1978) *Time to Get Out of the Bath, Shirley*. London: Cape.

Burningham, J. (1984) *Granpa*. London: Penguin/Puffin.

Butt, D., Fahey, R., Spinks, S. and Yallop, C. (1995) *Using Functional Grammar: An Explorer's Guide*. Sydney: National Centre for English Language Teaching and Research.

Butterworth, C. (1988) *Ants*. London: Macmillan.

Byars, B. (1970) *The Midnight Fox*. London: Faber.

Byars, B. (1974) *The Eighteenth Emergency*. London: The Bodley Head.

Callow, J. (1995) Visual literacy: some observations. Unpublished Master of Education Independent Study and Report, University of Sydney, Sydney.

Callow, J. (ed.) (1999) *Image Matters: Visual Texts in the Classroom*. Sydney: Primary English Teaching Association.

Callow, J. and Unsworth, L. (1997) Equity in the videosphere, *Southern Review*, 30(3): 268–86.

Cannon, J. (1995) *Stellaluna*. Mascot, Sydney: Koala Books.

Carter, R. (1990) The new grammar teaching, in R. Carter (ed.) *Knowledge about Language and the Curriculum*. London: Hodder and Stoughton.

Chambers, A. (1983) *The Present Takers*. London: Bodley Head.

Chambers, A. (1985) *Booktalk*. London: The Bodley Head.

Chapman, B., Perry, L. and Stead, K. (1989) *Science 9*. Milton, Queensland: Brooks.

Charman, A. (1992) *Science through Energy*. London: Franklin Watts.

Christie, F. (1997) Curriculum macrogenres as forms of initiation into a culture, in F. Christie and J.R. Martin (eds) *Genre and Institutions: Social Processes in the Workplace and School*. London: Cassell.

Christie, F. (2000) The language of classroom interaction and learning, in L. Unsworth (ed.) *Researching Language in Schools and Communities*. London: Cassell.

Clark, J. (1992) *Hands on Geography: Mining to Minerals*. London: Franklin Watts.

Claybourne, A. (1994) *How Do Bees Make Honey?* London: Usborne.

Clemence, J. and Clemence, J. (1987) *Electricity*. Sydney: Macdonald.

Cochrane, J. (1987) *Water Ecology*. Hove: Wayland.

Coffin, C. (1996) *Exploring Literacy in School History*. Sydney: Metropolitan East Disadvantaged Schools Program, New South Wales Department of School Education.

Coffin, C. (1997) Constructing and giving value to the past: an investigation into secondary school history, in F. Christie and J.R. Martin (eds) *Genre and Institutions: Social Processes in the Workplace and School*. London: Cassell.

Collerson, J. (1994) *English Grammar: A Functional Approach*. Sydney: Primary English Teaching Association.

Collerson, J. (1997) *Grammar in Teaching*. Sydney: Primary English Teaching Association.

Cooper, E. (1988) *First Facts: Insects*. London: Macmillan.

Cope, B. and Kalantzis, M. (eds) (2000) *Multiliteracies: Literacy, Learning and the Design of Social Futures*. Melbourne: Macmillan.

CSIRO (1994) *Insects – Little Creatures in a Big World*. Sydney: CSIRO Education.

Curriculum Corporation (1994a) *English – A Statement on English for Australian Schools*. Carlton, Victoria: Curriculum Corporation.

Curriculum Corporation (1994b) *English – A Curriculum Profile for Australian Schools*. Carlton, Victoria: Curriculum Corporation.

Dahl, R. (1974) *Fantastic Mr Fox*. Harmondsworth: Puffin.

Davidson, J. (2000) Young movie makers, *Practically Primary*, 5(2): 8–9.

Davies, F. and Greene, T. (1984) *Reading for Learning in the Sciences*. Edinburgh: Oliver and Boyd.

Davies, L., Leibe, F. and Matthews, J. (1987) *Bright Ideas Teacher Handbooks: Language Resources*. Marlborough, UK: Scholastic.

Department for Education and Employment (DfEE) (1998) *The National Literacy Strategy: Framework for Teaching*. Sudbury: DfEE Publications.

Derewianka, B. (1990a) *Exploring How Texts Work*. Sydney: Primary English Teaching Association.

Derewianka, B. (1990b) Rocks in the head: children writing geology reports, in R. Carter (ed.) *Knowledge about Language and the Curriculum: The LINC Reader*. London: Hodder and Stoughton.

Derewianka, B. (1998) *A Grammar Companion for Primary Teachers*. Sydney: Primary English Teaching Association.

DeVreeze, D., Lofts, G., Preuss, P. and Gilbert, K. (1992) *Jacaranda Science and Technology*, Vol. 1. Brisbane: Jacaranda Press.

Doonan, J. (1993) *Looking at Pictures in Picture Books*. Stroud: Thimble Press.

Drew, D. and Pride, M. (1997) *Insects*. Melbourne: Addison Wesley Longman.

Dubosque, D. (1998) *Draw Insects*. New York: Scholastic.

Eggins, S. (1994) *An Introduction to Systemic Functional Linguistics*. London: Pinter.

Elley, W.B., Barham, I.H. and Wylie, M. (1976) The role of grammar in a secondary school English curriculum, *Research in the Teaching of English*, 10(1): 5–21.

Ellyard, D. (ed.) (1996) *Discoveries: Weather*. Sydney: Allen and Unwin.

Fairclough, N. (ed.) (1992) *Critical Language Awareness*. London: Longman.

Fairclough, N. (ed.) (1995) *Critical Discourse Analysis: The Critical Study of Language*. London: Longman.

Farndon, J. (1992) *Eyewitness Explorers: Weather*. Sydney: HarperCollins.

Feez, S. and Joyce, H. (1998) *Writing Skills: Narrative and Non-fiction Text Types*. Sydney: Phoenix.

Fitzgerald, S. (1990) *Chippendale: Beneath the Factory Wall*. Sydney: Hale and Ironmonger.

Fitzpatrick, J. (1984) *Magnets*. London: Hamish Hamilton.

Foltz, P. (1996) Comprehension, coherence and strategies in hypertext and linear text, in J. Rouet, J. Levonen, A. Dillon, A. and R. Spiro (eds) *Hypertext and Cognition*. Hillsdale, NJ: Erlbaum.

Freebody, P. and Luke, A. (1990) 'Literacies' programs: Debates and demands in cultural context, *Prospect*, 5: 7–16.

French, S. (1981) *Cannily Cannily*. Harmondsworth: Puffin.

Fresch, M. (1994) Australian children's literature, *The Dragon Lode*, 12(2): 1–3.

Garton, J. (1997) New genres and new literacies: the challenge of the virtual curriculum, *Australian Journal of Language and Literacy*, 20(3): 209–21.

Gay, M. (1999) *Stella – Star of the Sea*. London: Allen & Unwin.

Gee, J. (1990) *Social Linguistics and Literacies: Ideology in Discourses*. London: Falmer Press.

Gell, R. (1987) *The Greenhouse Effect* (video). Box Hill, Victoria: Box Hill College of Technical and Further Education.

Gleeson, L. (1987) *I am Susannah*. Sydney: Angus and Robertson.

Gleeson, L. (1999) *Hannah and the Tomorrow Room*. Ringwood, Victoria: Puffin.

Gleeson, L. and Greder, A. (1999) *The Great Bear*. Sydney: Scholastic.

Goodman, S. and Graddol, D. (1996) *Redesigning English: New Texts, New Identities*. London: Routledge.

Goodwyn, A. (1998) Adapting to the textual landscape: bringing print and visual texts together in the classroom, in A. Goodwyn (ed.) *Literary and Media Texts in Secondary English – New Approaches*. London: Cassell.

Gordimer, N. (1972) *Livingstone's Companions: Stories*. London: Cape.

Graham, B. (1990) *Grandad's Magic*. Ringwood, Victoria: Penguin.

Graham, B. (1992) *Rose Meets Mr Wintergarten*. Ringwood, Victoria: Viking.

Graham, J. (1990) *Pictures on the Page*. Melbourne: Australian Reading Association.

Green, B. (1988) Subject-specific literacy and school learning: a focus on writing, *Australian Journal of Education*, 32(2): 156–79.

Green, B. and Bigum, C. (1993) Aliens in the classroom, *Australian Journal of Education*, 37(2): 119–41.

Halliday, M.A.K. (1973) *Explorations in the Functions of Language*. London: Edward Arnold.

Halliday, M.A.K. (1978) *Language as a Social Semiotic: The Social Interpretation of Language and Meaning*. London: Edward Arnold.

Halliday, M.A.K. (1985) *An Introduction to Functional Grammar*, 1st edn. London: Edward Arnold.

Halliday, M.A.K. (1993a) The act of meaning, *Applied Linguistics Association of Australia Occasional Paper*, 13: 42–61.

Halliday, M.A.K. (1993b) The analysis of scientific texts in English and Chinese, in M.A.K. Halliday and J.R. Martin (eds) *Writing Science: Literacy and Discursive Power*. London: Falmer Press.

Halliday, M.A.K. (1994a) *An Introduction to Functional Grammar*, 2nd edn. London: Edward Arnold.

Halliday, M.A.K. (1994b) Metaphor as semogenic process. Paper presented at the Workshop on Scientific Discourse, University of Sydney, September.

Halliday, M.A.K. and Hasan, R. (1985) *Language, Context and Text: Aspects of Language in a Social-Semiotic Perspective*. Geelong: Deakin University Press.

Halliday, M.A.K. and Martin, J.R. (eds) (1993) *Writing Science: Literacy and Discursive Power*. London: Falmer Press.

Halliday, M.A.K. and Matthiessen, C.I.C.M. (1999) *Construing Experience Through Meaning: A Language-based Approach to Cognition*. London: Cassell.

Hammond, J. (1990) Is learning to read and write the same as learning to speak?, in F. Christie (ed.) *Literacy for a Changing World*. Hawthorn: Australian Council for Educational Research.

Hasan, R. (1985) *Linguistics, Language and Verbal Art*. Geelong: Deakin University Press.

Hasan, R. (1995) The conception of context in text, in P. Fries and M. Gregory (eds) *Discourse in Society: Systemic Functional Perspectives*. Norwood, NJ: Ablex.

Hasan, R. (1996) Literacy, everyday talk and society, in R. Hasan and G. Williams (eds) *Literacy in Society*. London and New York: Longman.

Hathorn, L. and Rogers, G. (1994) *Way Home*. Sydney: Random House.

Heffernan, D. and Learmonth, M. (1983) *The World of Science – Book 4*. Melbourne: Longman Cheshire.

Heffernan, D. and Learmonth, M. (1988) *The World of Science*, 2nd edn, vol. 1. Melbourne: Longman Cheshire.

Heffernan, D. and Learmonth, M. (1989) *The World of Science*, 2nd edn, vol. 2. Melbourne: Longman Cheshire.

Heffernan, D. and Learmonth, M. (1990) *The World of Science*, 2nd edn, vol. 3. Melbourne: Longman Cheshire.

Hemsley, W. (1990) *Hands on Science: Jellyfish to Insects*. London: Franklin Watts.

Hillocks, G. (1986) *Research on Written Composition: New Directions for Teaching*. Urbana, IL: ERIC and NCRE.

Hillocks, G. and Smith, M.W. (1991) Grammar and usage, in J.M. Flood, D. Jensen, D. Lapp and J. R. Squire (eds) *Handbook of Research on Teaching the English Language Arts*. New York: Macmillan.

Hoban, R. (1982) *The Flight of Bembel Rudzuk*. London: Methuen/Walker.

Hoffman, M. (1986) *Animals in the Wild: Wild Cat*. Sydney: Ferguson.

Hollindale, P. (1995) Children's literature in an age of multiple literacies, *The Australian Journal of Language and Literacy*, 18(4): 248–58.

House, A. (n.d.) *The Greenhouse Effect and Global Warming*. Helensburg, New South Wales: Know Ware.

Howard, P. (1993) *Basic Skills: Grammar and Punctuation Level 1(Yrs 3–4)*. Sydney: Coroneos.

Howley, P. (1996) Visual literacy: semiotic theory, primary school syllabus documents and classroom practice. Unpublished Bachelor of Education Honours, University of Sydney, Sydney.

Hughes, S. (1981) *Alfie Gets in First*. London: The Bodley Head.

Humphrey, S. (1996) *Exploring Literacy in School Geography*. Sydney: Metropolitan East Disadvantaged Schools Program, New South Wales Department of School Education.

Hunt, P. (2000) Futures for children's literature: evolution or radical break. *Cambridge Journal of Education*, 30(1): 111–19.

Hutchins, P. (1968) *Rosie's Walk*. Harmondsworth: Penguin.

Hutchins, P. (1978a) *Don't Forget the Bacon*. Harmondsworth: Puffin.

Hutchins, P. (1978b) *The Wind Blew*. Harmondsworth: Puffin.

Hutchins, P. (1985) *You'll Soon Grow into Them, Titch*. Harmondsworth: Puffin.

Hutchins, P. (1986) *The Very Worst Monster*. Harmondsworth: Puffin.

Iedema, R. (1995) Political newsreporting: the media as 'secondary orality', *Social Semiotics*, 5(1): 65–100.

Iedema, R. (1997) The structure of the accident news story, *Social Semiotics*, 20(2): 95–118.

Iedema, R., Feez, S. and White, P. (1994) *Media Literacy*. Sydney: NSW Department of School Education, Metropolitan East Region Disadvantaged Schools Component.

James, R. (1999) Navigating CD-Roms: An exploration of children reading interactive narratives, *Children's Literature in Education*, 30(1): 47–63.

Janks, H. and Ivanic, R. (1992) Critical language awareness and emancipatory discourse, in N. Fairclough (ed.) *Critical Language Awareness*. London: Longman.

Jennings, P. (1994) *Unbearable!: More Bizarre Stories*. London: Puffin.

Jennings, P. and Gouldthorpe, P. (1994) *Grandad's Gifts*. Ringwood, Australia: Puffin/Penguin.

Johnson, T. and Louis, D. (1985) *Literacy through Literature*. Sydney: Methuen.

Kamil, M. and Lane, D. (1998) Researching the relation between technology and literacy: an agenda for the 21st century, in D. Reinking, M. McKenna, L. Labbo and R. Kieffer (eds) *Handbook of Literacy and Technology: Transformations in a Post-typographic World*. Hillsdale, NJ: Erlbaum.

Keeping, C. (1970) *Through the Window*. Oxford: Oxford University Press.

Keifer, B. (1995) *The Potential of Picturebooks: From Visual Literacy to Aesthetic Understanding*. Englewood Cliffs, NJ: Merrill/Prentice Hall.

Kelleher, V. (1979) *The Forbidden Paths of Thual*. London: Kestrel.

Kelleher, V. (1981) *The Hunting of Shadroth*. London: Kestrel.

Kemp, G. (1981) *The Clocktower Ghost*. Harmondsworth: Puffin.

Kidman Cox, R. and Cork, B. (1980) *Butterflies and Moths*. London: Usborne.

Kindersley, D. (1994) *Eyewitness Encyclopedia of Science* (CD ROM). London: Dorling Kindersley.

Klein, R. (1984) *Hating Alison Ashley*. Ringwood: Puffin.

Knobel, M. and Healy, A. (eds) (1998) *Critical Literacies in the Primary Classroom*. Sydney: Primary English Teaching Association.

Knowles, M. and Malmkjaer, K. (1996) *Language and Control in Children's Literature*, 1st edn. London: Routledge.

Kress, G. (1995a) *Making Signs and Making Subjects: The English Curriculum and Social Futures*. London: University of London, Institute of Education.

Kress, G. (1995b) *Writing the Future: English and the Making of a Culture of Innovation*. Sheffield: National Association of Teachers of English.

Kress, G. (1997) Visual and verbal modes of representation in electronically mediated communication: the potentials of new forms of text, in I. Snyder (ed.) *Page to Screen: Taking Literacy into the Electronic Era*. Sydney: Allen & Unwin.

Kress, G. (2000) Multimodality, in B. Cope and M. Kalantzis (eds) *Multiliteracies: Literacy Learning and the Design of Social Futures*. Melbourne: Macmillan.

Kress, G. and van Leeuwen, T. (1990) *Reading Images*. Geelong: Deakin University Press.

Kress, G. and van Leeuwen, T. (1996) *Reading Images: A Grammar of Visual Design*. London: Routledge.

Lafferty, P. (1989) *Hands on Science: Wind to Flight*. London: Franklin Watts.

Lafferty, P. (1990) *Hands on Science: Burning and Melting*. London: Franklin Watts.

Lankshear, C. (1994) *Critical Literacy*. Belconnen, Australian Capital Territory: Australian Curriculum Studies Association.

Lankshear, C. (ed.) (1997) *Changing Literacies*. Buckingham: Open University Press.

Lankshear, C., Snyder, I. and Green, B. (2000) *Teachers and Technoliteracy*. Sydney: Allen & Unwin.

Lawrence, D.H. (1971) *The Fox and the Virgin and the Gypsy*. London: Heinemann.

Lemke, J. (1998a) Metamedia literacy: transforming meanings and media, in D. Reinking, M. McKenna, L. Labbo and R. Kieffer (eds) *Handbook of Literacy and Technology: Transformations in a Post-typographic World*. Hillsdale, NJ: Erlbaum.

Lemke, J. (1998b) Multiplying meaning: visual and verbal semiotics in scientific text, in J.R. Martin and R. Veel (eds) *Reading Science: Critical and Functional Perspectives on Discourses of Science*. London: Routledge.

Leu, D. and Kinzer, C. (2000) The convergence of literacy instruction with networked technologies for information and communication, *Reading Research Quarterly*, 35(1): 108–27.

Lewis, C.S. (1950) *The Lion, the Witch and the Wardrobe*. London: Fontana.

Lockwood, D. (1996) *I, the Aboriginal*. Sydney: Landsdowne.

Lonsdale, M. (1993) Postmodernism and the picture book, *English in Australia*, 103: 25–35.

Loves, J. (1992) *Operation Insect Watch*. Melbourne: Collins Dove.

Luchinni, F. (1996) The ontogenesis of critical literacy in the junior secondary English classroom. Unpublished Master of Education Dissertation, University of Sydney, Sydney.

Luke, C. (2000) Cyber-schooling and technological change, in B. Cope and M. Kalantzis (eds) *Multiliteracies: Literacy Learning and the Design of Social Futures*. Melbourne: Macmillan.

Lunzer, E. and Gardner, K. (1984) *Learning from the Written Word*. Edinburgh: Oliver and Boyd.

Macaulay, D. (1994) *The Way Things Work*. London: Dorling Kindersley.

Macdonald, F. (1997) *I Wonder Why Romans Wore Togas and Other Questions About Ancient Rome*. London: Kingfisher.

MacLulich, C. (1996) *Insects*. Sydney: Scholastic.

MacLulich, C. (1998) *Ants*. Sydney: Scholastic Australia.

Macken, M., Kalantzis, M., Kress, G., Martin, J.R. and Cope, B. (1989) *A Genre-based Approach to Teaching Writing, Years 3–6, Book 1: Introduction*. Sydney: Directorate of Studies, NSW Department of Education and Literacy and Education Research Network.

Macken, M. and Rothery, J. (1991) *Developing Critical Literacy: A Model for Literacy in Subject Area Learning*. Sydney: Metropolitan East Region Disadvantaged Schools Program, New South Wales Department of School Education.

Macken-Horarik, M. (1996) Literacy and learning across the curriculum: towards a model of register for secondary school teachers, in R. Hasan and G. Williams (eds) *Literacy in Society*. Harlow: Addison Wesley Longman.

Macken-Horarik, M. (1998) Exploring the requirements of critical literacy: a view from two classrooms, in F. Christie and R. Misson (eds) *Literacy and Schooling*. London: Routledge.

Mackey, M. (1994) The new basics: learning to read in a multimedia world, *English in Education*, 28(1): 9–19.

Martin, J.R. (1984) Types of writing in infants and primary school. Paper presented at the Fifth Macarthur Reading/Language Symposium, Macarthur Institute of Higher Education, Sydney July.

Martin, J.R. (1989) *Factual Writing: Exploring and Challenging Social Reality*. Oxford: Oxford University Press.

Martin, J.R. (1991) Intrinsic functionality: implications for contextual theory, *Social Semiotics*, 1(1): 99–162.

Martin, J.R. (1992) *English Text: System and Structure*. Amsterdam: Benjamins.

Martin, J.R. (1993a) Genre and literacy – modelling context in educational linguistics, *Annual Review of Applied Linguistics*, 13: 141–72.

Martin, J.R. (1993b) Life as a noun: arresting the universe in science and humanities, in M.A.K. Halliday and J. R. Martin (eds) *Writing Science: Literacy and Discursive Power*. London: Falmer Press.

Martin, J.R. (1993c) Literacy in science: learning to handle text as technology, in M.A.K. Halliday and J.R. Martin (eds) *Writing Science: Literacy and Discursive Power*. London: Falmer Press.

Martin, J.R. (1993d) Technology, bureaucracy and schooling: discourse resources and control, *Dynamics*, 6(1): 84–130.

Martin, J.R. (1995a) Reading positions/positioning readers, *Prospect: A Journal of Australian TESOL*, 10(2): 27–37.

Martin, J.R. (1995b) Text and clause: fractal resonance, *Text*, 15(1): 5–42.

Martin, J.R. (1996) Evaluating disruption: symbolising theme in junior secondary school narrative, in R. Hasan and G. Williams (eds) *Literacy in Society*. London: Longman.

Martin, J.R. (1997) Analysing genre: functional parameters, in F. Christie and J.R. Martin (eds) *Genres and Institutions: Social Processes in the Workplace and School*. London and Washington, DC: Cassell.

Martin, J.R. (2000) Close reading: functional linguistics as a tool for critical discourse analysis, in L. Unsworth (ed.) *Researching Language in Schools and Communities: Functional Linguistic Perspectives*. London: Cassell.

Martin, J.R. (in press) Fair trade: negotiating meaning in multimodal texts, in P. Coppock (ed.) *The Semiotics of Writing: Transdisciplinary Perspectives on the Technology of Writing*: Begijnhof, Belgium: Brepols.

Martin, J.R. and Rothery, J. (1993) Grammar: making meaning in writing, in B. Cope and M. Kalantzis (eds) *The Powers of Literacy*. London: Falmer Press.

Martin, J.R. and Veel, R. (eds) (1998) *Reading Science: Critical and Functional Perspectives on Discourses of Science*. London: Routledge.

Martinec, R. (1999) Cohesion in action, *Semiotica*, 1/2: 161–80.

Matthiessen, C. (1995) *Lexicogrammatical Cartography: English Systems*. Tokyo: International Language Sciences.

McDonald, L. (1999) A case study of an apprenticeship in critical reading. Unpublished PhD, University of Sydney, Sydney.

McKee, D. (1987) *Not Now, Bernard*. London: Arrow.

Meek, M. (1988) *How Texts Teach What Readers Learn*. Stroud: Thimble Press.

Michaels, W. and Walsh, M. (1990) *Up and Away: Using Picture Books*. Melbourne: Oxford University Press.

Microsoft (1992–94) *Microsoft Encarta 95* (CD ROM).

Miller, B. (1995) Teaching critical literacy: current issues and some secondary school perspectives. Paper presented at the 21st National Conference of the Australian Reading Association, Confronting Literacies, Darling Harbour, Sydney, July.

Miller, B. and Howie, M. (2000) Critical literacy research project: using SLF to apprentice the students into the senior high school curriculum. Paper presented at the the 27th International Systemic Functional Linguistics Congress, University of Melbourne, 9–14 July.

Miller, B., Perry, B., Farmer, P., Long, M. and Roffe, S. (1999) The language of mathematics: contextualisation or confusion, *Literacy Learning: Secondary Thoughts*, 7(2): 10–18.

Miller, L. and Olsen, J. (1998) Literacy research oriented toward features of technology and classrooms, in D. Reinking, M. McKenna, L. Labbo and R. Kieffer (eds) *Handbook of Literacy and Technology: Transformations in a Post-typographic World*. Hillsdale, NJ: Erlbaum.

Miller, T. (1998) Visual persuasion: a comparison of visuals in academic texts and the popular press, *English for Specific Purposes*, 17(1): 29–46.

Misson, R. (1998) Telling tales out of school, in F. Christie and R. Misson (eds) *Literacy and schooling*. London: Routledge.

Moline, S. (1995) *I See What You Mean*. Melbourne: Longman.

Moore, P. (1999) Reading and writing the internet, in J. Hancock (ed.) *Teaching Literacy Using Information Technology*. Newark, DE: International Reading Association.

Morgan, S. and Bancroft, B. (1996) *Dan's Grandpa*. Freemantle, Western Australia: Sandcastle.

Morimoto, J. (1983) *The White Crane*. Sydney: William Collins.

Morris, A. and Stewart-Dore, N. (1984) *Learning to Learn from Text: Effective Reading in the Content Areas*. Sydney: Addison Wesley.

Morton, L. and Murakami, Y. (1989) *The Fox*. Flagstaff, AZ: Northland.

Mosel, A. (1968) *Tikki Tikki Tembo*. Sydney: Scholastic.

Munsch, R. (1994) *The Paper Bag Princess* (CD ROM). Buffalo, NY: Discis.

Muspratt, S., Luke, A. and Freebody, P. (eds) (1997) *Constructing Critical Literacies*. Sydney: Allen & Unwin.

National Professional Development Program (1997) *Literacy for Learning in Years 5–8*. Sydney: Open Training Education Network.

New London Group (2000) A pedagogy of multiliteracies: designing social futures, in B. Cope and M. Kalantzis (eds) *Multiliteracies: Literacy Learning and the Design of Social Futures*. Melbourne: Macmillan.

New South Wales Board of Studies (1998a) *English K–6 Modules*. Sydney: New South Wales Government.

New South Wales Board of Studies (1998b) *English K–6 Syllabus and Support Documents*. Sydney: New South Wales Government.

New South Wales Department of Education and Training (1997) *Basic Skills Test: Year 5*. Sydney: New South Wales Government.

New South Wales Department of Education and Training (1999) *English Language and Literacy Assessment*. Sydney: New South Wales Government.

Nicoll, V. and Unsworth, L. (1990) *Dimensions Teachers' Book Level II*. Melbourne: Nelson.

Nodelman, P. (1988) *Words About Pictures: The Narrative Art of Children's Picture Books*. Athens, GA: University of Georgia Press.

Norman, L. and Young, N. (1998) *Grandpa*. Sydney: Margaret Hamilton Books.

O'Brien, R. (1975) *Z for Zachariah*. New York: Atheneum.

Ogborn, J., Kress, G., Martins, I. and McGillicuddy, K. (1996) *Explaining Science in the Classroom*. Buckingham: Open University Press.

O'Halloran, K. (1999) Interdependence, interaction and metaphor in multisemiotic texts, *Social Semiotics*, 9(3): 317–38.

Oppenheim, J. and Broda, R. (1998) *Have You Seen Bugs?* New York: Scholastic.

Oram, H. (1984) *Angry Arthur*. Harmondsworth: Puffin.

Ormerod, J. (1985) *The Story of Chicken Licken*. London: Walker Books.

Osborne, R. and Freyberg, P. (1989) *Learning Science: The Implications of Children's Science*. Auckland: Heinemann.

O'Toole, M. (1994) *The Language of Displayed Art*. London: Leicester University Press.

Park, R. (1988) *Playing Beatie Bow*. Harmondsworth: Puffin.

Paterson, K. (1977) *Bridge to Terabithia*. Harmondsworth: Puffin.

Perera, K. (1984) *Children's Reading and Writing*. Oxford: Blackwell.

Pettigrew, M. (1986a) *Music and Sound*. London: Franklin Watts.

Pettigrew, M. (1986b) *Simply Science: Planet Earth*. London: Franklin Watts.

Polias, J. (1998) *Teaching ESL through Science*. Adelaide: South Australian Department of Education, Training and Employment.

Pople, M. and Williams, M. (1990) *Science to Sixteen*. Oxford: Oxford University Press.

Potter, B. (1987) *The Tale of Peter Rabbit*. Harmondsworth: Penguin.

Pownall, E. (1982) *Australia from the Beginning*. Sydney: Collins.

Prain, V. (1998) Picture books in secondary English, in A. Goodwyn (ed.) *Literary and Media Texts in Secondary English*. London: Cassell.

Queensland Department of Education (1994) *English in Years 1 to 10: Queensland Syllabus Materials*. Brisbane: Department of Education, Queensland.

Queensland Department of Education (1995) *English 1–10 Syllabus: A Guide to Analysing Texts*. Brisbane: Queensland Government Printing Office.

Quin, R., McMahon, B. and Quin, R. (1995) *Teaching Viewing and Visual Texts – Secondary.* Melbourne: Curriculum Corporation.

Quin, R., McMahon, B. and Quin, R. (1996) *Teaching Viewing and Visual Texts – Primary.* Melbourne: Curriculum Corporation.

Quin, R., McMahon, B. and Quin, R. (1997a) *The Big Picture: Reading Visual Language.* Melbourne: Curriculum Corporation.

Quin, R., McMahon, B. and Quin, R. (1997b) *In the Picture: Reading Visual Language.* Carlton, Victoria: Curriculum Corporation.

Quirk, R. and Greenbaum, S. (1993) *A University Grammar of English.* London: Longman.

Rassool, N. (1999) *Literacy for Sustainable Development in the Age of Information.* Clevedon: Multilingual Matters.

Ravelli, L. (2000) Getting started with functional analysis of texts, in L. Unsworth (ed.) *Researching Language in Schools and Communities: Functional Linguistic Perspectives.* London: Cassell.

Richards, G. (1978) *Classroom Language: What Sort?* London: George Allen and Unwin.

Robertson, M. and Poston-Anderson, B. (1986) *Readers' Theatre: A Practical Guide.* Sydney: Hodder and Stoughton.

Robson, P. (1992a) *Science Workshop: Magnetism.* London: Franklin Watts.

Robson, P. (1992b) *Science Workshop: Water, Paddles and Boats.* London: Franklin Watts.

Rothery, J. (1994) *Exploring Narrative in Video: A Unit of Work for Junior Secondary English.* Sydney: Metropolitan East Disadvantaged Schools Program, New South Wales Department of School Education.

Rothery, J. (1996) Making the changes: developing an educational linguistics, in R. Hasan and G. Williams (eds) *Literacy in Society.* London: Longman.

Rothery, J. and Stenglin, M. (2000) Interpreting literature: the role of appraisal, in L. Unsworth (ed.) *Researching Language in Schools and Communities: Functional Linguistic Approaches.* London: Cassell Academic.

Roughsey, D. (1973) *The Giant Devil Dingo.* Sydney: Collins.

Rowling, J.K. (1997) *Harry Potter and the Philosopher's Stone.* London: Bloomsbury.

Rowling, J.K. (1998) *Harry Potter and the Chamber of Secrets.* London: Bloomsbury.

Rowling, J.K. (1999) *Harry Potter and the Prisoner of Azkaban.* London: Bloomsbury.

Rowling, J.K. (2000) *Harry Potter and the Goblet of Fire.* London: Bloomsbury.

Rubinstein, G. (1994) *Foxspell.* Melbourne: Hyland.

Scales, D. (1981) *Rigby Moving into Maths: Teachers' Resource Book.* Melbourne: Rigby.

Sealey, A. (1996) *Learning about Language.* Buckingham: Open University Press.

Selsam, M. and Hunt, J. (1982) *A First Look at Dinosaurs.* New York: Scholastic.

Sendak, M. (1962) *Where the Wild Things Are.* London: The Bodley Head.

Sendak, M. (1973) *In the Night Kitchen.* London: The Bodley Head.

Seventy, V. (1984) *Animals in the Wild: Penguin.* Sydney: Ferguson.

Shirato, T. and Yell, S. (1996) *Communication and Cultural Literacy: An Introduction.* Sydney: Allen & Unwin.

Simmelhaig, H. and Spenceley, G. (1984) *For Australia's Sake.* Melbourne: Nelson.

Simon, N. (1987) *Vanishing Habitats.* London: Franklin Watts.

Sloan, P. and Latham, R. (1985) *Bats.* Sydney: Methuen.

Smith, R., Curtin, P. and Newman, L. (1996) Kids in the kitchen: the social implications for schooling in the age of advanced computer technology: Hobart. Paper presented at the Australian Association for Research in Education Annual Conference, November.

Southall, I. (1971) *Josh.* Sydney: Angus and Robertson.

Stannard, P. and Williamson, K. (1991) *Science Now, Book 3.* Melbourne: Macmillan.

Stephens, J. and Watson, K. (eds) (1994) *From Picture Book to Literary Theory*. Sydney: St Clair Press.

Street, B. (1984) *Literacy in Theory and Practice*. Cambridge: Cambridge University Press.

Sustainable Solutions (1995) *Australian Home Greenhouse Scorecard*. Melbourne: Environmental Protection Authority (Victoria).

Taylor, B. (1989) *Science Starters: Bouncing and Bending Light*. London: Franklin Watts.

Taylor, B. (1990) *Science Starters: Water at Work*. London: Franklin Watts.

Taylor, B. (1991) *Science Starters: Air and Flying*. London: Franklin Watts.

Taylor, B. (1992) *Young Discoverers: Weather and Climate*. London: Kingfisher.

Thomson, G. (1996) *Introducing Functional Grammar*. London: Edward Arnold.

Thomson, R. (1988) *Eyes*. Sydney: Franklin Watts.

Thurton, R. (1999) Review, *Magpies Magazine*, 14(1): 41.

Travers, D. and Hancock, J. (1996) *Teaching Viewing: Ten Units of Learning with Visual Texts*. Adelaide: South Australian Department of Education and Community Services.

Tudball, L. (ed.) (1991) *Australian Perspectives: Australian History for Senior Students*. Milton, Queensland: Jacaranda.

Ubisoft. (n.d.) *Payuta and the Ice God*. London: Ubisoft Multimedia.

Unsworth, L. (1993a) Choosing and using information books in junior primary science, in L. Unsworth (ed.) *Literacy Learning and Teaching: Language as Social Practice in the Primary School*. Melbourne: Macmillan.

Unsworth, L. (1993b) Managing the language program: children's literature in the primary school, in L. Unsworth (ed.) *Literacy Learning and Teaching: Language as Social Practice in the Primary School*. Melbourne: Macmillan.

Unsworth, L. (1993c) Multiple semiotic sources as scaffolding for young children's emergent reading of picture-story books, *Australian Review of Applied Linguistics*, 16(2): 1–14.

Unsworth, L. (ed.) (1993d) *Literacy Learning and Teaching: Language as Social Practice in the Primary School*. Melbourne: Macmillan.

Unsworth, L. (1996) How and why: recontextualising science explanations in school science books. Unpublished PhD, University of Sydney, Sydney.

Unsworth, L. (1997a) Scaffolding reading of science explanations: accessing the grammatical and visual forms of specialised knowledge, *Reading*, 31(3): 30–42.

Unsworth, L. (1997b) Some practicalities of a language-based theory of learning, *Australian Journal of Language and Literacy*, 20(1): 36–52.

Unsworth, L. (1997c) 'Sound' explanations in school science: a functional linguistic perspective on effective apprenticing texts, *Linguistics and Education*, 9(2): 199–226.

Unsworth, L. (1999a) Developing critical understanding of the specialised language of school science and history: a functional grammatical perspective, *Journal of Adolescent and Adult Literacy*, 42(7): 508–27.

Unsworth, L. (1999b) Explaining school science in book and CD ROM formats: using semiotic analyses to compare the textual construction of knowledge, *International Journal of Instructional Media*, 26(2): 159–79.

Unsworth, L. (1999c) Teaching about explanations: talking out the grammar of written language, in A. Watson and L. Giorcelli (eds) *Accepting the Literacy Challenge*. Sydney: Scholastic.

Unsworth, L. (ed.) (2000) *Researching Language in Schools and Communities: Functional Linguistic Perspectives*. London: Cassell.

Unsworth, L. and O'Toole, M. (1993) Beginning reading with children's literature, in L. Unsworth (ed.) *Literacy Learning and Teaching: Language as Social Practice in the Primary School*. Melbourne: Macmillan.

Van Allsburg, C. (1985) *The Polar Express*. London: Andersen.

van Leeuwen, T. (1991) Conjunctive structure in documentary film and television, *Continuum*, 5(1): 76–114.

van Leeuwen, T. (1996) Moving English, in S. Goodman and D. Graddol (eds) *Redesigning English: New Texts, New Identities*. London: Open University Press/Routledge.

van Leeuwen, T. (1999) *Speech, Music, Sound*. London: Macmillan.

van Leeuwen, T. (2000) It was just like magic – a multimodal analysis of children's writing, *Linguistics and Education*, 10: 273–305.

van Leeuwen, T. and Humphrey, S. (1996) On learning to look through a geographer's eyes, in R. Hasan and G. Williams (eds) *Literacy in Society*. London: Addison Wesley Longman.

Vaughan, P. (1988) *The Greenhouse Effect* (video). London: BBC.

Veel, R. (1997) Learning how to mean – scientifically speaking: apprenticeship into scientific discourse in the secondary school, in F. Christie and J.R. Martin (eds) *Genres and Institutions: Social Processes in the Workplace and School*. London: Cassell Academic.

Veel, R. (1998) The greening of school science: ecogenesis in secondary classrooms, in J.R. Martin and R. Veel (eds) *Reading Science: Functional and Critical Perspectives on the Discourses of Science*. London: Routledge.

Veel, R. (1999) Language, knowledge and authority in school mathematics, in F. Christie (ed.) *Pedagogy and the Shaping of Consciousness: Linguistic and Social Processes*. London: Cassell Academic.

Veel, R. and Coffin, C. (1996) Learning to think like an historian: the language of secondary school history, in R. Hasan and G. Williams (eds) *Literacy in Society*. London: Longman.

Victor-Pujebet, V. (n.d.) *Lulu's Enchanted Book*. Hove: Wayland.

Wagner, J. (1977) *John Brown, Rose and the Midnight Cat*. Ringwood, Victoria: Penguin/Puffin.

Ward, B. (1987) *Life Guides: Alcohol Abuse*. London: Franklin Watts.

Warshauer, M. (1999) *Electronic Literacies: Language, Culture, and Power in Online Education*. Mahwah, NJ: Lawrence Erlbaum.

Watson, K. (ed.) (1997) *Word and Image*. Sydney: St Clair Press.

Watson, V. (1996) The left-handed reader in linear sentences and unmapped pictures, in V. Watson and M. Styles (eds) *Talking Pictures: Pictorial Texts and Young Readers*. London: Hodder and Stoughton.

Watson, V. and Styles, M. (eds) (1996) *Talking Pictures: Pictorial Texts and Young Readers*. London: Hodder and Stoughton.

Wells, G. (1994) The complementary contributions of Halliday and Vygotsky to a 'Language-based Theory of Learning', *Linguistics and Education*, 6(1): 41–90.

Wells, R. (1978) *Noisy Nora*. London: Fontana, Picture Lions.

Wheatley, N. (1982) *Five Times Dizzy*. Melbourne: Oxford University Press.

Wheatley, N. (1985) *The House That Was Eureka*. Melbourne: Viking, Kestrel.

White, M. (1980) *Mindwave*. Sydney: Methuen.

White, P. (1997) Death, disruption and the moral order: the narrative impulse in mass media hard news reporting, in F. Christie and J. Martin (eds) *Genres and Institutions: Social Processes in the Workplace and School*. London: Cassell.

White, P. (2000) Media objectivity and the rhetoric of news story structure, in E. Ventola (ed.) *Discourse and Community: Doing Functional Linguistics*. Tubingen: Gunter Narr Verlag.

Whyman, K. (1989) *Hands on Science: Sparks to Power Stations*. London: Franklin Watts.

Wild, M. and Brooks, R. (2000) *Fox*. Sydney: Allen & Unwin.

Wild, M. and Tanner, J. (1989) *There's a Sea in my Bedroom*. Ringwood, Victoria: Puffin.

Williams, G. (1987a) Rumpelstiltskin's Secret. Paper presented at the Annual Conference of the Victorian Reading Association, Ballarat, September.

Williams, G. (1987b) Space to play: the analyses of narrative structure in classroom work with children's literature, in M. Saxby and G. Winch (eds) *Give Them Wings: The Experience of Children's Literature*. Melbourne: Macmillan.

Williams, G. (1993) Using systemic grammar in teaching young learners: an introduction, in L. Unsworth (ed.) *Literacy Learning and Teaching: Language as Social Practice in the Primary School*. Melbourne: Macmillan.

Williams, G. (1998) Children entering literate worlds, in F. Christie and R. Missan (eds) *Literacy in Schooling*. London: Routledge.

Williams, G. (2000) Children's literature, children and uses of language description, in L. Unsworth (ed.) *Researching Language in Schools and Communities: A Functional Linguistic Perspective*. London: Cassell.

Wilson, L. (2000) Christian reads N64, *Practically Primary*, 5(2): 5–7.

Winton, T. (1998) *The Deep*. Freemantle, Western Australia: Sandcastle.

Wong, O. (1991) *Hands-on Ecology*. Chicago, IL: Children's Press.

Wood, L. and Rink, D. (1991) *Bats*. Mankato, MN: Creative Education.

Woodside, D. (1993) *Masters of the Night Sky*. Gosford, New South Wales: Bookshelf.

Wray, D. and Lewis, M. (1997) Teaching factual writing: purpose and structure, *Australian Journal of Language and Literacy*, 20(2): 131–9.

Wright, P. (1986) *The Space Race*. London: Franklin Watts.

Wyatt-Smith, C. and Cumming, J. (1999) Examining the literacy demands of the enacted curriculum, *Literacy Learning: Secondary Thoughts*, 7(2): 19–31.

Index